TREATISE

ON

THE DENTAL ART,

FOUNDED

ON ACTUAL EXPERIENCE.

Illustrated by two hundred and forty-one figures in Lithography, and fifty-four Wood Cuts.

BY F. MAURY,

DENTIST OF THE ROYAL POLYTECHNIC SCHOOL.

Translated from the French,

WITH NOTES AND ADDITIONS,

BY J. B. SAVIER,

DOCTOR OF DENTAL SURGERY.

MILFORD HOUSE
BOSTON

This Milford House book is an unabridged
republication of the edition of 1843.

Published in 1972 by MILFORD HOUSE INC.
85 Newbury Street, Boston, Massachusetts

Library of Congress Catalogue Card Number: 72-92721
Standard Book Number: 0-87821-025-3

Printed in the United States of America

TO

C. A. HARRIS, M. D., D. D. S.

PROFESSOR OF PRACTICAL DENTISTRY IN THE BALTIMORE
COLLEGE OF DENTAL SURGERY,

As a memorial of respect and esteem for his professional
worth, and zeal in behalf of the Dental
Profession, by which its interests
have been enhanced and its
character elevated, and as
a tribute of grateful
affection,

This volume is inscribed

By his Friend,

THE TRANSLATOR.

PREFACE.

THE reputation of the author of this Treatise entitles his opinions upon the various subjects connected with the science of dental surgery to deference and respect, and it is believed will win for the present version of it a favourable reception.

The translator has endeavoured to give a faithful interpretation of the views of his author, and would have preferred essaying no farther than this, did not the many improvements made in this department of the curative art within a few years past render it necessary that he should omit or condense certain passages that would in the present condition of the science be of no profit, and to append notes to others to explain or to refute whatever appeared ambiguous or erroneous.

Of the *third part* he need only remark, that although it contains information of value to every dentist, it would not serve as a guide in the department of the art to which it is devoted. The necessity of other information was therefore so manifest that the Treatise of Dr. Solyman Brown, the most complete upon this subject extant, has been levied upon to atone for this deficiency.

The translator also makes his acknowledgments of the obligations he is under to the various other authors whose writings he has without ceremony appropriated to his use. He has made such selections with his best discrimination, and it is his highest hope that in his humble vocation of translator and compiler his labours may prove of utility to the members of his profession.

J. B. S.

Baltimore, December, 1842.

CONTENTS.

PART I.

ANATOMY AND PHYSIOLOGY.

DENTAL PATHOLOGY.

PART II.

DENTAL HYGIENE AND THERAPEUTICS.

PART III.

MECHANICAL DENTISTRY, OR ODONTOTECHNY, AND THE MECHANICAL MEANS OF REMEDYING LESIONS OF THE PALATINE ARCH.

PART I.

ANATOMY AND PHYSIOLOGY.

TREATISE.

PART I.

ANATOMY AND PHYSIOLOGY.

THE MOUTH AND ITS APPENDAGES.

THE mouth is an oval cavity placed between the jaws, bounded laterally by the cheeks, anteriorly by the lips, posteriorly by the palate, superiorly by the palate bones and the palatine processes of the superior maxillary bones, and inferiorly by the tongue and buccal membrane.

As the anatomy of this cavity should precede the description of its various diseases, we deem it necessary to examine briefly its different parts, and also their respective functions; for, without such examination, it would be as difficult to understand the nature of its diseases as it would be to arrest their progress by the judicious employment of hygienic and therapeutical means, or to perform the operations to be hereinafter described.

The Lips, or Anterior Walls of the Mouth.

The lips are two symmetrical, membranous, moveable folds, which flatten from without inward; they are situated in front of the maxillary bones, and separated by a transverse slit, called the opening of the mouth. The skin, hair, muscles, sebaceous glands, mucous follicles, cellular tissue, arteries and veins, capillaries and lymphatics, nerves, and a mucous membrane, form the tissues of their organization. The lips are also composed of muscular fibres, so arranged as to enable them to execute the different movements necessary in the performance of their functions.

The skin which covers the exterior of these organs is thin, very fine, and of a serous tissue; it adheres strongly to the subjacent parts by a cellular tissue, which contains no fat, and in the male subject at puberty is covered with beard. The mucous membrane which lines the mouth is reflected over their borders, and gradually blends with the skin. This membrane is remarkable for its redness and its strong epidermis; it covers numerous mucous follicles, the orifices of which are within the lips.

The muscles of the lips have each a peculiar form and a distinct point of insertion. Some of these are common to both lips, and others appertain to one only. The first class are the zygomaticus major, depressor anguli oris, caninus, buccinator, and the orbicularis oris; the second class are the levator labii superioris alæque nasi, levator proprius, and the zygomaticus minor, which act upon the superior lip, and the muscles of the chin, the action of which is upon the lower lip, (Pl. I. Fig. 1.)

The arteries of the lips are branches of the external carotid, especially the labial, the sub-mental, the mental, the buccal, the sub-orbital, the alveolar, and the transversalis facii.

Their veins follow the course of these arteries, and empty into the jugulars.

Their nerves are branches of the sub-orbital, the mental, and the facial nerves.

With respect to their lymphatics, they enter into the formation of ganglions situated under the chin.

The Palate, or Posterior Wall of the Mouth.

The palate is a species of moveable partition. It is soft, wide, thick, and of a quadrilateral figure, attached above to the palatine arch, on the sides to the walls of the pharynx, on each side by two folds of the buccal membrane; below it is free, and is called the pillars of the palate. These pillars are separated from each other, by a mass of muciparous follicles, which are called the *amygdalæ*.

The posterior opening of the mouth is situated under the palate; it is bounded by the root of the tongue, the palate, its pillars, the palatine roof, and the tonsils.

The palate is composed of a mucous and a muscular coat; the first, which forms a species of duplicature, in which the muscular coat is contained, is continuous anteriorly with the membrane of the mouth, and posteriorly with that of the nasal fossæ. This membrane is lined with a great quantity of mucous follicles, of a yellow colour, very serous, round, and forming of themselves nearly the thickness of the uvula.

The second, or muscular coat, is formed by the azygos uvula and the internal and external palato-pharyngeus, the pterygo-staphylius, the salpingo-staphylius and the glosso-staphylius. The use of these muscles is to move the soft palate.

Its arteries are branches of the labial, the palatine, and the superior pharyngeus.

Its veins unite with those of the tongue and pharynx, and empty into the internal jugular.

Its nerves are furnished from the ganglion of Meckel and the glosso-pharyngeus.

The Cheeks, or Lateral Walls of the Mouth.

The cheeks, which do not constitute distinct organs, form the lateral walls of the mouth. They are flattened transversely, broad, of a quadrilateral figure, and their thickness varies in different individuals. They have exteriorly no distinct limits, but are continuous with the inferior eye-lid above, and below they descend to the base of the jaw. They are limited anteriorly by the wings of the nose, and posteriorly by the posterior border of the rami of the jaws. Interiorly they are bounded above and below by duplicatures of the mucous membrane of the mouth; posteriorly by the anterior pillars of the palate, and anteriorly by the commissures of the lips. Their external surface may be either convex or concave; on their internal surface are scattered numerous buccal glands, and opposite the space between the second and third molares the ducts of Steno are situated, one on each side.

The cheeks are composed of three distinct coats, the dermoid, the muscular, and the mucous coats.

The first, or *dermoid*, is very fine, and in male adults is partly covered with beard.

The second or *muscular,* is composed of the muscles already named, namely, the buccinator, the masseter, the zygomatici major and minor, and a portion of the platysma-myoides, (Pl. I. Fig. 1.)

The third, or *mucous,* is thinner in the cheek than in any other part of the mouth. The molar glands are situated posteriorly, between the buccinator and masseter muscles. They are composed of agglomerations of sub-mucous follicles, the excretory orifices of which are opposite the last molar tooth.

The arteries of the cheek are branches of the labial, transversalis facii, buccal, superior alveolar, and sub-orbital arteries.

Their veins correspond to their arteries, and empty into the two jugulars.

Their nerves are branches of the suborbital, facial, buccal, masseter and cervical plexus.

The Palatine Roof, or Superior Part of the Mouth.

The palatine roof, or superior part of the mouth, is a species of paraboloid arch; it is horizontal, slightly concave, immovable, traversed longitudinally by a medial line of a whitish colour and slightly depressed, and terminating in front between the incisores by a slightly elevated tubercle corresponding to the inferior orifice of the anterior palatine foramen. The palatine roof is surrounded by the superior teeth, which we will hereafter describe in detail.

The *osseous* portion of the palate is formed by the superior alveolar arch, the palatine processes of the superior maxillary bones, and the palate bones.

Its *mucous membrane* is thinner and of a lighter colour than in any other part of the mouth; at its anterior part, which is the thicker part, it presents transverse ridges varying in number and extent. Smooth at its posterior part, this membrane is covered with numerous holes which are the excretory orifices of mucous follicles situated between it and the osseous wall of the palate. It is continuous in front and upon the sides with the gums, and is a species of fibro-mucous tissue, reddish, firm, destined to cover the two sides of the alveolar arch, and accurately fills up the spaces between the teeth the necks of which it surrounds. This tissue, the nature of which is little understood, is identified in some manner with the periosteum of the two alveolar arches, and is continued exteriorly with the internal membrane of the cheeks and lips.

The gums appear to be formed of a pulpous and fibrous layer, which is reflected over the mucous membrane. They are highly vascular.

The arteries of the gums, like those of the palate, are branches of the palatine, alveolar, sub-orbital, labial, and buccal; those of the inferior gums are, more especially, branches of the mental and sub-mental arteries. Their veins are from the internal and external jugulars, and their nerves are furnished by the palatine, facial, sub-orbital, superior and inferior dental, and the naso-palatine ganglion.

The Base, or inferior Part of the Mouth.

The inferior part of the mouth is larger posteriorly than anteriorly, and forms beneath the tongue a duplicature called the frænum linguæ. Here are seen the inferior jaw, surrounded by its teeth; the tongue, which occupies the entire space between the branches of the jaws; and the mucous membrane, which invests the whole.

The Tongue.—The tongue is a symmetrical organ, almost entirely muscular, of a flat, oblong form, rounded at its border and point, thick in its centre, but more so at its base; it occupies the mouth, the cavity of which it fills when the jaws are closed. It extends from the os hyoideus and the epiglottis as far as the posterior part of the incisores. It is anatomically divided into two faces, two borders, and two extremities, (the dental extremity, or its point, the hyoidean extremity, or its base.)

The tongue is chiefly formed of a peculiar tissue of muscles, and of a mucous membrane, which is a continuation of the lining membrane of the mouth. These muscles are the hyo-glossus, genio-glossus, stylo-glossus, superficial and deep-seated linguals, and the transverse and vertical linguals.

The floor of the mouth, beneath the tongue, is formed by the following muscles: the genio-hyoideus, the mylo-hyoideus, the digastricus and the platysma-myoides, and finally by the skin. The nerves which are distributed to the floor of the mouth are the linguals, the glosso-pharyngeus, the hypo-glossus, the facial, the superficial cervicals, and a branch of the inferior dental nerve. The arteries are the sub-linguals, inferior palatine, and sub-mental. Veins and many lymphatic plexi are also observed here.

~~~~~~~~~~~~~~~~~~~~

THE DIFFERENT PARTS THAT ENTER INTO THE FORMATION OF THE MOUTH.

The Bones.

The bones that enter into the formation of the mouth are the superior maxilla, which forms the whole of the superior jaw; the palate bones, situated posteriorly; the inferior jaw; and the teeth. The development of the teeth presents peculiar phenomena, which we will explain in the chapter devoted to the description of these little organs, when we will endeavour to omit nothing either in relation to their structure or the mechanism of their eruption.

Muscles of the Mouth.

Some of these muscles appertain to the walls of the mouth, and others form a part of this cavity as they enter into the formation of organs which constitute it.

The following muscles are under the jaws in the base of the mouth: 1, platysma-myoides; 2, digastricus; 3, mylo-hyoideus; 4, genio-hyoideus. These draw the jaw downward and backward.

There are also: 5, stylo-glossus; 6, genio-glossus; 7, hyo-glossus; 8, deep and superficial linguals; also, the transverse and vertical linguals which Dr. Gerdy has recently discovered, and which appertain solely to the tongue.

There are other muscles that belong to the cheeks and lips: 1, the temporal; 2, the masseter; 3, the pterygoideus internus, which constitutes the levator of the inferior jaw; 4, the pterygoideus externus; 5, the two zygomatici; 6, the two levators of the superior lip; 7, the canini; 8, the two depressors of the lips, which, as their names indicate, are the movers of the lips;

9, muscle of the chin; 10, the buccinator; 11, the labial. (Pl. I. Fig. 1.)

The muscles of the soft palate may also be named here, viz: glosso-staphylius; 2, palato-pharyngeus; 3, salpingo-pharyngeus; 4, peristaphylus; 5, azygos-uvulæ. These comprise all the muscles of the mouth.

Nerves.

The nerves which are distributed to the different parts of the mouth, already described, are branches of the fifth, seventh, eighth and ninth pairs.

The branches of the fifth pair, which supply the different parts of the mouth with nervous fillets, are the superior and inferior maxillary. (Pl. I. Fig. 2, Pl. II. Fig. 2.) The first of these branches furnishes the posterior and anterior dental nerves, and forms the spheno-palatine ganglion. The second, the masseter, deep temporal, buccal, pterygoid, superficial, temporal, lingual and inferior dental nerves. (Pl. I. Fig. 2, Pl. II. Fig. 1.)

The portio dura of the seventh pair, or the facial nerve, distributes to the cheek the buccal and malar branches, and under the chin it sends off the mental and submental branches. (Pl. I. Fig. 2.)

The eighth pair sends off the glosso-pharyngeus, which is distributed in the mouth.

The ninth pair, or the great hypo-glossal, is exclusively distributed to the tongue.

Arteries.

The arteries that nourish the different parts of the mouth are branches of the external carotid; they are the lingual, the musculo-palatine, the sub-mental, the tonsillaris, the inferior labial and its two coronaries, the inferior dental, the masseter, the buccal, the alveolar, the sub-orbital, the superior palatine, and the spheno-palatine. (Pl. II. Fig. 2.)

Veins.

The veins follow the course of the arteries and receive the same names, but they are more numerous and more complicated. (Pl. II. Figs. 1, 2.)

Salivary Glands.

The salivary glands we shall speak of as accessories of the mouth are the parotid, the sub-maxillary and the sub-lingual.

The parotid Gland.—This gland, the largest of all the salivary glands, is situated on the side of the face between the mastoid process of the temporal bone and the ramus of the lower jaw, the external auditory conduit, and the mastoid apophysis of the temporal bone. It presents the form of an irregular pyramid inverted, and extending vertically from the zygoma to the angle of the jaw.

It is nourished by branches of the transversalis facii and the anterior auricular arteries. The veins distributed to this part return into corresponding trunks. Its nerves derive their origin from the facial, the inferior maxillary branches, and the cervical plexus. As regards its lymphatics, they are very numerous and enter into ganglions situated behind the angle of the jaw. The use of the parotid gland is to secrete the saliva.

The sub-maxillary Gland.—This gland is smaller and not so solid as the preceding; it is of an irregular ovoidal form, flattened upon three of its sides, and bifurcated in front. It is situated on the internal side of the branch and body of the lower jaw, in the space between the two bellies of the digastric muscle, and bears a strong resemblance in colour, consistency, and internal structure, to the parotid.

It receives its nourishment from branches of the facial and lingual arteries.

Its veins are branches of the neighbouring venous trunks, and its nervous twigs are supplied by the lingual and inferior dental nerves and the sub-maxillary ganglion.

This gland, like the parotid, secretes a great quantity of saliva, which is carried into the mouth by a canal called the duct of Wharton.

The sub-lingual Gland.—This gland is of an ovoidal form, slightly flattened transversely, and resembling an almond divested of its shell. It is situated in the substance of the inferior portion of the mouth under the anterior part of the tongue.

Its organization is the same as that of the other salivary glands. It is red and firm, and the lobes or lobules of which it is composed are smaller than those of the sub-maxillary gland. It has about twenty excretory ducts of extreme tenacity occupying different situations. Some pierce the mucous membrane, covering the floor of the mouth, and others have their orifices upon the lateral parts of the frænum of the tongue. Two or three, and even more, have been known to open into the duct of Wharton.

Its arteries are branches of the labial and sub-mental.

Its nerves are furnished by the inferior maxillary and the hypo-glossal.

Its use is the same as the preceding glands.

As we designedly neglected to give the history of the teeth, when treating of the superior and inferior walls of the mouth, we will now notice them in a particular manner.

THE TEETH IN GENERAL.

The teeth, together with the alveoli in which they are implanted, and the jaws, constitute the dental apparatus, properly so called. The first of these are the hardest and most compact bones of the body. " They form," says Beclard, "upon the alveolar arch, by an uninterrupted series, two curved paraboloid lines, which are called the *dental arches*. These being unequal, the *superior* represents the large extremity of an oval, and the *inferior* the small extremity of the same oval. The superior arch overlaps the inferior. The free border of each dental arch is thin and simple in front, thick and double on the sides, where the teeth are larger and furnished with two rows of tubercles.

The teeth differ in structure and mode of growth and nutrition, from other bones of the body; and, although they resemble them in their chemical and physical properties, they differ from them in many other respects. They vary in number at different periods of life, are partly exposed to the atmosphere, and often drop out during old age. They are covered with an enamel of pearly whiteness, which is peculiar to them, and which assumes, according to the temperament of the individual, a blue, yellow, or gray hue.* Together with these there

* The colour, shape, and size of the teeth are not only indicative of the temperament of the individual, but they indicate their liability to decay. For a

is another hue very common to the teeth, but not so distinct; it is slightly red, which is caused by the artery and vein which penetrate the little orifice at the extremity of each root, (Pl. II. Fig. 2,) and nourish the dental pulp found at the middle of the interior of the crown. (Pl. IV. Fig. 4.) The teeth generally assume a slightly vertical direction. They are of the form of an irregular cone, their crowns representing the base and their roots, single or double, pierced at their extremities, and buried in their sockets, representing the summit of the cone. (Pl. VI. Fig. 3.)

Each tooth has a part called the *crown*, projecting beyond its alveolus and covered with a thick enamel. This, in a healthy state, protects the tooth from the impressions of heat and cold. The crown is surrounded by a slight depression called the *neck*, around which the gums adhere and separate it from an articular portion, called the *root*, which is buried in the alveolus. The roots may be single, double, triple, quadruple, and sometimes quintuple, according to the class of teeth, (Pl. VII. Figs. 11, 18, 24,) and are covered with a thin periosteum or vascular membrane which lines the alveolus and becomes a means of securing the teeth by a species of articulation known among anatomists as *gomphosis*, resembling the union of a nail with a board into which it has been driven.

There are in the human mouth, when second dentition is completed, thirty-two teeth. These are divided into classes, uniform within themselves, and having corresponding sides in contact. (Pl. VII. Figs. 11 to 26.)

The teeth are thus classified, viz:—*Incisores, Cuspidati, Bicuspides* and *Molares.* It will be perceived by their respective shapes (Pl. VII. Figs. 1 to 26) that nature intended them for different uses. The incisores, situated in front, are intended to cut similarly to a pair of scissors; the cuspidati appear to be destined to seize and tear aliment like those of carnivorous animals; and the bicuspides and molares, flattened upon the crown and provided with conical tubercles, are to grind animal and vegetable aliment.

---

full description of the appearances of the teeth, and their local and constitutional indications, the reader is referred to Professor Chapin A. Harris' Treatise on the Physical Characteristics of the Teeth and Gums, Chap. II.—S.

The Incisores.—The incisores are divided into superior and inferior centrals and laterals. They are eight in number, four in each jaw, occupying the anterior and smaller portion of the arch. Their bodies are quadrilateral, narrower and thicker near the root than at its extremity, convex, smooth and polished in front, and concave and narrow behind. They have upon each side a triangular surface, contiguous to the neighbouring tooth, and separated from the root by a neck presenting anteriorly and posteriorly the form of a paraboloid border. These teeth have always single roots, which are long, conical and pointed, compressed laterally, and fluted lengthwise upon each side. At their points there is a foramen, through which pass a nerve, artery and vein.

The two superior central incisores are always larger and stronger than the superior laterals, and the latter somewhat exceed the inferior in size and strength. The axis of each of the four superior incisores, situated below and in front, is a little inclined toward its fellow, and the external border of their bodies is rounded near the gums, while their extremities are brought down to a cutting edge. (Pl. VII. Figs. 11, 12.)

The inferior incisores, we have already said are narrower and not so strong as the preceding. The centrals are a little smaller than the laterals. The edges of the inferior are inclined obliquely inward, a disposition, says Garriot, that is caused by the friction produced upon their anterior surfaces by the superior teeth. Their axis is vertical, their roots longer, narrower and more deeply fluted than those of the superior incisores. (Pl. VII. Figs. 19, 20.)

The Cuspidati.—The cuspidati are four in number, two in each jaw, one on each side of the four incisores. They have a conical body, are very convex anteriorly, a little irregularly concave posteriorly, and terminating in a point or tubercle which is often beyond the level of the other teeth. Their roots are single, but much longer and thicker than those of the incisores, and the extremity is sometimes separated into two branches, having the appearance of two united, (Pl. VIII. Fig. 19.) They are flat and rough upon their sides, and, like the incisores, their necks have anteriorly and posteriorly two curves.

3

The superior cuspidati are the longest of all the teeth. Their roots often penetrate the base of the sub-maxillary bone.

The inferior cuspidati are smaller, and situated upon a more anterior plane than the adjoining teeth. (Pl. VII. Figs. 13 and 21.

The Bicuspides.—These occupy the lateral part of the mouth, four in each jaw, and are placed posterior to the cuspidati. Their bodies, the greatest dimension of which is in length, slightly resemble the cuspidati. They are cylindrical anteriorly and posteriorly, flattened laterally, larger at their external than at their internal sides, and are surmounted by two short conical tubercles, one external, large and prominent, the other internal, small and less elevated. These tubercles are more prominent upon the superior than upon the inferior bicuspides, and there are between them two uneven depressions.

The root of the bicuspides is flat, deeply fluted anteriorly and posteriorly. The first two superior and the four inferior bicuspides have generally one single root; but the two posterior superior have each two roots, which have at their extremities two foramina, through which pass nerves and vessels. The necks of these teeth describe a more irregular circle than the preceding. (Pl. VII. Figs. 14, 15, 22, 23.)

The Molares.—The largest of all the teeth terminate the dental arches, and are twelve in number, six in each jaw. Their bodies are slightly cubical, short, partly round, but flattened posteriorly and anteriorly: their surface is surmounted by four or five tubercles with corresponding depressions, so arranged that when the jaws are closed the tubercles of the molares of the upper jaw are adapted to the depressions of those of the lower jaw, and *vice versa.* These tubercles are separated from each other by deep winding grooves. The roots of these teeth are shorter than those of the bicuspides, and are divided into three, four, and sometimes five branches, through each of which pass a nerve, artery and vein. These branches may be more or less straight or curved, long or short, smooth or unequal, and sometimes, after diverging, they approach each other in such a manner as to embrace a part of the alveolus.

The neck is well marked. But the three molares differ so much from each other as to require a separate examination.

The first is the largest of the three molares, and has upon its crown generally four, and sometimes five tubercles, three externally and two internally. The root of this tooth in the superior jaw is triple or quadruple, while that in the inferior is only double. (Pl. VII. Figs. 16, 24.)

The second molar is smaller than the preceding, is provided in the inferior jaw with four tubercles separated by a crucial groove which is less regular in the superior molar, the body of which is of a rhomboidal figure. Its root has three branches, two external and united, one internal and very divergent. (Pl. VII. Figs. 17, 25.)

The third molar, commonly called the *wisdom tooth*, bears much resemblance to the second molar, but is smaller, and its axis is directed more inward. Its crown is round and furnished with three or four tubercles. Its root is generally single, grooved longitudinally, short, conical: sometimes it has the appearance of two, three, and even four fangs united partially or totally. (Pl. VII. Figs. 18, 26.)

Teeth of First Dentition.

The teeth named thus in contradistinction to those which have already been described, are seen in children of from three to four years of age, and are twenty in number, ten in each jaw, when the first denture is complete. They differ so materially from those of second dentition as to require a separate description. They have, according to their form and use, been divided into incisores, cuspidati and molares. Those in the superior are generally stronger than those in the inferior jaw. The *deciduous incisores* and *cuspidati*, (Pl. VII. Figs. 1, 2, 3,) differ but little from the permanentes. They are smaller, and of an azure blue; they are brittle, and have long roots previous to their destruction by the teeth of replacement.

The four *temporary molares* are of a different form from those which succeed them, and can only be compared to the permanent molares, from which however they greatly differ in conformation. The first molar of the superior jaw is larger than the cuspidati, and has upon its crown five tubercles, three

internally and two externally; its root has three divisions, two
of which are united, (Pl. VII. Fig. 4.)   The second is larger
and rounder than the first, and has five tubercles upon its
crown, which is cylindrical, three upon its outer and two upon
its inner part; it has three diverging roots, and near its neck
a peculiar prominence. (Pl. VII. Fig. 5.) The two molares of
the inferior jaw are smaller and have generally only two roots
very strong and short. (Pl. VII. Figs. 9, 10.)

The teeth of first dentition are usually of a bluish white
colour. The incisores and cuspidati are much smaller than those
of the second denture, (Pl. VII. Figs. 1, 2, 3, 6, 7, 8, 11, 12,
13, 19, 20, 21,) and their cutting edge is thinner, and their
bodies rounder and more swollen, particularly the outer part.
In regard to their chemical composition, they differ but little
from the adult teeth.   They have perhaps a little less of the
phosphate of lime, as may be seen in the following table, in
which we give the results obtained by Mr. Phelps of the
analysis of the teeth at different periods of life:—

	Temporary Teeth.	Adult Teeth.	Roots of Teeth.	Enamel of Teeth.
Phosphate of lime,	62	64	58	78
Carbonate of lime,	6	6	4	6
Cartilage,	20	20	28	0
Water and loss,	12	10	10	16

STRUCTURE OF THE TEETH.

Although anatomists and physiologists do not agree upon
the nature of the different substances that enter into the composition of the teeth, they in general acknowledge three distinct parts, namely, first, the *enamel*, which covers the body of
the tooth; second, the osseous part, or that which is called
bone; third, the dental pulp, a gelatinous substance which fills
the cavity of the tooth.

Enamel of the Teeth.—The enamel of the teeth is a peculiar
substance, semi-transparent, bearing a slight resemblance to
porcelain; its colour in different subjects, and even in the different teeth of the same subject, varies from a milky white-

ness to a brown or yellow. It is smooth and polished, analogous to no other tissue of the system, and so durable that it resists the action of those causes which generally destroy bone. "It envelops the body of the tooth," says Beclard, "and becomes thinner at the neck, where it terminates. Its texture is fibrous; the fibres press against each other, and are directed from the circumference to the centre of the tooth, to which they adhere by their extremities." These fibres are fine, adhering to each other by their lateral surface, and in proportion to their length is the thickness of the enamel.

The enamel of the teeth, with regard to its hardness, can only be compared to blue steel. It is capable of resisting fire, and produces fire when struck with the above named metal.

It varies much in thickness; sometimes it forms the greater part of the crown, at other times is very thin. It is always thickest upon the tubercles or eminences of the teeth. When submitted to the action of fire it will become at first dark, and afterward tarnish, crack, become pliable after having resisted the heat for a longer period than the bone is capable of. When placed very near the fire it splits and drops off. In acid it dissolves into a light and white formless flake. The following is the analysis given by Berzelius of the different portions of the materials which enter into its composition:

Phosphate of lime, ...85.3
Carbonate of lime, ...8.0
Phosphate of magnesia, ...1.5
Membranes, soda and water, ...0.2

In speaking of the analysis of the teeth in general, we gave the analysis of the enamel as obtained by M. Pepys, who differs from Berzelius simply in denying with M. Hatchett the existence of cellular and cartilaginous tissues in this substance. Fourcroy, Vauquelin, and Berzelius are of an opposite opinion; for they have discovered in it a great quantity of these tissues. The enamel contains no vessels, and when once destroyed cannot be reproduced. M. Cuvier, adopting the opinion of Hunter, thinks that this substance is entirely inorganic.

3*

Osseous Part of the Teeth.—This substance is of the form
and nearly the entire size of the tooth, the root of which it
forms exclusively. The neck is the largest part of the bony
substance of the body. It has less tenacity, and is not so brittle
as the enamel, and contains a cavity which occupies the centre
of the crown, and is prolonged, gradually diminishing to the
extremity of the root. The texture of the bone is extremely
dense, and in it there can be discovered neither traces of vessels nor cellular medullary.* This substance is of a yellow

---

* The opinion expressed by the author on this subject is, with scarcely an
exception, now discarded by intelligent writers on dental physiology. "That
the teeth presses vitally," says Thomas Bell, "that they are connected by
their organization with the general system, having nerves, blood vessels, and
absorbents, and are analogous in this respect to other bones, is a truth so
strongly attested by all the phenomena they present, whether in a healthy or
a diseased state, that it is difficult to imagine upon what grounds it can have
been controverted, or even doubted, by any one whose opinions are deduced
from observation or experiment .... I have on purpose, by breaking a
tooth immediately after extraction, when the pain and inflammation had been
severe, found *distinct red patches*, in the *very substance of the bone.*"

"In certain varieties of asphyxia," Dr. H. H. Hayden remarks, "the appearances of the teeth are not only singular, but highly instructive, in a physiological point of view especially. They are almost uniformly tinged red.
If examined immediately after death, they present a deep pink hue; if some
time after, the tint is darker.—The different shades of colour, however, will
generally depend in a great measure upon the age of the person and the
violence of the death: for instance, the bony structure of the teeth of young
persons is far more transparent and vascular than those of persons advanced
in years. These appearances are particularly observable in the teeth of such
as have been drowned, and more especially in those that have been hanged.—
They are, moreover, met with in the teeth of refractory bullocks that have
been forcibly drawn into the slaughter house by means of a rope round the
neck."

"On examining the teeth," continues the same writer, "for the purpose of
ascertaining, if possible, the nature of these appearances, I found, on splitting
them open through the roots, or fangs (which ought to be done from the edge
of the crown, so as not to touch or disturb the vessels of the tooth) the whole
nervous pulp turgid, almost black, and even surrounded with blood. From
this condition of the vessels, one might be led to suppose that the red tint
of the teeth was reflected through the bone. But on removing the nerve, I
found that the *bony substance of the tooth was literally injected with the colouring matter of the blood.* And this so effectually as to render every effort to
return it to its natural whiteness, perfectly ineffectual."

If farther proof were required on this subject, it could be supplied from
the pages of the "American Journal of Dental Science," in which may
be found reports of several cases in point made by Professor Harris and
others.—S.

tinge, and more compact than other bone, which appears to be owing to the great quantity of the phosphate of lime that it contains. The teeth appear to be formed of bony plates encased in each other, and adhering so strongly as to be inseparable; an arrangement not plainly manifested in their roots. When fractured, the teeth have generally a fine aspect. The dental bone withstands the air, but when submitted to the action of acid, its earthy part dissolves, and a compact, dense parenchyma remains, having neither a fibrous nor an areola aspect. When submitted to the action of fire it becomes black, burns, and leaves a hard, pliable, white residue, which is not the case with the enamel when submitted to the same process.

The osseous part of the teeth, submitted to a critical analysis by Berzelius, furnishes the following results:—*

Phosphate of lime, ...	61.95
Fluate of lime, ...	2.10
Phosphate of magnesia, ...	1.05
Carbonate of magnesia, ...	5.30
Soda and chloride of soda,...............	1.40
Cartilage, blood vessels and water, ...	28.00

Dental Pulp.—We discover in the axis of a tooth a cavity which is continuous with the canal of the root, or canals, if there be more than one root. This cavity, which occupies the centre of the tooth, where it is largest, is filled in a fresh state with a soft, grayish substance called the dental pulp. "A species of ganglion," says M. J. Cloquet, "possessing great sensibility, and which is continuous with the vascular and nervous pedicle that enters through the root of the tooth, and which bears some resemblance to a bud. (Pl. IV. Fig. 4.) This pulp, or *pulpous kernel,* of the tooth, is only, according to Beclard and the generality of anatomists, a papilla of the mucous membrane of the mouth, which forms gums and lines the alveoli, and in the bottom of these cavities sends off in that of the ivory a swollen prolongation which entirely fills it.

* The analysis of the teeth is seldom attended with like results; but there is sufficient uniformity to predicate the modes of treatment suggested by a knowledge of their composition. Therefore we deem it unnecessary to exhibit here the minute differences between the above statements and those founded upon the experiments of others.—S.

This papilla is provided with nervous and vascular rami, which distribute themselves particularly upon its surface; and the part that it performs in the mode of development of the teeth is not less important than that which it is destined to fulfil in their nutrition. It has been, from its great sensibility, compared to the gelatinous substance of the labyrinth of the ear. It is indeed by means of the dental pulp that we distinguish the differences of heat and cold.

DEVELOPMENT OF THE TEETH.

The teeth are not formed like other bones of the skeleton in a cartilaginous mould; they are preceded in their development by organs called germs, and those of the deciduous teeth are visible in the fœtus of about two months. (Pl. III. Figs. 6 to 15.) " These germs," says Beclard, " consist of membranous follicles situated under the gums in the groove that commences to present itself along the jaws, where they form by their series two arches, a superior and an inferior, the germ of the cuspidatus excepted, which occupies a place anterior to the arch. But these alveolar arches, continuing to increase, at the epoch of the eruption of the teeth, the cuspidatus is found to be in a line with the rest.

" This follicle, at first very small, but rapidly increasing, is ovoidal, or of the form of an olive. It is buried in the midst of pulpous cellular tissue. By one of its extremities, which is deep-seated, it is connected to a vascular and nervous pedicle: by the other, which is superficial, it is connected to the under part of the gum, and has probably at this part a porous or imperceptible orifice of communication with the surface of that membrane.

" The cavity of the follicle is at first of the same figure as the follicle itself, and occupies its whole extent. It is filled with a colourless limpid fluid, but containing some flakes. Its consistency is mucilaginous, but not viscous." At a more advanced period," the same author continues, " the follicle contains a species of vascular and nervous papilla of the same form, which, issuing from its deep extremity, and vegetating, to use the expression, in its interior, almost entirely fills it.

It nevertheless holds to the adherent extremity of the follicle by a pedicle, and the whole of its remaining surface is free and bathed in liquor. The liquor diminishes in quantity in proportion to the increase of the papilla or dental pulp. The alls of the follicle are formed by a double membrane, the external leaf of which is white, opaque, tenacious, and fibrous, and covers the other, which is very vascular.* The papilla itself is again covered by a part of the internal membrane. The follicle, and the papilla, which fills it in a great measure, increase until the period of *ossification*, and then the summit of the papilla is of the form of the tooth."

The germ of the tooth being thus formed, we soon discover upon the surface of the serous membrane the development of a point of ossification which resembles a small osseous shell. It commences in the incisores and cuspidati in one point, in two distinct points in the bicuspides, and in the molares in four or five, according to the number of tubercles upon their crowns.

Ossification commences upon each dental pulp of the lower jaw a little sooner than upon the corresponding ones of the upper, and almost simultaneously upon corresponding pulps in the same jaw. The hard, or ossific part of the tooth, shows itself at a period between the third and sixth months, the first, which are the incisores, beginning to ossify at about the end of the third and fifth months, and the posterior molares at the end of the sixth.

The following, according to Beclard, is the order in which the teeth commence to ossify: 1, central incisores; 2, lateral incisores; 3, first molares; 4, cuspidati; 5, second molares. This order, however, is not constant, as the anterior molares sometimes take precedence of even the lateral incisores.

---

* A variety of opinions is entertained among physiologists upon this point. "Where the pulp," says J. Hunter, "is very young, as in the fœtus of six or seven months, this membrane itself is pretty thick and gelatinous. We examine it best in a new-born child, and we find it made up of two *lamellæ*, an external and an internal: the external is soft and spongy, without any vessels; the other is much firmer and extremely vascular, its vessels coming from those that are going to the pulp of the tooth."

Dr. Blake, on the contrary, does not admit the vascularity of the internal lamella, but says that the external is "full of vessels."

"In several preparations, which are minutely injected, taken from the human subject, and also from the fœtal calf, I have found both the *lamellæ* to be very vascular."—Fox.

The bony part of the tooth is first formed, and is seen occupying the summit of the dental papilla, and resembling a small cap, single upon the incisores and cuspidati and multiple upon the molares. This little cap, which is the form of the free extremity of the tooth, is the bony larva soon to be covered with enamel. It continues to enlarge until it entirely covers the papilla.

"In teeth in which the papilla is divided, as in the molares," adds Beclard, "the little bony caps increase in size until their borders meet each other, and uniting form one cap having as many eminences as the pulp. It also increases in thickness interiorly; that is to say upon the side next the papilla, which diminishes in proportion to the increased thickness of the cap, a phenomenon that has given rise to the opinion that ossification results from a transformation of the papilla into bone by a calcareous deposition in its tissue. This is altogether contrary to the generally received opinions of modern anatomists, who believe that ossific matter is deposited upon the surface of the pulp, and is not a transformation of its tissue.

As the formation of the ivory of the crown increases, the enamel at first forms upon its surface, and then upon the neck of the tooth. It presents at first a very thin layer, very incomplete, composed of distinct granulations, which afterward unite into a rough, pliable layer, which gradually becomes smooth, increases in thickness, and becomes extremely hard. There are several opinions entertained with regard to the formation of the enamel. Some have supposed that, like the bone, it is deposited by the dental pulp, and that the material of which it is formed traverses the bone and transudes through it; others, and they are the more numerous, regard the enamel as deposited upon the surface of the bone by either the liquor in which the body of the young tooth is bathed, or by the internal membrane of the capsule. We will add, that the bone of the root differs essentially from that of the body of the tooth.

"After the formation of the enamel," says M. J. Cloquet, "the tooth increases interiorly by the addition of new bony layers. Its cavity elongates and contracts as its walls increase in thickness; the root forms itself by gradually encompassing the pedicle of the pulp, which soon finds itself enclosed in a kind of conical tube. When there are to be several roots to the tooth, it insensibly separates at its neck into two, three or four divisions, according to the number of roots that it is destined to have, and it is precisely where these divisions occur that the base of each root is formed which afterward continues to elongate.

MECHANISM OF THE ERUPTION OF THE TEETH.

"As the tooth developes itself upon its pulp by the addition of new layers upon its internal surface," says Beclard, "it lengthens, and the top of its crown rises from the bottom of the alveolus in order to approach the gums. Its summit soon presses against the external membrane of the follicle, which is thus ruptured, as also is the gum to which this adheres. An absorption is now produced which permits the tooth to escape. When the crown has only one point, it makes but a single opening, and the eruption of the tooth is affected by its enlargement: but when it has several points, it forms as many openings as there are tubercles, and there remains between these points a portion of gum which is finally destroyed. (Pl. V. Fig. 4.)

The *dental matrix,* or membranous follicle, continues with the tissue of the gums by a narrow canal, and as the tooth rises this canal is dilated; but contracts in length, until the tooth appears upon the surface of the gums. (Pl. IV. Fig. 1.)

"When the tooth has escaped through the gum, the external membrane of the follicles, which has ceased to cover its crown, continues to envelop the root, as it unites to the walls of the alveolus, forming what is called the *alveolo-dental* periosteum. This is nothing more than the prolongation of the gum, with which it continues to the level of the neck of the tooth."

The eruption of the teeth takes place at two or three principal epochs of life.

The first, is the eruption of the teeth of children, which are twenty in number. It is called *first dentition.* The second eruption, or *second dentition,* consists of twenty-eight teeth, twenty of which replace those of first dentition, and eight make their appearance posterior to the bicuspides; and, finally, the *wisdom teeth* make their appearance.

These different eruptions of the teeth present phenomena too remarkable not to merit particular consideration, which they shall receive when we shall have pointed out the nerves, arteries, and veins which form a part of the dental organs proper, and the numerous anomalies that the teeth present in their number, position, structure, &c. &c.

The nerves of the teeth are branches of the fifth pair, or trigeminus. The superior teeth receive their branches from the second branch (superior maxillary:) this nerve, as is known, before entering the sub-orbital canal, gives off two branches, called the *posterior dentals*. The first, or the *internal*, gives off a twig, which, running into a canal in the wall of the maxillary sinus, communicates with the dental, and the other pierces the substance of the bone to reach the roots of the three molares. The *posterior external dental* is sometimes distributed to these roots, after having pierced their alveoli. This same superior maxillary nerve, after having traversed the sub-orbital canal, gives off, near its external orifice, the *anterior dental* nerve, which, after passing along the groove of the maxillary sinus, communicates with a branch of the posterior dental, and is distributed to the bicuspides, cuspidati, and incisores.

The inferior teeth receive their sensibility from the *inferior maxillary*, the third branch of the trigeminus. After having supplied the neighbouring muscles and the tongue with nervous fillets, this branch penetrates the canal of the inferior jaw, and gives off twigs to all the teeth. Under the first bicuspides, a branch of this nerve escapes outward through the anterior mental foramen, to be distributed to the inferior lip. (Pl. I. Fig. 2.)

The arteries of the teeth follow the course of the nerves. The superior are branches of the alveolo sub-orbital; and the inferior are derived from the internal maxillary. They consequently have their origin from the external carotid. It has been ascertained that the inferior dental artery has three divisions; one, near the inferior border of the bone, appears to be the vessel that nourishes it; the others are distributed to the pulps of the teeth of first and second dentition. (Plate II. Fig. 2,) and (Plate VI. Fig. 2.)

The veins of the teeth follow the course of the arteries. The inferior has its own canal, under that of the artery. (Plate

II. Figs. 1 and 2.)   As to the anomalies that are met with in the teeth of the human subject, they, as well as their varieties are very numerous. (Pl. VIII. Figs. from 1 to 23.)

Varieties of Number.—The circumstances under which, by an unnatural development, more than sixteen teeth are sometimes seen in each jaw, are very rare.   It more frequently happens that this number is incomplete.   Some persons, particularly women, never cut their wisdom teeth.   At other times they have a supernumerary molar, or incisor, but this is still more unfrequent. (Pl. IX. Fig. 9,) and (Plate X. Fig. 1.)

Varities of Form.—The superior incisor teeth are sometimes bent in the form of a bayonet; (Pl. IX. Fig. 10;) and sometimes they have double roots.   At other times teeth are met with of an unnaturally large size, (Pl. VIII. Figs. 3, 20, 22, 23.)

Varieties of Position.—The annals of medicine have furnished us with remarkable examples of this species of anomaly. In fact, teeth have been met with situated transversely in their sockets, others piercing the alveolar border or the palatine arch.   They are sometimes developed in the very substance of the maxillary bone above the palate (Pl. XIII. Fig. 12,) and even in the pharynx.   Albinus speaks of two extremely large and long teeth that were concealed in the bodies of the nasal apophyses of the superior maxillary bones, with their crowns pointing upward and their roots downward.   The anatomical cabinet of the Faculty of Medicine in Paris contains a somewhat similar specimen.   This truly curious and unique case, was furnished by Professor Marjolin.   It is carefully preserved, and displays two supernumerary incisores situated in the substance of the base of the maxillary bone.   The bodies of these two teeth were inverted, and the root of the right central incisor presented the form of a bayonet. (Pl. IX. Figs. 1, 2, 3, 4.)

M. Dentz, dentist to the King of Holland, sent us from Amsterdam several teeth which present very remarkable anomalies. Among these different pathological specimens was a superior jaw, in which the right central incisor pointed toward the wings of the nose. (Pl. IX. Fig. 5.)

Varieties of Structure and Consistency.—These are generally

4

very numerous and nearly always dependent upon morbid
causes.   (Pl. XII. Figs. 16 to 21.)

Uses of the Teeth.—The teeth, in a healthy state, possess a
hardness far greater than other bones of the body; they contribute, each one respectively, to mastication, each class having
its peculiar office in this process; they are necessary in the
operation of perfect digestion; they assist in the articulation of
words; and they are ornamental.   Man possesses the most
beautiful and regularly arranged denture of all animals.

Now that we have terminated our general remarks upon the
teeth, and briefly pointed out their structure, mode of development, mechanism of eruption and use, we shall briefly review
the different phenomena that accompany their emancipation
from the alveoli.

MECHANISM OF THE ERUPTION OF THE TEETH OF FIRST DENTITION.

Although at birth, and some months after, the teeth are not
visible, their formation has commenced some time previously.
(Pl. V. Fig. 1.)

" The germs of the deciduous teeth," says the learned anatomist heretofore quoted, " exist in the fœtus of two months'
gestation.   They commence to ossify about four and a half
months after conception, or the middle of gestation.   Ossification first commences upon the inferior incisores, and then upon
the superior; afterward upon the cuspidati and molares, following the order of their eruption.

" Though the teeth are far advanced at birth, they are
enclosed in their alveoli and covered by the gums.   It is very
rare that any of the teeth have protruded through the gums at
this period; it is generally not until the sixth or eighth month
that they commence to appear.   (Pl. V. Fig. 2.)

Until the fourth month of birth, the jaws, and the compact
tissue which covers them, experience no change; but in proportion as their organization progresses, their changes are more
obvious.   The alveoli are prolonged ; the *bony borders* of which

they are constituted enlarge and keep pace in height with their increasing diameter. The tooth acquiring greater dimensions, can no longer be retained in its socket, and hence rises and perforates the alveolar portion of the membrane, the pulpous tissue which constitutes the gum, and the mucous membrane that covers them." At this epoch, it is vulgarly said that the child *cuts* its *teeth*. The expression is highly improper, as it is always the teeth that cut the gums. "This perforation," says M. J. Cloquet, "is ordinarily effected with difficulty, because that triple layer is gradually thinned as the tooth advances. The tooth having escaped, the membranous tissues continue to unite to each other by their borders adhering together at its neck, and forming a circular pad which adds to its solidity.

The age at which the eruption of the teeth of children begins is variable. Cases are related of children having one or two of their teeth at birth; they sometimes are one or two years old before any of them make their appearance. I had under my care in Bagneres, in 1810, a young girl, aged seven years, whose inferior incisores had never appeared; the space left for them was wide enough for three teeth, and the alveolar border, at this point, was very low and narrow:

The eruption of the teeth of first dentition is gradual, and they generally appear in pairs, a longer or shorter time elapsing between the eruption of each pair. The two inferior central incisores appear first; about two months after the two superior central incisores; then the inferior and superior lateral incisores appear in about an equal space of time. Some months later the inferior, and then the superior cuspidati make their appearance through the gums. It often happens that the cuspidati do not appear until after the first molares, or at the same time with them. Finally, usually from two years and a half to three and a half, we discover the second molares. First dentition is then completed, and the child possesses the twenty teeth of which we have spoken in treating of the teeth in general. (Pl. V. Figs. 2, 3, 4, 5, 6.) It may be concluded from what we have said, that the teeth of first dentition appear in the following order, at the different epochs annexed.

The four central incisores, the inferior appearing first,

		at from 5 to 10 months of age.
The four lateral incisores,	"	9 to 16 " "
The four cuspidati,	"	14 to 23 " "
The four first molares,	"	20 to 31 " "
The four last molares,	"	27 to 40 " "

The above is the order in which teeth of first dentition usually appear, but we repeat that it is liable to variations.

MECHANISM OF THE ERUPTION OF THE TEETH OF REPLACE-MENT, OR SECOND DENTITION.

In second dentition thirty-two permanent teeth appear in the jaws, of which twenty are called teeth of *replacement*, because they replace those that have been shed, and twelve are new.

"The germs of the teeth of the second denture," says M. J. Cloquet, "are visible in the fœtus of three or four months' gestation. Those of the twenty teeth of replacement are placed behind the follicles of first dentition, and the remaining twelve are situated posteriorly in the substance of the jaw."

The germs of both dentures are included in the same cavities of the jaws, before the formation of the walls of the alveoli. When these partitions, at first membranous, commence to ossify, distinct osseous cells are formed for each class of follicles, which are thus formed, occupying separate cavities. The dental vessels nourish both classes of follicles. Dr. Rousseau, who had charge of the anatomical works of the National Historical Museum of Paris, has endeavoured several times to discover the dental follicles of which we speak. This able anatomist has instituted for this purpose the most minute investigations; and although on account of the extreme tenuity of these follicles he was not able to discover them, he nevertheless with M. J. Cloquet, admits their existence.

"The germs of second, like those of the first dentition, adhere to the gums by a full or canaliculated elongation, which is simply the dental canal, or the appendage of the membrane of the follicle. (Pl. IV. Fig. 1.) This canal, in order to reach the gum, passes through a little opening that is seen in the maxillary bone, behind each deciduous tooth, upon the posterior part of the alveolar border. These small openings, are very perceptible at the level of the incisores and cuspidati.

"As the teeth of second dentition advance, those of the first denture become loose, detach themselves or drop out spontaneously, almost entirely deprived of their roots ; but if they are extracted as soon as they become loose, a great portion of their roots will still be found unabsorbed.

When we examine the cause of these phenomena with attention, we observe that the teeth of second dentition are placed below and behind the alveoli of those of the first denture. (Pl. V. Figs. 4, 5, 6.) In advancing, they press against the posterior walls of the alveoli of the deciduous teeth; this pressure at first occasions a thinning of the walls, and afterward the perforation of the osseous partition. The permanent teeth gradually introduce themselves into the alveoli of the deciduous teeth through the opening, and soon cause atrophy of their vessels and absorption of their roots.

The absorption of the partition of the alveoli and of the roots of the perishable teeth, does not appear to be occasioned by the simple pressure exercised by the permanentes. The generality of anatomists admit, with Bourdet, Laforgue, and others, that the absorption is effected by a vascular organ, a kind of absorbent apparel that covers the crown of the teeth of second dentition. It is a species of fleshy bud, or of red vascular membrane, which is placed between the crowns of the permanent and the roots of the deciduous teeth, in such a manner as to prevent their immediate contact.

The following is the order in which the permanent teeth appear through the gums:—

About the seventh year, the first molar appears, at the posterior part of the jaws. (Pl. VI. Fig. 2.) The deciduous teeth commence at the same time to loosen and drop out, generally between the sixth and eighth years, in the order of their eruption. (Pl. VI. Fig. 1.) The incisores and cuspidati of the superior and inferior jaws are successively replaced by teeth similar to themselves. The two molares drop out, and are replaced by the two bicuspides. From about the eleventh to the thirteenth year the second bicuspides appear, one on each

4 *

side, behind the first. From the twelfth to the fourteenth year the second molares appear. The mouth is then provided with twenty-eight teeth.

We have subjoined the following table, by which we can, at a glance, discover the different periods at which the teeth of the second denture make their appearance.

The four first molares, and	} from 6 to 8 years.
The two inferior central incisores,	
The two superior central incisores,	" 7 to 9 "
The four lateral incisores,	" 8 to 10 "
The four first bicuspides,	" 9 to 11 "
The four cuspidati,	" 10 to 12 "
The four second bicuspides,	" 11 to 13 "
The four second molares,	" 12 to 14 "

Hence it is not until the twelfth or fourteenth year that second dentition is completed. Finally, from the eighteenth to the thirtieth year, and sometimes at a later period, the four last molares, commonly called the *wisdom teeth*, make their appearance through the gums. (Pl. VI. Fig. 3.)

These last, as we have seen, do not make their appearance at periods as uniform as the others, but generally between the twenty-third and twenty-fifth years. Very often two only are cut; sometimes only one; and sometimes they are never cut. This often happens among women, and may depend upon the maxillary bones being shorter in them than in men; or it may be occasioned by a mal-position of the tooth. These teeth are not very regular: they present two or three very short roots, united to one another, and permit only half their crowns to be visible. Sometimes they crowd upon the preceding tooth, and at other times are thrown out of the arch. They are often of an unnaturally small size, but sometimes are extremely large; and at times have strange forms. (Pl. VIII. Figs. 2, 3, 23.) M. Dumoutier, Assistant Anatomist in the Medical School of Paris, presented us with a superior jaw, in which there were two wisdom teeth placed the one above the other. (Pl. X. Fig. 1.) Our friend, Dr. Tesse, dentist in Douai, sent us a wisdom tooth of late growth, having two crowns united, and but one small root. (Pl. VIII. Fig. 7.) We will return to this subject of anomalies of the teeth in treating of *irregularities*.

It will be perceived, from what we have said, that there are, for all the teeth, fifty-two germs; twenty for the teeth of the first denture, and thirty-two for those of the second.

"When the process of first dentition is going on, the alveolar arches are but partially developed. The deciduous teeth are at first crowded together; but the branches of the jaws continue to elongate, and at the period of second dentition, as they are much enlarged, these teeth are found remote from each other. The maxillary bones have then increased in depth and diameter; but as the permanent incisores are very large, they generally force the cuspidati out to occupy places anterior to them. The branches of the jaws continuing to increase at a later period and the two bicuspides being smaller than the two molares that preceded them, there is sufficient space for them, and these teeth arrange themselves regularly in the alveolar arches. (Pl. VII. Figs. 4, 5, 9, 10, 14, 15, 22, 23.)

" As the teeth are emancipated from the gums, the space between the two jaws increases and the face requires greater dimensions in its vertical direction. The branches of the maxillary bones are redressed, their angles become more prominent, and the maxillary tuberosity sinks down after the emancipation of the wisdom tooth. (Pl. VI. Fig. 3.)

"When all the teeth have appeared, the two arches form by their reunion a paraboloid figure. The superior is wider than the inferior, which it overlaps when the jaws are approximated. The free border or edge of the dental arch is undulated. It is uniform in the anterior part, which is formed by the incisores and cuspidati; posteriorly it presents two rows of eminences, in consequence of the largeness of the molares and the arrangement of their tubercles. With regard to these eminences the external is sharper than the internal, in the superior jaw. The contrary is the case in the inferior." (J. Cloquet, Anatomy of Man.)

The only appreciable changes that the teeth undergo after their complete formation, are the ossification of the pulp or papilla that fills their cavities, and which, when ossifying, contracts a little; and the gradual wearing down of their crowns.

The teeth, after having been worn down more or less, whether they experienced accidents and vicissitudes or not, often drop out before old age. The dental vessels and nerves finally become obliterated, and the opening of the dental canal closes. The teeth may then be regarded as bodies foreign to the alveoli that contain them. The walls of these cavities contract imperceptibly upon the roots of the teeth and gradually expel them.

When all the teeth have been lost, the inferior jaw no longer retains its position, but naturally approaches the superior, and is carried farther forward and upward, so that the face becomes shorter and the chin more prominent. This gives a peculiar appearance to the physiognomy of old persons. The alveolar border, thus deprived of teeth, undergoes remarkable changes. The bottom of the sockets fill up, their walls approximate, the alveoli finally disappear entirely, and the dental border presents only a flattened surface. (Pl. VI. Fig. 4.) The gums gradually acquire a great degree of firmness, and perform, though with more difficulty, the important functions of the teeth, considered as the principal agents in mastication.

FIRST AND SECOND DENTITION, AND THE MEANS OF PREVENTING EVILS THAT MAY RESULT THEREFROM.

The evils that generally accompany first dentition are very numerous, and it may be truly said that, from the formation of the first rudiment of the dental pulp until the completion of the teeth of first and second dentition, nature is continually at work. Dentition, however, is not a disease, though it often disposes the subject to a number of certain morbid affections; but this operation of nature, remarkable for its process of ossification, is sometimes critical to children. During the first two or three years this operation is wonderful, and the morbid phenomena that then present themselves, are necessarily in proportion to the difficulty that the teeth experienced in rising from their alveoli. Sometimes indeed dentition is so calm and easy, that it is not perceptible. This happens generally among children of strong constitution. At other times, on the contrary, it is very laborious, and is accompanied by maladies that dispel all hope of the recovery of the child.

Among the diseases that present themselves at this period, some appertain to the local efforts of dentition and are precursors of this process. They are salivation, or ptyalism, inflam-

matory swelling and pain in the gums, aphthæ, or certain
inflammations of the lining membrane of the mouth. The
others may be considered as purely sympathetic affections.
They are convulsions, vomiting, diarrhœa, cutaneous eruptions,
&c. &c. After what has been stated, it may be inferred that
the emancipation of the deciduous teeth is more or less serious
according to the extent of the disorders attendant upon it.

The appearance of the deciduous teeth is generally manifested by a slight heat in the gums, a greater flow than usual of the
saliva, and an irritation somewhat painful, that causes the child
to put his finger or any thing that he may happen to have in
his hand, into his mouth. The circular border of the gum
flattens, and the nose is often the seat of a very troublesome
itching sensation, which produces frequent sneezes: alvine de-
jections are more or less abundant, and an increased flow of
urine supervenes. The motions of the child are rapid, and it
manifests great impatience and fretfulness; is agitated during
sleep, and frequently starts with loud and plaintive shrieks.
The part of the gum through which the tooth is about making
its way is swollen, becomes red, smooth, and distended, and
finally becomes white as the tooth approaches its surface. This
species of tumefaction is sometimes circumscribed, but when
several teeth are making their appearance at the same time it
is often extended over the whole jaw. The slightest pressure
upon the gums of the child now creates pain; but the tooth
does not long delay coming forth, and so vanishes all suffering.

Thus far, this is the natural process; but these symptoms,
which present nothing alarming, are not always so favourable.

When dentition is difficult, new derangements are experienced between the fourth and the eighth months, and they
portend the disorders that may accompany them. Digestion is
impaired; the child becomes fretful; his nervous susceptibility is
increased; the milk that is given as his nourishment is readily
thrown up; he is troubled with a serous, yellow, or green
diarrhœa, or an obstinate constipation; the flow of saliva becomes more abundant; the gums are extremely sensitive and
much tumefied; and there is an engorgement of the parotid and
other salivary glands. Sometimes there will be paralysis of
the inferior extremities; convulsions often manifest themselves

successively in several parts of the body. Such symptoms are always serious, and appear to be produced by the darting pains in the nervous fibres of the periosteum and gums. There is frequently fever, agitation, groaning, fright, delirium, &c.; and, if prompt relief is not obtained, it is seldom that the child survives a series of phenomena so alarming. We shall treat more particularly of several of these evils, and although their treatment comes under the province of the medical practicien, we shall point out, in a brief manner, the course that should be pursued under such circumstances.

Salivation, or Ptyalism.—Salivation, which ranks first among the local affections of first dentition, so far from being a symptom that should be feared, is, on the contrary, a natural and very salutary effect of dentition; and, if it becomes injurious, it is only from its length and intensity. As it tends to favour the suppleness and the dilatation of the gums, and to prevent pain and inflammation of these parts, we should endeavour to preserve and excite it whenever it may be suppressed by any cause; for the instant it is suppressed, the sufferings of the child become greater, and sometimes the result has been the engorgement of the sub-maxillary glands. It is proper, in such cases, to use slight frictions upon the gums of the little patient when his sufferings increase: it even appears that this pleases him, since it often is sufficient to prevent his crying, and dispels the troublesome itch created in the gums. These frictions should be made with mucilages of marsh-mallow, or gum Arabic sweetened with honey or sirup. The parts that are painful should be rubbed, either with the finger or a thin piece of marsh-mallow root, or with fine linen soaked in honey. Large figs, cooked in milk, or mashed between the fingers, are also appropriate.

But if friction upon the gums of children be not hurtful to them, it is not so with the pressure sometimes applied to these parts, by means of hard and polished bodies, to facilitate the exit of the teeth, under the erroneous idea that these little bones, in coming through the gums, mechanically pierce them: hence the inconsiderate use of corals, or other hard bodies, that are put into the mouths of children to soften their gums.

They are useless, even though they should not occasion any injurious effects; but the gums are hardened by the irritation thus produced by continued friction: and so far from diminishing, by their use, the evils that we wish to prevent, they only augment them. The parts becoming more irritable, the nervous system participates in the local affection, and many diseases common at this period of life are thus excited.

When the child appears desirous of biting something, if we wish to employ friction, we can substitute for the hard bodies of which we have spoken a crust of bread, root of boiled marsh-mallow, piece of liquorice wrapped in fine linen and dipped into a strong decoction of barley-water, sweetened and aromatised with a few drops of the flowers of orange, or any other liquid. This, by relaxing and softening the tissues of the gums, diminishes the irritation. This mode of friction occasions none of those inconveniences which are ordinarily produced by those composed of harder bodies.

The flow of saliva may still be kept up by keeping the child warm, and moistening his mouth with mucilaginous drinks. It may also be increased by using upon the sides of the mouth fomentations, with decoctions of marsh-mallow.

M. Bollet, an accoucheur, advises, under such circumstances, to place upon the child sleeves of prepared flannel, to be worn from birth to the fourth or fifth year of age. These sleeves, sewed together to a border of the same material, cover the shoulders and reach as far as the fore-arm. We have several times advised the employment of these, and discovered that their efficacy depended entirely upon the quantity of perspiration excited in the parts with which they were in contact. This is a proper means to favour the disgorgement of the salivary glands: it is also for the accomplishment of the same end that we advise warm baths.*

* A writer in the Cyclopedia of Practical Medicine observes: "The injury which the constant use of these sweet and stimulant ingredients must do to the stomach, renders their employment very objectionable.

"The management of infants during teething when the process is going on in a favourable manner, is very simple, and rarely calls for the interference of the physician. The child should be much in the open air, and well exercised, and the bowels kept free. The employment of the cold bath or cold sponging daily, followed by gentle friction over the surface of the body, is

Inflammatory Swelling and Pain in the Glands.—The tissue of the gums at the period of dentition is often very tender, of a livid red, or nearly violet colour, dry, shining and very painful to the touch.   These swellings are then accompanied with redness and burning heat of the cheeks, tumefaction of the face, and great thirst.   The child is also affected with drowsiness, and is interrupted in its sleep by agitated movements and repeated cries.—Fever supervenes, which is continued or intermittent, and which has received the name of *fever of dentition.*

Although this phlogosis of the gums is considered only a local affection, it is nevertheless true that the digestive organs generally sympathize with it.   In fact, in a very short time, the general health becomes sensibly impaired; and if we have not recourse to proper treatment, the little patient may be exposed to great danger; as that which was considered only a local affection soon becomes a constitutional disease very difficult to cure.

Under such circumstances, it is proper to administer soothing lotions to the child, or to the nurse, if the child has not been weaned.   If these prove insufficient to keep the bowels open, we should have recourse to clysters and laxative drinks, such as whey, water sweetened with honey, decoction of prunes, &c.   We should also persist in the use of derivatives, which will diminish the cerebral congestion and prevent convulsions or drowsiness.   Pediluviums, simple or compound, and cataplasms, emollient or slightly stimulating, placed upon the inferior extremities, and, above all, the application of two or three leeches behind the ears, according to the age of the child, are the means that are highly useful under such circumstances. If the painful swelling of the face does not diminish, and if the part continues red and distended, and has the appearance of being elevated by the crown of the tooth, it is then expedient to have recourse to incision of the gums.   The pain and ge-

very useful; and all means should be taken to support the tone of the system at a just medium.   The breast should be given to it often, but not long at a time, and thus the attendant thirst will be quenched and the gums kept moist and relaxed, and their irritation soothed, without the stomach being overloaded.   The health and diet of the nurse should at this period be particularly attended to, and all stimulant food and drinks avoided."—S.

neral swelling, after this operation, is often known to disappear as if by enchantment. In some cases, however, it contributes to augment the nervous symptoms, by the irritation which it produces in the parts, the sensibility of which has already been very much increased by the efforts of dentition.

This operation, so useful in many cases, should not, as is often the case, be practised without judgment, lest the dental capsule be opened before the tooth has sufficiently advanced in ossification. It is absolutely useless during the eruption of the incisores, but very proper when the molares are about making their appearance through the gums; as these teeth, on account of their tubercles, and the size of their crowns, meet with more resistance from the tissue of the gums. When the tooth is nearly through, and the gums are distended so as to assume a white colour, the operation may be performed without any inconvenience, since it assists the tooth in surmounting the resistance of the soft parts that surround it.

This operation is performed with a very small lancet blade, a little curved, mounted and fixed with a spring upon a steel shank, and adapted to a handle, (Pl. XIV. Fig. 4,) or with a flat hook having two cutting sides. An assistant holds the head of the child; his mouth is kept open with the left hand of the operator, who with his right introduces the first mentioned instrument between the cheeks and gums; he plunges it horizontally in the external side of the gum, and describing a semicircle, elevates the flap of gum that may prevent the eruption of the tooth. The flat hook which we mentioned, is so constructed as to be introduced into the mouth without any fear of injuring the child. This instrument may serve to cut away a portion of the gum.*

* The operation of lancing the gums in dentition is one that cannot be too strongly recommended; its beneficial effects are observed after all other means have failed. "There exists much causeless opposition to this practice, and the objections of its opponents, though they have been shown to be groundless, are again and again reiterated, and, to one unacquainted with the subject, not without some seeming plausibility."

"By some it is objected, that, though the opening of the gum may afford temporary relief, yet the cicatrix, formed by the healing of the wound, forms a greater obstacle to the exit of the tooth, than the parts, when left to themselves, ever do. Now, any one who is at all conversant with the subject, knows, that in four cases out of five, where the operation is necessary, the

5

This mode of operating is preferable to the longitudinal incision, which is very painful, and requires frequent repetition.

We shall now point out the means necessary to subdue the principal sympathetic disorders which depend upon first dentition.

Convulsions.—Some children, during dentition, are almost constantly affected with spasms, which are preceded by a sort of general irritation and frequent tremours of the limbs. The pain becoming more intense, produces slight convulsions, which, in very nervous children, may be repeated, prolonged, and become so violent, as to produce death. Children most subject to these nervous affections, are usually thin, of feeble, excitable, or sickly parents. Fat, fresh, rosy, strong, and vigorous children, are also liable to convulsions; and it is observed that this happens most frequently during the erruption of the molares.

These convulsions may be more or less extended; sometimes they are confined to the muscles of the eyes and face; at other times they extend to the superior, but rarely to the inferior extremities. Sometimes they are transient, and the child quickly recovers the use of his limbs; and again the paroxysm may be prolonged for a considerable period.

teeth are so far advanced, that on the collapsing of the edges of the wound, their crowns immediately protrude: and even when the wound does unite, the soft and spongy cicatrix much more readily yields to the action of the absorbents, than the unpunctured gum ever would have done.''

"Another objection is founded upon a supposition that the enamel, at this period, is in a soft and amorphous state, and that, consequently, the teeth may be injured by contact with the knife. But as the parts of the enamel that are exposed to the instrument usually attain their hardness before this operation is required, this objection is without foundation. In short, I have never known any injury to result from it, either in my own practice, or in that of others; nor can those that are opposed to it bring facts to support their opposition.

"This practice often succeeds after all others have failed. I have frequently known children, after having suffered the greatest agony for days and weeks, until they were reduced to mere skeletons, to obtain immediate relief without the aid of any other remedy than this, which at once removes the cause; whereas, the others only counteract the effects of suffering, and can, therefore, only be considered as palliatives, that may assist nature in her struggle with disease, but cannot always prevent her from sinking in the contest.'' (*Professor C. A. Harris' Dental Art.*)—S.

In other respects the treatment of the sympathetic convulsions of dentition differs but little from that applicable to convulsions from other causes, and should be treated according to the state of the child's system; but generally they terminate the instant the teeth appear through the gums. During the paroxysm, we should make use of such remedies as have a direct influence over it. Thus we should give the child fresh air, put salt into its mouth, apply cold water to its face and forehead, and immerse its hands or feet in water warmed or slightly stimulating.

When there is fever, and manifest symptoms of plethora, a leech should be applied behind each ear, or at the angles of the jaws. As regards anti-spasmodics, such as the water of the flowers of orange, ether, camphor, opium, &c., they are all useful for children of feeble constitution.

We shall say but a few words upon the popular use of collars of amber, the grains of pæony, the root of valerian, the heads of vipers, or any similar charms accredited by the ignorant and credulous. These are incapable of injury, and as their employment may, under such circumstances, calm the restless imagination of some mothers, their use may be allowed without inconvenience.

Diarrhœa, accompanied by Vomiting.—We cannot pay too much attention to the vomiting and diarrhœa that take place during dentition; they are sometimes the precursors of serious diseases of the brain and abdominal organs. " Diarrhœa occurs sometimes alone; but oftener vomiting accompanies it or promptly succeeds it in such manner, that in most cases the one may be regarded as only the first stage of the other."— (*Guersent, Dict. de Med.*) These two principal symptoms united, constitute a particular disease, which is especially observable among children, from the third or fourth month until the end of first dentition, and, which is much more frequent during the emancipation of the cuspidati, bicuspides and molares. It is met with in every class of society; and is believed to be more prevalent among infants who have been weaned very early, or whose regimen has been badly directed.

In the first stage of this disease the diarrhœa is extremely abundant, serous, yellow, or oftener greenish. It is sometimes inodorous, at other times it is fetid; the abdomen is distended, round and sonorous, and the child is sad, dejected, and fretful. The preceding symptoms are accompanied by vomiting, at first serous and transparent, and afterwards greenish, which is nearly always preceded by a slight dry cough. At this period the eyes are encircled, sunken, and somewhat dimmed, and have a heavy appearance; the febrile exacerbations, more or less observable, are irregular; the green vomiting and intestinal evacuations become still more abundant at this stage of the disease, and afterward diminish. As the disease progresses, the debility and emaciation become great, and the child dies of convulsions, preserving nearly always its consciousness to the last moment of its existence.

"The course of the disease sometimes varies: the intervals between the vomitings are often long, which is a favourable sign. In some cases the diarrhœa precedes the vomiting several days, or even a week; at other times, the vomiting and diarrhœa supervene nearly at the same time, and the child perishes in the course of three or four days."—(Guersent.)

In the first stage of this affection, the longest duration of which is from thirty to forty days, light diet, soothing and mucilaginous drinks, injections, fomentations, and emollient cataplasms, will be sufficient to arrest the violence of the symptoms: the same mode of treatment is employed with advantage in the second stage, by combining with them baths, opiate injections, and also emollient vapours to the abdomen, or application of laudanum to the same part. In serious cases, that is, when there exists manifest prostration of the vital energies, it is necessary to use sinapisms and blisters upon the extremities, nape of the neck, and even upon the abdomen if the alarming symptoms are not promptly alleviated.

Constipation.—Constipation is a very serious symptom during dentition. New and serous milk of a healthy nurse is at first the best remedy. Tepid baths answer a good purpose, when there is heat in the primæ viæ; and we may, without inconvenience, excite evacuations with mild purgatives, such as an infusion of one drachm of senna in the juice of prunes sweetened with sugar or honey.

If there is painful tension of the abdomen, or constipation, soothing injections are indicated, and also emollient fomentations to the part.

Cutaneous eruptions that occur during dentition require no particular treatment; they disappear on the protrusion of the tooth through the gums; these eruptions consist of little scaly tetters that have their seat upon the face or behind the ears. We, however, should not confound them with erysipelatous erythema, and which is nearly always the result of the bad management of the child by its nurse.

SECOND DENTITION, AND THE EVILS THAT ACCOMPANY IT.

The evils that present themselves during the second, are not so serious as those that accompany the first, dentition. As to the sympathetic affections to which children are mostly disposed at the epoch of second dentition, which comprises the removal of the twenty deciduous teeth, their replacement by the permanent, and, according to our division, the eruption of the four molares, are congestions, nasal hemorrhages, a mucous and sometimes sanguineous ptyalism, engorgement of the glands, diseases of the eyes and ears, scaly eruptions, and farinaceous tetters of the face, which disappear as promptly as they appear; but they at this period do not experience catarrh, and inflammatory serous diarrhœa.

The molting of the temporary teeth, which precede second dentition, scarcely ever occasions any sensible disturbance in the economy. It has, however, been noticed that this secondary process appears to favour the development of scrofula and rachitis, and, it is rare that it is not accompanied by local or general evils, which are always proportioned to the temperament, strength, or feebleness of the child.

In proportion as the teeth of second dentition are developed, the roots of the deciduous teeth, and often the interior of their crowns, are found to be destroyed; and, as there is no trace of

5*

the roots left, it is presumed that they are gradually decomposed, and, assuming a fluid consistency, are afterward taken into the general circulation.   The absorption of the temporary roots is a curious process in the development of second dentition.   It sometimes commences at the point, and progresses to the neck of the tooth, which, becoming loose, falls out, or may be easily taken from its socket, to which it is very slightly attached, since, in most cases, the fingers are sufficient for its extraction.

There are circumstances under which nature deviates from her usual course.   These are, for example, when the roots of the temporaries, not having been destroyed, the permanentes are turned from their natural situations.   This occasions irregularities in the dental arch, which it would always be easy to avoid if the injudicious tenderness of parents did not cause the operation to be too long delayed; being in hopes, from day to day, that the tooth will drop out, they thus allow the permanent tooth to deviate from its place in such manner that it is difficult to replace it.   In such a case, we should explain to the parents of the child that there is no danger, and by means of a simple operation, timely performed, serious consequences will be prevented.   We should then extract the temporary teeth, one after another, to bring the permanentes into their proper places.

This operation is not only necessary in order to prevent evils that may arise without it, but in some measure becomes indispensable to obtain a regular arrangement of the permanent teeth, which may always be accomplished by care being taken to make sufficient room for their convenient arrangement.   As some children loose their teeth sooner than others, frequent examinations of their mouths should be made; and when the temporary teeth commence to be loosened, we should still continue our examinations; for no period of life demands more attention than that of the replacement of the deciduous teeth.

THE EVILS THAT ACCOMPANY THE ERUPTION OF THE THIRD
MOLAR TEETH.

Adults are sometimes not more exempted than children from
the serious evils of dentition. These often manifest themselves during the eruption of the third molares or *wisdom
teeth:* evils which more particularly happen when the other
teeth are very close, as there is but little space between the
coronoid apophysis and the second molar.

It often happens that these teeth are cut without the consciousness of the patient; but it is not always the case, and their
eruption sometimes produces evils more or less serious. These
appear to depend upon the thickness of the osseous substance,
through which the teeth have to pass. With some persons
the pain is very acute, and frequently continues for several
weeks, and sometimes for two or three years, as the tooth is
making its entire appearance. Fluxions also supervene, followed by suppuration of the gums; and the contraction of the
muscles of the part is such, that it is painful for the patient to
open his mouth.

Some persons, during the eruption of the third molar, are
affected with continued or irregular intermittent fever, with
nervous symptoms about the breast or head.

These fevers, after having resisted all remedies, generally
disappear, and also most of the nervous symptoms, on the
eruption of the teeth, which may be assisted by removing
the portion of the gum that covers them. This operation,
practised in time, immediately dispels the spasms, or the acute
pains, the causes of which the patient did not suspect. To
remove the portion of the gum that covers the decayed tooth
we make use of the instrument, (as in Plate XIV. Fig. 4.)

If the mouth has been contracted so that it cannot be opened
sufficiently wide, we should apply leeches behind the ears,
prescribe pediluviums and an application of cataplasms with
flaxseed and a decoction of poppy heads. If it be possible for
the patient to open his mouth a little, we should introduce in
it a small quantity of barley-water, or a large fig.

Under other circumstances, though the tooth has sufficiently appeared through the gum, we should not on that account hesitate to extract it, to remedy this evil, because its presence restrains the movements of the opposite jaw. If, however, it cannot be extracted, and there is urgent necessity for its removal, by taking away the anterior tooth we will alleviate the pain, and the remaining tooth will come into the place of the one that has been extracted.

DENTAL PATHOLOGY.

HAVING spoken of the different diseases which manifest themselves at the period of the eruption of the teeth, we shall now occupy ourselves with the examination of the diseases of the dental organs, proper; and, to proceed methodically in the classification of their various affections, we will divide them, according to Professor Marjolin, into three principal sections. Thus, in the first, we shall speak especially of the anomalies that they present in their *arrangement,* and vices of *form* of the *dental arches,* having made known the different anomalies that they present in their number and situation. We will examine in the second section the diseases proper to their *substance:* and, in the third, the different affections of the parts adjacent to them.

SECTION I.

ARRANGEMENT OF THE TEETH.

"The arrangement of the teeth," says M. Marjolin, "may present several kinds of irregularities. Some depend solely upon the mal-direction of the teeth, and others are the effect of an unnatural size of the dental arch."

The first of these irregularities is called *obliquity of the teeth,* and may be anterior, posterior, lateral or rotary. The deciduous teeth scarcely ever present a mal-arrangement, and among the permanentes the anterior teeth are more prone to it than the posterior. Several causes produce obliquity of the permanent teeth; such as, for example, a disproportion between their size and the space which they should occupy. (Pl. XI.

Fig. 1;) the protracted molting of some of the deciduous teeth; the presence of any tooth, that diminishes the space which should be filled by the new tooth; the existence of a supernumerary tooth; and organic diseases of the alveolar ridge. This evil is often announced by the setting on edge or the loosening of an adjoining deciduous or permanent tooth, and the obliquity of a tooth is often occasioned by the position of other teeth. The dental arch sometimes becomes deformed, and, under certain circumstances, lesions of the tongue and cheek are the result.

The following is the manner by which this vice of dental conformation may be remedied.

When at the commencement of second dentition, there is manifested, anterior or posterior to the inferior or superior cuspidati, a prominence indicating the presence of the permanent tooth, the deciduous cuspidati should be extracted, whether loose or not,* and others must be extracted as soon as those of replacement appear. If the extraction of two, three, or four temporary teeth should not afford sufficient room for the same number of permanentes, we should not be too hasty in removing the next temporary tooth for fear of allowing too much space to the permanent tooth, which would encroach upon the place that should be occupied by the next tooth of replacement. The dentist should attentively inspect the eruption of the second teeth, and not extract the deciduous unless he is assured that those of replacement will only have the necessary space for their good arrangement. When the inferior and superior incisores, and also the cuspidati, or the first bicuspides, are entirely through the gums, we should examine if the jaw be sufficiently developed to contain the teeth so as not to be crowded together. If it be not well developed, we should extract the first bicuspides,† and the teeth, then standing sufficiently apart, will not occasion the decay of each other, but will assume positions adapted to them.

---

* It frequently occurs that the growth of the permanent incisores is more rapid than the destruction of the roots of the temporary teeth, and that the former emerge through the gums behind the latter. In such cases the temporary incisores should also be extracted.

† The second bicuspides are the teeth proper to be sacrificed if the irregularity be slight, as the absence of these teeth cannot so easily be perceived.

But, in case of obliquity of divergence, we should be cautious in extracting the adjoining tooth, since this unseasonable extraction would make the deviation greater and the separation of the teeth more extensive.

The incisores and the cuspidati frequently assume an oblique position. There are dentists who pay so little regard to the symmetry of the mouth, that they do not hesitate to sacrifice a superior or inferior lateral incisor in order to allow sufficient place for the adjoining teeth to arrange themselves properly, either by the efforts of nature, or by the use of ligatures. It would be better to extract in the first instance the two first bicuspides, or only one, according to the exigency of the case, and then place a ligature of raw silk of the proper size around the cuspidatus and attach it to the first molar. The ligature should be renewed daily; and in about two or three weeks the cuspidatus will have occupied the place of the tooth that had been extracted.*

* "The most frequent kind of irregularity, resulting from a narrowness of the jaws, is the projection of the cuspidati. These teeth, with the exception of the second and third molares, are the last of those of the second denture that are cut, and are consequently more liable to be thrown out of the arch than any of the others, especially when it is so much contracted as to be almost entirely filled before they make their appearance. The common practice, in cases of this kind, is to remove the cuspidati. But as these teeth contribute more than any others, except the incisores, to the beauty of the mouth, and can, in almost every case, be brought to their proper places, the practice should certainly be discarded.

"Therefore, instead of removing these teeth, room should be made for them by extracting the two bicuspides. Much judgment, however, is requisite to determine which class of these teeth to remove. If between the first bicuspides and the lateral incisores, there be spaces of one-half the width of the cuspidati, the second bicuspid should be extracted instead of the first; but if there be no such spaces, the first should be drawn; for although these might be carried far enough back, after the removal of the second, to admit the crowns of the cuspidati between them and the lateral incisores, yet still there would not be a perfect harmony of arrangement, for the fangs of these teeth would still cross each other; so that those of the bicuspides would be found deeply seated in the arch while those of the cuspidati would be thrown forward so much, that they would occasion considerable prominences in the gums that cover their alveoli; which, in consequence, would be gradually absorbed, and thus the teeth would be loosened and caused to drop out."

In addition to the foregoing recommendation, which is extracted from Dr. C. A. Harris' "Dental Art," we would advise the correction of the irregular growth of the incisores by means of the extraction of the bicuspides also, pos-

We should be very careful in attaching the second bicuspid to the cuspidatus alone; this latter tooth having the stronger root, the former will be drawn toward it, and the object of the operator will be defeated. When the cuspidatus has been regulated we must bring the lateral incisor into its proper position by the same method. The space between the tooth now to be removed and that to which the ligature is to be attached for this purpose is wider by the distance of a tooth, and thus advantage will be had from the greater contractility of the ligature. The dentist who reasons on this will know the method by which teeth that overlap each other can be brought into their natural position.

The last operation of the kind that came under our practice, was performed upon the young Canaris, the son of the intrepid Greek mariner of that name. This boy, aged nine years, had his right central incisor overlapping more than one-half of the left, and the lateral of the same side equally overlapped the central. We extracted the deciduous cuspidatus, and after placing a ligature around the second molar and lateral incisor, the latter was brought into the desired position, and we had only to place a similar ligature around the central incisor and the second molar, and in five days after, it no longer overlapped its neighbour. We continued ligatures for three months, being careful to renew them frequently, in order to retain the teeth in their proper positions.

When a tooth protrudes from its socket beyond the level of the rest, we employ the ligature to restrain it, by passing it first around the tooth, then over its crown, and finally attaching it around the neighbouring teeth in such manner as to produce vertical pressure upon the affected tooth. (Pl. XI. Fig. 7.*) The tension of the cord, thus continued, presses the tooth so as to force it into the place that we wish it to occupy; and

terior or anterior, according to the exigency of the case. When this is done, however, the application of ligatures becomes necessary, to be applied first upon the cuspidati, and after upon the mal-directed tooth.

* The object cannot be attained in the manner recommended by our author. No means can produce the effect desired that do not possess power at least equal to the pressure of antagonizing teeth against each other. We believe the best advised remedy to be the reducing of the length of the mal-directed tooth by means of filing, and its restoration to its place by means of force applied laterally.

this object being effected, we permit the ligature to remain upon it for a few months simply to keep the tooth in its new position. It often happens that these ligatures slide under the gums, which, becoming considerably inflamed, recede from the neck of the teeth and cause them to become loose. We remedy this inconvenience by the application of a hook upon those teeth which the ligatures are most liable to denude in this way.

This species of hook has two curves: one is to be applied upon the crown or cutting edge of the tooth; the other reaches very near the neck of the tooth, and is fixed so as to prevent the ligature from slipping nearer than it is desired toward the gums. By means of this little fixture, the ligature then answers better than if its whole pressure was directed upon the root (Pl. XI. Figs. 3 to 6.) We advise, whenever it is possible, the placing of the ligature upon the molares, because these teeth are better capable of retaining it than the cuspidati which have the form of an inverted cone.

We shall not now speak of partial luxation of the teeth, as a means of replacing them in a more suitable position: this procedure is not always without danger. We will mention, however, that we have greater hopes of success from this operation when performed a short time after the eruption of the deviated teeth, and in a period little more advanced in life, that is to say, from eight to fourteen years. In fine, whenever the obliquity of the teeth cannot be remedied, we should, as far as possible, correct the bad effects that may result from its presence. Hence, we may extract those that are too much deformed, or which injure the tongue, the cheeks or lips. We may even without inconvenience, excise the crowns of some of these teeth, if they cannot be extracted. *

The mal-directions that the dental arches may present are, *prominence, recession,* and *inversion.*

Prominence scarcely ever exists except where the jaws are too narrow to allow of a proper arrangement of the teeth. In such a case, the dental arches are very oblique, and projected

* We would here state that luxation and excision are means that should never be resorted to. No enlightened practicien of the present day will tolerate such practices. We will have occasion in the second part of this work to speak more at large upon this subject.—S.

6

anteriorly; they appear very long, and sometimes seem to follow the direction of the teeth. (*Marjolin.*) The central incisores are then projected so far forward and are so crowded together, that the mouth has more resemblance to that of a beast than to that of a human being.

This mal-disposition of the teeth, of which examples are found among some nations, is sometimes hereditary; but its progress may be arrested by following the procedure which we have proposed; that is, by being particular to extract the first right and left bicuspides, and by the application of ligatures so as to draw the cuspidati into the place previously occupied by the bicuspides. The four incisores afterwards yield of themselves, and the jaw gradually assumes a more agreeable form. The different metallic plates that are recommended for the correction of this evil, rarely produce favourable results; even metallic ligatures are not in such cases as valuable as the silken ones, which are more flexible and more easily adapted. We prefer raw silk or hemp ligatures; and when the teeth are brought to the place we wish them to occupy, we maintain them in that position, by means of a thread of aloes which is soaked for half an hour in hot water. This thread, one of the best ligatures that a dentist can use, distends itself, and in this manner we can employ it without fear of forcing the tooth to take a different direction from that which is desired.

There are cases in which we cannot employ ligatures to bring the teeth into the places that they should have at first occupied; for example, an individual twenty or thirty years of age, who has one or more teeth situated behind the alveolar arch. The dentist, in the first place, should ascertain if the spaces between the teeth on the right and left of the mal-placed organ are sufficient to admit of these last being easily brought into proper position. Should it not be the case, he will file, as low down as the root, each one of them upon the lateral surface, and facing that tooth which he will afterward luxate from behind forward, to bring it into the circle of the neighbouring teeth.[*]

---

[*] The period of life most congenial to the correction of irregularities of the teeth is the fourteenth year. The alveolus is at this age pliant, and, if it be impaired by the removal of the tooth, reparation is soon made by an osseous deposite, and the tooth itself is more readily made to assume the

The key, or other instrument, in skilful hands, suffices to perform the operation and to effect a good result; but we also perceive that this luxation should be done slowly, and that the tooth should be released as soon as it is upon a level with the others. The tooth, being properly placed, very often remains in its new position without the assistance of ligatures. These should, however, be employed when they appear necessary.

The dentist, who has sufficient command over his movements, will perform this operation with confidence, and will always succeed. A few weeks suffice for the alveolar border that has been forced from the tooth to approach it, and become as solid as it was previous to the operation. We have often had occasion to practise this operation in the several schools to which we are attached as dentist.

" *Recession* is," continues M. Marjolin, " a vice of conformation opposite to the preceding. The anterior teeth are obliquely inward: it occasions deformity, difficulty of pronunciation, premature wearing away of the anterior parts of the teeth, and sometimes even ulceration of the inferior gums, rubbed by the contact of the superior teeth. This requires the filing, more or less, of the cutting edge of the teeth that cause the deformity.

Inversion of the Dental Arches.—When the superior teeth shut within the circle of the inferior, and if even their tubercles are not regularly adapted, they are said to be inverted.

desired position. If this operation be attempted at a period so late as is recommended by our author, the chances of success will be unfavourable.

In relation to the use of the file in those cases Mr. Bell observes: " If the irregularity be very slight, and the want of space trifling, it will be sufficient to pass a very thin file between several of the teeth, so as not to deprive any of them of the whole thickness of the enamel, and in this way considerable space will be gained by the approximation of all the teeth so treated, and the irregular tooth be brought into its place by moderate pressure; but if the want of space be so great as to afford no hope of its being remedied by this mode, it often becomes necessary to sacrifice one of the permanent teeth."

Professor C. A. Harris, in his lectures, repudiates the use of the file in these cases, as the contact of the filed surfaces of the teeth, affording lodgment for extraneous matter, would hasten their decay. We cannot but regard this as a valid objection, and would at least advise much circumspection to be exercised by those who would persist in the mode above recommended.—S.

The anterior parts of the superior teeth are thus often worn away, while in the natural state the contrary occurs. This want of regularity in the teeth, which we will call *menton de vieillard*, (old man's chin,) and not *jimber-jaw*, (Pl. XI. Fig. 8, and Pl. IV. Fig. 9,) may be remedied, particularly in children. Whenever the superior incisores and cuspidati alone shut behind the inferiors, we may bring them forward by means of an *inclined plane*, invented by M. Catalan in 1808. This instrument consists of a metallic plate attached to the inferior teeth, which projects some lines, and which is inclined in such a manner as to push forward the corresponding superior teeth. We cannot but admire a process so ingenious. In able hands it possesses great advantages; and whenever it can be properly applied, from ten to twenty days are sufficient to establish the teeth in their proper places. We have observed, that, to put this in execution, we should wait at least until the four lateral incisores have entirely come through the gums, in order to offer a sufficient hold to the plate that is to be attached to them.

Our method consists in applying a sufficiently large ligature to the two inferior central incisores in such manner that the tension of the ligature may force them back. When these two are replaced we are in like manner to replace the other two incisores; (Pl. XI. Fig. 8,) but if we wish to regulate the cuspidati, and the inferior alveolar border be more developed than the superior, it is necessary, previously, to extract the two first inferior bicuspides, first, to allow the preceding teeth the facility of taking the desired direction, and secondly, not to prevent the lateral incisores from taking their proper situation. There is no need of employing any thing to prevent the jaws from closing, as the pressure exercised by the ligatures is sufficient to prevent the inferior jaw from pressing against the superior.

The dental arches, it will be perceived, themselves form a part of the irregularities of which we treat, as, also, do *supernumerary* teeth. These, as their name indicates, are not a portion of the regular complement: they are larger and differ very much in their form from the other teeth, which is always relative to the position they occupy in the mouth. We have seen them in the superior jaw only. They are generally situated between the two central incisores, (Pl. IX. Fig. 9,) the cuspidati, the first or second bicuspides; sometimes above or at the sides of the molares, below the soft palate, and behind the central incisores, the lateral incisores, the cuspidati, or the first bicuspides. Those that are placed between the central incisores have their crowns rounded and pointed, and the root equally round. (Pl. VIII. Fig. 16.) Generally, these teeth are not more than two-thirds of the size of the laterals. We have extracted some that were nearly as large as the cuspidati. (Pl. VIII. Fig. 6.) The supernumerary teeth that are situated between the cuspidati, and between or at the sides of the bicuspides, have the same form as these teeth, but they are smaller; and those that are sometimes found near the third molar bear greater disproportion to these.

The supernumerary teeth, situated behind the central incisores, generally come in pairs; they are nearly as large as those teeth. The root has a peculiar curve, and the crown has the shape of a double crown. (Pl. VIII. Figs. 6 and 11.) As to those that are placed behind the laterals or cuspidati, they are nearly as strong as these last, and present as a particular characteristic upon their root and upon their crown, three faces well developed, which terminate in a single point.

SECTION II.

DISEASES OF THE DENTAL SUBSTANCE.

Among the various diseases that affect the dental organs, some attack the hard structure, others involve the soft. Thus, we find in the first series, *denudation, fracture, atrophy, decomposition of the enamel, discoloration, caries of the teeth, destruction of the roots,* and even their *exostosis.* The second series presents *inflammation of the dental pulp,* its *fungosity,* its *ossification,* and the different *dental neuroses.* The third includes the diseases of the teeth relative to their connexions, *loosening, luxation, denudation of the roots, concretions* which are formed

6*

upon the teeth, &c. We will also arrange in this series *odontalgia,* or *tooth-ache.*

As we have already well established our principal divisions, we shall now give in detail the particulars of each disease.

Denudation of the Teeth.—Although the teeth, in their natural structure, are much stronger and more compact than any of the other bones of the human body, they present a number of circumstances during life which contribute to produce denudation; such, for example, as their bad organization; chemical influence from certain aliments; their friction during mastication (Pl. XIII. Figs. 3, 4;) the use of dentifrices that are not sufficiently pulverized, those composed of acids, stiff brushes (Pl. XIII. Fig. 5;) the use of pipes made of clay (Pl. XIII. Fig. 6;) the habit of chewing on one side; the action of cracking substances with the teeth capable of breaking the enamel (Pl. XIII. Fig. 2;) gnashing the teeth during convulsive affections of the muscles of the jaws, &c. There are some persons who, during sleep, experience habitual convulsive movements, which occasion friction of the teeth, and produce very soon a wearing down of their substances.*

This organic lesion, in which the dental substance is more or less destroyed, takes place in the teeth of most animals; it is attendant upon age, and manifests itself in all individuals. "It is," says M. Duval, "partial or total, vertical or horizontal; it occasions a change of volume and form of the teeth, which

---

* Of denudation of the teeth, J. Hunter observes: "From its attacking certain teeth rather than others, in the same head, and a particular part of the tooth, I suspect it to be an original disease of the tooth itself, and not to depend on accident, way of life, constitution, or any particular management of the tooth."

"That Mr. Hunter has mistaken the cause of this denuding process," says Dr. E. Parmly, "is evident from the following fact, which seems to indicate that this disease results from the condition of the fluids of the mouth. I have seen many examples in which artificial human teeth have suffered this denuding process exactly in the same manner as the original teeth in the same mouth. But the following instance seems to settle the question beyond all doubt. A gentleman who had lost his teeth, partly from this cause, came to us about four years ago from a considerable distance, to procure artificial substitutes. A set of human teeth of the best quality were accordingly provided, which, in the course of three years and a half, on his return to us, were found to be grooved from the surface to the central cavity."—S

are not then easily recognised." We will add, that several particular circumstances may diversify this mode of denudation; and it has been noticed that the incisores are worn away much more promptly in the absence of the molares; but these last are frequently thus affected. The part of the tooth that has been denuded is never reproduced; but in proportion as the crowns wear away, there appears to be a process of ossification going on in the dental cavity, which does not always prevent these teeth from becoming sensitive by the contact of cold, heat, or acids. The denuded part is never the subject of disease unless it contains a cavity.

By an examination of the interior of denuded teeth, M. Rousseau, whom we have several times quoted in the course of this work, discovered not only the same variety of colours as in the grinding surface, but, moreover, a new ossified substance, that formed and increased at the part worn away, and which he called *osselet* (small bone.) (Pl. X. Fig. 4.) This substance, yellower than the other parts of the teeth, is, like them, transparent and brittle; it does not form a regular structure, detaches itself from the dental cavity, by separating all at once from it; and the sides that correspond to this cavity are much more sensitive than its internal surface.

In endeavouring to remedy the inconveniences that result from denudation of the teeth, we are governed by the cause that produces the affection. If, for example, a tooth become denuded by friction with its antagonist in the opposite jaw; or if it press upon such as may be diseased, or even if the different forms of the tooth occasioned by denudation produce deformities that injure the adjacent soft parts, we should cut it away with the file. Supposing that badly prepared dentifrices have occasioned the evil, we should suspend their use. When the tooth is very much denuded, or has become very painful, we must expose, with a drill, the cavity resulting from that alteration; and afterward destroy the nerve with a hot iron,*

---

* It will be perceived that the actual cautery is a favourite remedy with our author. It has indeed been popular, and good effects have often resulted from its use; but still, as it is productive of much pain, as the inflammation resulting from its use in the destruction of the dental nerve is often serious, and, especially, as recent investigations have supplied an agent at once more

and plug the cavity. If this operation is impracticable, we should cauterize the crown of the painful tooth, which will for a long time render it insensible. Persons who gnash their teeth should place a piece of linen or any other kind of soft substance between the jaws, to prevent the teeth from rubbing upon each other.

Cracking of the Teeth.—This is, properly speaking, a small superficial fracture, (Pl. XIII. Fig. 2,) and does not produce

potent and safe for effecting this object, we are prepared in unqualified terms to condemn the mode above recommended. The importance of this subject will justify us in laying somewhat ample contributions upon accredited authorities for the purposes of elucidation.

Professor C. A. Harris says: "The use of cautery may often be successful, but inasmuch as it almost always produces inflammation in the investing and alveolar membranes, I cannot unreservedly recommend it." *Dental Art*, p. 171.

Dr. W. E. Ide, of Ohio, in a communication to the American Journal of Dental Science (March, 1842) remarks: "A safe and efficient agent for destroying the nerves of teeth has ever been a desideratum. Among the various things that have at different times been suggested for this purpose, none has been more unqualifiedly lauded by some and condemned by others, than ARSENIC. In the 'Guide to Sound Teeth,' published by Dr. Spooner of New York, in 1836, public attention was first called to its use, and its qualities are extolled in no measured terms. In a work soon after published by Dr. Burdell, its use is condemned as cruel, ineffectual, and dangerous. In volume I. p. 227, Journal of Dental Science, Dr. S. Brown says: 'Of all the remedies which have hitherto been generally made known to the profession in this country, arsenic is unquestionably the most prompt, safe, and effectual, when properly applied.' The opinions of such men as these, surely no one acquainted with his profession will treat with disrespect: but, as these doctors disagree, it may be difficult for the inexperienced to decide. As the matter now stands we fear that some may wholly discard a valuable remedy, while others may use it so indiscriminately as frequently to fail of the beneficial results that might otherwise be obtained. In the hands of the above mentioned gentlemen who have recommended it, it has doubtless been so judiciously used as to be unattended by the objections that have elicited this communication: but others, as we have done, may use it in a manner to make a caution not altogether unnecessary.

"We have used it pretty freely for more than three years, and though we find it a remedy of much value, and one for which we have been unable to find a substitute, its use has sometimes been attended by effects that should be known to the inexperienced. One objection that has been urged against it is, that the use of a poison so virulent as arsenic, cannot be unattended by danger. If properly used, I conceive this objection can never be valid, as the quantity necessary to produce the most desirable result can never be productive of any serious consequences. The power of the remedy should only

any morbid alteration of the tooth. It is produced by very many causes. It may, indeed, be often occasioned by gnashing the teeth, by accident, by biting hard bodies during mastication, and is often caused by endeavouring to crack solid substances with the incisores, and sometimes by the use of the file. The pain, at the time of the accident, is more or less acute according to the extent of the injury, and the tooth is for some time after susceptible of the impressions of heat, cold, acids, or the friction of hard bodies upon it. Such injured

be a caution to the inexperienced against the use of a quantity that may be as unnecessary as dangerous. A second objection has been founded on the pain which is said to result from its application to an exposed nerve.

"In our first experiments we used simply three parts of arsenic and one of acetate or sulphate of morphine, and, contrary to our expectations, in nearly all cases where the nerve was much exposed, the application was attended by a considerable amount of pain. When the nervous pulp of a molar tooth was denuded and inflamed, the pain was often excruciating. More recently we have used equal parts of arsenic and morphine. A small quantity of this, say one-fifteenth or twentieth of a grain, is sprinkled on a piece of cotton that has previously been saturated with kreosote, and carefully applied to the exposed nerve, after as much of the foreign matter as practicable has been cautiously removed from its surface. Over this, white wax is to be applied in a manner to prevent pressure, and the whole permitted to remain five or six hours. If the preparation is applied to more than one tooth at the same time, the patient should be cautioned against swallowing his saliva, lest nausea to a greater or less extent be the consequence. Since having used the kreosote, we have found the amount of pain to be very materially diminished, but never entirely wanting, if the nervous pulp is much exposed. Where the bony parietes of a tooth is sensitive to such a degree as to make its preparation for a plug painful, this sensibility can always be perfectly removed, and with no pain, by this application. But this practice is not unfrequently followed by results which constitute the chief objection that we desire to point out in this communication. As is recommended by many at the present time, it was our former practice to apply it in all cases where the nervous sensibility of a carious tooth was such as to make its preparation for a plug painful. In teeth that are highly organized, especially in young persons, every dentist knows that a carious surface may be exquisitely sensitive though the nervous pulp may not be exposed. This is especially the case with the incisores and cuspidati. In such cases, as we have before said, the application of arsenic will entirely remove the morbid sensibility for the time, and the tooth can be plugged with the greatest facility. But it often occurs that, in a few days, the whole tooth becomes so exquisitely sensitive, as to be affected by the slightest change of temperature. If the enamel is thin and transparent, the tooth assumes a purple or reddish brown colour, and the investing membrane of the fang becomes more or less inflamed, as is indicated by pain in occlusion of the jaws. Where the absorption of the poison is slight, this appearance

parts are generally filed in order to prevent their angles from injuring the soft parts of the mouth that may come in contact with them, and to give the tooth a more agreeable form.

Fractures of the Teeth.—Fractures of the teeth differ from the foregoing, inasmuch as the lesion of the former is more extensive than that of the latter. It may occur at the crown, root, or neck of the tooth; and its direction may be transverse or oblique. (Pl. XIII. Fig. 7.) These fractures, as is seen,

subsides in a few days, and the tooth is restored to its original colour. In other cases, where the morbid effect was more marked, the inflammatory symptoms have continued from one to two months, when the tooth would become perfectly destitute of vitality. The purple colour would then be changed to a dark brown, that permanently destroys the beauty of the tooth. In one or two instances I have removed plugs that have been in such a tooth for two years or more, and not the slightest trace of vitality has been discovered. The nerve and blood vessels through the whole dental canal have been completely destroyed, though they could have been in contact with the preparation only through the medium of absorption. If the enamel of a front tooth is partially transparent, and the patient young, indicating activity of the absorbents, he should bear the pain of having it prepared for a plug without the use of arsenic, rather than endanger its beauty. If the tooth be opaque there is little danger of absorption taking place; but in this case the bony parietes are rarely so sensitive as to render any application necessary. If in the above cases we do not entirely discard the use of arsenic, it would probably be better to continue its application to a particular tooth not more than one hour, and then proceed immediately to cleanse and plug. By this practice absorption may be, to some extent at least, prevented, and the desirable results partially, if not wholly obtained.

"If the nervous pulp of an incisor or cuspidatus is exposed, especially in a young person, it is better to destroy it by thrusting a small instrument up the dental canal, as by this means the portion of vitality which is derived from the external periosteum will, for a time at least, be retained."

In commenting on the foregoing, Dr. C. A. Harris remarks: "The effect which it (arsenic) has, when applied to the teeth of very young persons, as described by Dr. Ide, we have frequently noticed, and for the last two years have refrained from applying it to the teeth of very young subjects, unless urged to it by the most pressing necessity."

The following succinct description of the mode of applying arsenic is from the pen of Dr. J. J. Greenwood of New York:

" When a patient applies to me for the cure of toothache, I examine the tooth, and clean out the cavity, endeavouring to make bare the nerve, if practicable, with a small instrument. If the nerve bleeds, so much the better. I then wipe out the cavity with raw cotton, steeped in the essence of peppermint, laudanum, or alcohol. After which, I take raw cotton of sufficient size to stop up three-fourths of the cavity of the tooth. I dip the point into lauda-

affect different parts of the dental organs. Sometimes, indeed, only a portion, at other times the whole crown is affected. Under other circumstances, on the contrary, the fracture runs from the root to the neck of the tooth, which may be split from above downwards, or only fractured in that direction.

A violent blow, a fall upon the face, making a fulcrum of the tooth without necessary precaution in the extraction of a neighbouring one, rachitis, scorbutus, syphilis, or any other morbid affections susceptible of rendering the teeth brittle, are so many causes that may render the teeth liable to fracture. A tooth may often appear to an inexperienced eye to be sound, though it be more or less decayed in the interior of its crown, and although it may not occasion the least pain, the dental substance being protected, its weakest part may still be fractured by motions in mastication.

num, so as somewhat to saturate the cotton with it, that the mixture I shall mention may adhere to it. I then take upon the point of it, by touching the mixture, about the size of a large pin's head, and in no instance do I ever use more, however large the cavity in the tooth, but sometimes a smaller quantity. This I place in the cavity of the tooth, immediately in contact, if I can, with the nerve, and stop up the cavity with mastic, composed of Venice turpentine, heated, and mixed with calcined plaster of Paris and chalk. Feuchtwanger's Prussian cement for the teeth will answer, placed upon the raw cotton in the tooth, and sometimes mixed up with it so as to fill up the cavity, charging the patient to take it out in three days exactly, and in no wise to masticate on that side during the time. If patients will come to me, which they generally will do, I take it out for them, which I prefer to do, and wash out the cavity with alcohol. The tooth is by this time cured; but for fear there may remain an ichorous fluid oozing still from the dental canal, I leave it for three days longer, when the organ is fully prepared and ready for stopping. The symptoms of the efficacy of the cure are these, namely: the pain, after commencing, will endure for three or four hours, sometimes more, according to the irritability of the patient. After the acute pains have passed away, a soreness will continue for some time, accompanied by a looseness of the organ, occasioned by the inflamed state of the periosteum. This gradually dies away, and by the second or third day, in almost every case, disappears. If, when the raw cotton and the mastic are removed on the third day, the patient takes cold water in the mouth, and no pain arises from it, the cause is removed. This is the proof in all cases. I have been thus prolix in order that you may be supported by one who has tested its efficacy for years with success, and, indeed, I make use of no other remedy.

Mixture, to be placed in an ounce glass vial, with glass stopper.

℞.   Three parts arsenic

One   do.   acetate morphine. Misce.—S.

The impression of heat and cold, the action of acids, the rubbing of hard bodies, cause more acute pains upon fractured teeth than upon those that have only been cracked. This sensitiveness may last for several months, and even for years, according as the fracture is more or less extensive. It may even last until ossification has gone on in the internal side of the cavity of the tooth. Teeth thus affected often become yellow or blackish, and only decay when the fracture occasions a cavity, which is very rare. They are also as hard as the others. I have a lateral incisor that has been fractured in the middle of its crown for twenty-five years, and which has not for twenty years occasioned the slightest pain. It is as sound as my other teeth.

The means that are employed to obviate inconveniences which may result from a fracture of a tooth are generally simple, and their choice, in most cases, is left to the intelligence of the dentist: but, previously to adopting any measures, he should well examine that portion of the tooth that has been injured.

When the fracture has not reached the dental pulps, we cauterize the newly exposed part, that it may be less susceptible to the impressions of the atmosphere. If the pulp be nearly exposed, we must lay it entirely bare with a drill; we cauterize it, and also the nerve, and plug the cavity of the tooth. (Pl. XIII. Fig. 7.) When the fracture extends near to the neck, after having destroyed the sensibility of the tooth, we should prepare the root for the reception of an artificial crown, if it be in the anterior part of the mouth, or in other cases we should plug the root.*

If the fracture be lengthwise, and if it extend to the root of the tooth, we should immediately extract the loosened frac-

---

* The roots of the molares should never be permitted to remain in the mouth, as they will be a continual source of irritation to the gums, sockets and maxillary bones; and this irritation being often communicated to the nervous system, produces a general derangement of the whole economy. These objections do not so much apply to the roots of the incisores and cuspidati ; as these are known to remain for years without exercising any injurious influences, and they are, moreover, useful for the reception of artificial crowns. The remarks we have already made on the actual cautery will apply to the above.—S.

tured parts: their retention in the alveolus may produce violent pains, inflammations, abscesses, and many other evils. A similar operation is indicated in subjects of from ten to fifteen years of age, whose neighbouring teeth may approximate and close the aperture resulting from the loss of a fractured tooth. We cannot, therefore, be too careful in extracting, or in endeavouring to obtain a consolidation of fractured teeth, since, if they are left to themselves, an inflammation of the dental pulp, and of the alveolus, a cyst at the extremities of the roots, (Pl. IV. Fig. 3,) a fistulous abscess, a discharge of fetid pus, and finally caries, will nearly always result.

Erosion of the Teeth.—Erosion or atrophy of the teeth is a disease peculiar to their enamel, and which, in its development, presents three varieties, each of which we shall carefully examine.

The first variety of dental erosion consists in spots of a milky whiteness, or of a deep or light yellow, irregular, and situated in the enamel of the tooth, the polish of which it does not affect. These spots remain stationary, and nothing can efface them. The second variety is the most common of all. Like the first, it only affects the enamel, and it presents little crowded holes, resembling quilting, irregular depressions, whose surfaces are not always polished, or even transverse sinuosities, single or divided by prominent lines; (Pl. XII. Fig. 12;) the sinuosities are sometimes yellow, but often of the same colour as the enamel. As to the third variety of erosion, it differs very much from the preceding, for it affects the whole dental substance, particularly the bone of the tooth, which is only imperfectly developed. (Pl. XII. Figs. 7 and 8.) The tooth itself does not possess its whole dimensions; it is often entirely or nearly deprived of one of its parts. Sometimes its crown is reduced to one-third of its natural size; sometimes it is divided by a deep circular depression; at other times the grinding surface of a molar presents a kind of cavity. Under some circumstances it offers asperities, whose summits are covered with enamel, of which their base is totally deprived. It has been observed that the roots of eroded teeth

7

have sinuosities and prominent circular lines, are knotty and
very short.

These various species of erosion that attack the enamel of
teeth, produce sometimes such deep holes as to communicate
with the dental pulp: they often constitute a local disease of
the parts in connexion with the teeth, but oftener a general
affection, at the period of the formation of their enamel. It
appears that, at this time, nature, not possessing sufficient
vigour, is arrested in her operation. But, at the same time, the
osseous portion of the tooth is growing, and the enamel only
covers it as the health is re-established; if it again decline, the
enamel is again arrested in its formation. We witness teeth
that have three and four lines of erosion, (Pl. XII. Fig. 12,)
and we may say that the child has been sick as often as there
are lines upon his teeth. This malady may also be occasioned
by scrofulous or scorbutic affections, or by a disease contracted
by the fœtus in the womb of its mother, or communicated
during lactation. This atrophy is congenital, and is not produced by a consecutive alteration of the crown of the tooth
after its formation.

Although it is difficult to erase those kinds of alterations
resulting from dental atrophy, we should endeavour to combat
their causes, either by preventing them, or by arresting their
progress. This disease, however, requires no local treatment;
and the only advice that can be given, is to endeavour, by appropriate treatment, to eradicate the general affection that has
produced it; this appertains more properly to the medical
practice than to that of the Surgeon Dentist.

Decomposition of the Enamel.—This affection presents, like
atrophy of the teeth, three varieties. The first is the most
frequent, and manifests itself by some brown or blackish spots
which are developed upon the anterior face and the sides of
the crown. These spots may extend as far as the internal
face of the enamel, which, in most cases, preserves its polish,
or becomes rough by a slight wasting of substance. They are
produced, either by a disease of the dental pulp, or by great
pressure of the teeth incased in alveolar borders too narrow to
contain them, or, lastly, by the contact of decayed teeth.

This alteration of the enamel does not render the teeth painful, and is spontaneously arrested as soon as that which is affected ceases to be in contact with the diseased parts.

The second species of decomposition of enamel is easily known by the loss of its polish, the facility with which some particles of the part may be taken away, and by the extraordinary whiteness that the substance at first acquires, and which is afterward lost. This decomposition generally manifests itself near the anterior border of the gums, but may extend to the osseous substance: the teeth at first are very sensible to the impressions of heat and cold, and even to the conflict of solid bodies; they become yellow where the enamel is lost, and incrustations of tartar, or viscid secretions, more easily adhere to them. This disease is the commencement of a decay very hard to destroy; it shows itself particularly upon the external neck of the inferior molares, after long sickness, or in persons of a bilious temperament, whose teeth are continually bathed in viscous saliva. When this affection is slight, it disappears upon the re-establishment of health, and its progress is also diminished, by daily cleansing the teeth, particularly the diseased part, with a soft brush.

The third variety, which is difficult to recognise at the moment it shows itself, presents a superficial wasting of the enamel, at the anterior part of the crown, under the form of an oval or circular facet, which gradually increases in size or depth. This facet is at first as white as the enamel; it afterward assumes a yellow hue, and the denudation of the osseous part of the tooth that results from the disease, renders it sensible to the slightest touch: generally atrophy of the teeth alters the enamel, and sometimes disorganizes it. Independent of this it does not influence the diseases of the dental substance proper. The treatment of this third variety, consists in cutting away with a file the defective portion, or in plugging the cavity, should any exist.

Discoloration of the Teeth.—The teeth of first dentition are of a milky whiteness and very brilliant; but the hue of those of adults corresponds to the good or bad constitution of the subject;* they do not always present the same colour nor the same polish, and are, in certain individuals, of a bluish or opaque white. Young persons, who, from the period of ossification of second dentition, until the eruption of these teeth, are affected in their lungs, have generally long and thin teeth of a milky white enamel and transparent. Those, on the contrary, whose enamel is of an opaque or grayish white, and are shorter than the preceding, are indicative of a better constitution. When ossification is completed, and the enamel is of a whitish yellow, and the teeth short, particularly if the person be corpulent, good health is usually indicated.

During life the teeth may undergo alterations in colour, in the course of different affections to which man is subjected; but they soon resume their primitive colour when the disease has been of but short duration. If, however, the disease be manifested after the thirty-first year of age, it is probable that the teeth will preserve the hue that they assumed during its continuance. We shall not consider as discolorations of the teeth, those large blackish spots, and more particularly greenish ones, which are sometimes found near their necks. These spots are superficial, although a rugine cannot detach them like tartar: we can, however, destroy them by means of a piece of porous wood dipped in fine moistened pumice stone.

Teeth usually have a somewhat yellow hue. In order to whiten them, acids, cream of tartar, tobacco leaves, snuff, quinine, &c., have for some time been made use of.†

---

* The colour and density of the deciduous teeth are as much influenced by the state of the health of the mother and infant during the ossification of their crowns, as are those of the permanent ones, by the operations of the economy at a later period of life, at which they are undergoing solidification.—S.

† Of the injurious influences of acids upon the teeth, Mr. J. Snell remarks: "By the improper use of acids, that beautiful polish natural to the enamel is injured; and where the application is repeated, layer after layer is removed, or honey-combed pits and spots of brown appear, and the teeth become morbidly sensible to changes of temperature, pain being produced from cold air or water."

"The application of strong mineral acids," says T. Bell, "for the purpose of assisting in the removal of tartar, is to be deprecated as excessively injurious, as it dissolves the enamel and the earthy part of the bone wherever it comes in contact with them. The immediate effect of the treatment is to render the teeth beautifully white, but, in a short time, the surface of the enamel being made rough, and, as it were, eroded, they become again dis-

Caries of the Teeth.—The name *caries* has been given to the gradual destruction of a part or the whole of the dental substance.

This affection often commences upon the layer of enamel, which is thinnest nearest the bone of the tooth, (Pl. XII. Fig. 15;) it often shows itself in little black spots upon the lateral surface where the teeth are in contact with each other, or upon the little inequalities in the crown of the enamel, (Pl. XII. Fig. 14,) which very soon loses its transparency and colour. In this way the disease becomes visible. Its progress is sometimes so rapid that it occasions the destruction of the bone before its morbid influence has decomposed the enamel. As the disease of the bone deprives the enamel of its support, the slightest pressure in mastication breaks it, and then a cavity is found in the tooth, the size and depth of which imperceptibly increases until the disease penetrates the interior cavity. (Pl. XII. Figs. 10 and 19.) The membrane that lines the tooth, being then exposed to the action of the atmosphere, and aliment, and all external agents, becomes inflamed and irritable to such a degree as to produce pain, the intensity of which is always in proportion to the rapidity of the progress of the disease, to the thickness of the osseous substance of the tooth, and to the narrowness of the cavity. Pain is not always a proof of the progress of caries, for we observe teeth that have been completely destroyed without having given rise to the slightest inconvenience. Decay of itself is not painful: the diseases of the nerve alone produce the sensibility of the dental organ. It also is seen that one part, which is the seat of the disease, ceases, for a longer or shorter time, to be painful, and after-

coloured, and, if the application be frequently repeated, the bone is exposed, and gangrene is the inevitable consequence."

Knowing as we do that the same elements enter into the composition of dental tartar that compose the teeth themselves, and that hence the latter are just as susceptible to the action of any chemical agent as the former, it seems indeed astonishing that any intelligent person could be indiscreet enough to use such.

Whether tobacco be injurious to the dental organs or not is a controverted point. Be this as it may, however, its deleterious effects upon the gums, and upon the system generally, should induce us to condemn the use of it, without reference to the disgust that should be felt for so filthy a practice.—S.

ward becomes insensible for a long time, or even for ever after. This we have noticed, and presume it has not escaped the generality of dental observers.

No disease is more frequent or more serious than caries of the teeth, since, independently of the pain that it usually occasions, it tends to the destruction of the affected tooth. This is not uniformly the case, for we have seen caries spontaneously arrested, or remain stationary for a time, and even for ever.

Decay manifests itself upon the exterior of the teeth. The molares are more subject to it than the incisores or cuspidati: it generally attacks these upon their lateral surfaces, and scarcely ever upon their cutting edges or lingual faces. In the molares the little cavities on their grinding surfaces are generally the primitive seats of this disease. Incisores and cuspidati that are irregular are particularly subject to decay. It is rare for decay to affect the roots of the teeth; it is nearly always arrested when it reaches that portion of the dental organ. It is still more uncommon for it to penetrate to the extremity of the root: this part in most cases remains in all its integrity, while the rest of the organ has been entirely destroyed. The wisdom teeth, says M. Marjolin, when their eruption is prolonged, are sometimes decayed while they are coming through the gum; and it often happens that several corresponding teeth, of the same side, in the same jaw, are affected with caries at the same time, or at very short intervals, which can be explained rather by the density of their structure than by the distribution of the nerves that they receive.

The deciduous teeth, like those of replacement, are often affected with decay, either in consequence of sickness, or by a natural tendency. Generally, the incisores are the least exposed to this disease, and when they manifest it, it is generally in those of the upper jaw, the crowns of which are gradually destroyed as far as the gum without occasioning severe pain. The inferior molares are of all others the most subject to it, the disease makes rapid progress in these, and produces such suffering that extraction becomes necessary. They, however, are often retained without ever being attacked by disease.

As we have already said, decay commences sometimes in

the neighbourhood of the dental cavity.* It is developed upon the crown, under the enamel, and in the root, upon its surface. It never affects the sides of teeth started from their sockets, or a portion of a root for a long time denuded. It occurs in children, youths, and in mature age: but the teeth of old men, and even of men of fifty years of age, who are endowed with good constitutions, seldom decay. Those of women are more subject to it than those of men.

Decay of the teeth is so common that few persons, even among youths of good health, are altogether exempted from it. We have for this purpose collected facts that appear to us to leave no doubt upon this point. Situated as we were, as dentist in several boarding-schools, we examined the mouths of more than a thousand pupils, and can affirm that, of this number of persons, of whom more than five hundred were sixteen or twenty years of age, we met annually from five hundred and fifty to six hundred decayed teeth. Five hundred and fifty appears to be about the average number according to the examinations made every five or six months.

Authors have never agreed upon the true cause of decay. Hunter supposed it to be a hereditary disease, and regarded it as a kind of necrosis or mortification of the dental substance; and Fox thought that it was a defect in the primitive formation of the teeth. Some have thought that dental caries should be classed among ulcerous affections, while others are modest enough to say that they know of no reason why the teeth should decay. For us, we believe that the disease is produced by primary causes, and that the causes are both external and internal.

The external Causes of Decay are blows and contusions; all lesions of the teeth; the contact of cold air determining fluxions; the application of substances capable of altering the dental organ or increasing its nervous sensibility; the frequent use of acid drinks or aliment; the habit of taking at the same repast very cold and hot drinks; the constant presence of saliva upon a certain part of the enamel of the tooth; and, we may add, malformation; lateral pressure of the teeth against each

* See in a subsequent page our remarks upon *internal* decay.—S.

other; affections of the gums; malaria; the use of certain medicines, as mercury, acids, &c.; uncleanness; and such irregularities as permit viscous substances to penetrate their spongy parts, &c.

Among *the internal Causes of Caries*, we enumerate the weak and soft texture of teeth indicated by a milky whiteness, or bluish cast; congenital erosion; and organic or accidental diseases, such as scrofulous, syphilitic, gouty, rheumatic, variolous, scorbutic, acute or chronic inflammatory, gastric, nervous, adynamic affections, &c.; and precocious growth of the permanent teeth at the period of their formation.*

---

* "If it were true that inflammation was necessary to the disease, it would never occur except in living teeth, and it is notorious that dead teeth are as liable to its attacks as living ones. It exhibits, too, in these, all the phenomena that are manifested by it in the others. This is true, not only with regard to teeth that have lost their vascular connexion with the general system, and are still retained in the mouth, but also with those that are placed there by art, if fabricated from bone or ivory. The vitality of the teeth may influence the progress and character of the decay, though I am not certain that it does, but it is not, by any means, essential to it.

"If the decay of the teeth then is not referable to inflammation in their bony structure, to what is it to be ascribed? The inference is, that it is the result of the action of chemical agents, and when we take into consideration that the fluids of the mouth, when in a morbid condition, are capable of decomposing their enamels, if not possessed of more than ordinary density, and that the disease frequently commences upon this outer covering, the conclusion is at once irresistible. A most remarkable case of this description of caries (called by Mr. Hunter "*decay by denudation*,") is mentioned by Dr. Eleazar Parmly, in his notes to this gentleman's treatise on the teeth, published in the American Journal of Dental Science, in which the labial surfaces of several natural teeth, that had been artificially placed in the mouth, were attacked by it.

"It may, however, be asked, if caries of the teeth be produced by the action of external agents, how is it that the disease sometimes commences within the bony structure of the organs, and makes considerable progress there, before any indications of its existence are observable externally? I answer, that it never does commence within the bony structure of the organs; its attacks are always upon their external surfaces, sometimes upon the enamel, but most frequently upon the bone within the indentations on the grinding faces of the bicuspides and molares, and on the sides of the teeth at the points where they come in contact with each other, and where this outer covering is frequently so fractured by the pressure that is exerted upon it, that the juices of the mouth find ready access to the subjacent osseous tissue. The destruction of the organs may be gradually going on here for months and even years without any notable signs of its existence; the commencement

Without instituting a special examination into the characteristics of dental decay, arbitrary classifications of this disease
were made, as, for instance, external, internal, dry, humid, &c.
Such classifications were of course defective, and it was left for
that eminent dentist, M. Duval, to reform this.—He describes
seven species or varieties of decay, which he calls *calcareous,
peeling, perforating, black, deruptive, stationary, and wasting.*

First Species. Calcareous Decay.—This decay presents a slight
circular depression near the gum, where the enamel appears to
be of a whiter colour than in its natural state, brittle, irregular
resembling lime, and very sensitive. (Pl. XII. Fig. 1.) It frequently occurs in youth, or in the course of severe inflamma-

of the malady in these places has led many to suppose that it had its origin
within their osseous structure.

"But a still more absurd and ridiculous theory, in regard to the cause of
the disease, is advanced by Mr. Charles Bew: he attributes it to the arrest of
the circulation in the organ, ' by the lateral pressure of the teeth against
each other.'

"The exposure of the teeth, too, to sudden changes of temperature, as from
heat to cold, or cold to heat, has been regarded almost from time immemo-
rial as a cause of their decay; but no explanation of the manner by which it
produced the disease was attempted, until the promulgation of the doctrine
that it was the result of inflammation, when it was numbered among only
the *exciting causes.* The popular belief that cold is a cause of dental caries,
is traced back to Hippocrates, who in mentioning the parts of the body that
are injuriously affected by it, includes the teeth."

Delabarre, in alluding to this affection, observes: "Caries of the teeth is a
disease of their tissue, and not a simple decomposition proper to inert bodies.
As an ulcer in a soft part is easily healed in a healthy subject, so the cure of
this malady is effected with ease, in those of good constitutions. Caries, in
individuals of different constitutions cannot be of the same nature, because
their teeth have not the same solidity. Thus, those that are largely charged
with gelatine will be exposed to *odonto-malaria,* whilst those in which the
calcareous phosphate is present in large quantities, will not be attacked with
it as long as they preserve this advantage. But absorption being effected in
teeth as in other bones, (which their softening in the interior and below the
enamel, demonstrates,) consequently it follows, unless some external agent
may have had power to act on the osseous tissue, that we can estimate the
qualities of the humours by the nature of the caries that is manifested in
the teeth.

"The softening of the interior tissue can result only from a derangement
of the central ganglion; and this is caused by the arrival at this body of arterial blood deprived of the properties requisite to maintain it in a healthy
state.

tory diseases: it is arrested by age, and the altered part becomes yellow and sensitive. This decay may be the result of a congenital atrophy, or a blow upon the teeth. Its progress is slow, and art can afford no relief, except by widening the cavity to prevent the retention of viscous matter. It should be deeply cauterized* to dry up the soft parts and destroy its sensibility. Afterward, if the part be kept clean by means of a brush, we may hope to entirely destroy the disease, or at least to arrest its progress as long as the advice here given is followed.

"The incorrectness of the opinion advanced, by M. Delabarre that caries of the teeth consists in something more than a mere composition of this tissue, has been shown in the fact that dead teeth decay as readily as living ones, and that caries in them exhibits the same appearances that it does in those that are possessed of vitality; and between the manner of the arrest of the progress of this malady, and that of an ulcer in soft parts, there is no more sameness than there is between the two diseases. The cure in the one case is effected by the restorative powers of the body, whereas in the other, it is accomplished by the aid of art, the operations of the economy not contributing in the least to the restoration of the injury.

"The reason of the difference in the nature of caries of the teeth in individuals of different constitutions is, as M. Delabarre has justly remarked, because of the difference in the density of the organs, which is determined by the temperament or state of the general health at the time of their formation. I am compelled to differ with him in the opinion that softening of teeth that are not well provided with 'calcareous phosphate,' is owing to the removal of this earthy material by the absorbents, and that the disease is identical with that which, in other bones, is denominated *mollities ossium.* The action of the solvent agents that are concerned in bringing about that condition of the teeth designated caries, is facilitated by the softness of the organs, and hence the rapidity of decay in those that are of a very loose and spongy texture, and the rare occurrence of the malady in those that are endowed with great solidity. The decomposition, too, of their earthy salt is the more perfect, in proportion as they exist in small quantities. An impairment of the arterial blood, resulting from a 'disturbance of the central ganglion,' or any other cause, can have no agency in the decomposition or softening of the osseous structure of the teeth, except it gives rise to a morbid condition of the interior parietes of the salivary and mucous fluids of the mouth. The destruction of the interior parietes of a tooth never takes place while the pulp or central ganglion remains; but this sometimes inflames and separates, and gives rise to the formation of an acrid and very corrosive humour; and it is to the presence of this that the softening of the bone surrounding the dental cavity is attributable."—C. A. Harris on the Teeth, &c. &c.—S.

* We have in a previous place given our objections to the use of the actual cautery.—S.

Second Species. Peeling Decay.—The enamel, in the second species, which is nearly always accompanied by tetterous affections, assumes a yellow hue near the gum, becomes very brittle, and detaches itself from the tooth in small pieces. (Pl. XII. Fig. 3.) The bony substance, at first yellow, and afterward brown, is soft, and may be cut away in layers, and is very sensitive where the enamel still remains.

Third Species. Perforating Caries.—This kind of decay, the most frequent of all, shows itself indistinctly upon every part of the crowns of the teeth. The bony substance is often yellow or brown, softens, or becomes humid and fetid; the cavity increases with greater or less rapidity, and communicates exteriorly by a small opening. (Pl. XII. Fig. 6.) It also often presents the form of a funnel, or that of a canal; the diseased walls are sensible to the slightest impression of cold or solid bodies; and whenever inflammation propagates itself to the bulb of the tooth, when the pulp is exposed, the pain becomes insupportable. The osseous part is gradually destroyed, and the enamel being thus deprived of its support, soon breaks into fragments; and finally nothing but the root remains, which ordinarily ceases to be painful. In such a case, if the nerve be not exposed, the tooth should be plugged, after having all the decayed part removed. But when the nerve is entirely laid bare there remains no other remedy, if it be a tooth that had two or three roots, but extraction, or excision of the crown. (Pl. XV. Figs. 1, 2.)

Fourth Species. Black Decay.—This species of decay is not observed until from the fifteenth to the thirtieth year, particularly in individuals disposed to rachitis or consumption. It usually commences in a blackish spot, (Pl. XII. Fig. 4,) the circumference of which is of the same colour, and shows itself through the enamel, which at this point appears bluish, blackens, and is easily destroyed. This black spot occasions a cavity in the bony substance, which becomes dry, brittle, black, inodorous, and insensible. The disease makes rapid progress, and usually stops when it has reached the root of the tooth; but it may be prevented by pursuing, according to the morbid

condition of the tooth, the different procedures that I have indicated for other species of decay; that is, by plugging the
cavity, or by eradicating with the file the whole of the diseased part, so that it may not exercise any influence upon the
sound part.

Fifth Species. Deruptive Decay.—This generally attacks the
incisores of consumptive subjects. It manifests itself by a
yellowish spot with destruction of substance near the neck of
the tooth, and afterward extends itself obliquely and down-
wardly toward the root, (Pl. XII. Fig. 2,) by forming nearly
always a semicircular brownish furrow. The osteo-dental substance softens, and becomes sensible to the impression of heat
and cold, and to the contact of acids and solid bodies. The
disease makes great progress, and reaches the dental cavity;
the tooth ceases to be sensible, and it sometimes happens that,
the crown remaining entire, separates itself from the carious
root. We may save a tooth affected with this species of caries,
during the early stage of the disease, by filing all the decayed
part in such a manner as to prevent the retention of any viscous substance.

Sixth Species. Stationary Decay.—Each of the five kinds
of decay of which we have spoken may be called *stationary*,
when it is not thought necessary to remove the discoloured spot,
at each filing, to preserve the tooth, which has not really become decomposed. (Pl. IV. Fig. 7.) The name of stationary
decay has been applied more particularly to that species which
attacks the enamel of the teeth, without altering the part which
it covers. It develops itself all at once after severe constitutional indisposition, when convalescence has been very sudden; under other circumstances, they are determined by a too
great approximation of the teeth; but then it ceases to progress, as soon as the space which separates them becomes
wider, whether obtained by art or produced by the disease.

Seventh Species.—Decay resembling Denudation.—This last
species, difficult to discover at its commencement, because it as
often presents the appearance of decay that has been spontaneously arrested as that which is forming, has its seat upon the

grinding surface of the molar teeth. (Pl. XII. Fig. 11.) It manifests itself by a deep or superficial depression, whose bottom is sometimes upon a level with the neck of the tooth. This cavity is polished and single, oftener very yellow, but sometimes brownish, and the polish of its enamel may lead us to confound it with denudation of the teeth, if the inspection of the opposite teeth does not contradict this supposition.*

The setting on edge of the teeth, and their sensibility and pain, are insufficient to characterize decay. We are, nevertheless, often obliged to make use of the probe to assure ourselves of its existence whenever it has its seat upon the lateral surfaces of the teeth or near their roots; but in the majority of cases, simple inspection is sufficient to detect this disease. As to its prognosis, we perceive that it differs according to the number of the teeth that it affects, the character that it presents, and the nature of its causes. Hence in the treatment of caries in general, we should have two distinct objects in view, 1st, to preserve sound teeth from this disease, 2d, to remedy the disorders that have produced it, by endeavouring to entirely arrest their progress, by means of the remedies which we have indicated when speaking of each particular class of decay.

Destruction of the Roots of Teeth.—This disease often manifests itself in persons from forty to fifty years of age, of a bilious temperament; also, in persons whose constitution at this period of life undergoes a very great change; and we observe it too in certain women, still younger, whose health has become deranged after parturition. Its progress is slow, and only produces serious results after the space of two, three or four years.

Destruction of the roots of the teeth is the result of decomposition of the substance that surrounds them. Its principal

---

* Properly speaking, there is but one kind of dental caries, and the differences in the appearance of this disease, as has been correctly described by Professor Harris in the quotation we have just made in a note, from his treatise on the "Characteristics of the Teeth, Gums," &c. &c., are occasioned by the differences in the density of the teeth of different individuals, which determines the differences in their susceptibility of being acted upon by the causes that produced this affection.—S.

8

characteristics are, inflammation of the periosteum of the root, and suppuration of the integuments that envelop it. This inflammation afterward attacks the alveolar border; the root then becoming a foreign body in the alveoli, is insensibly expelled, or gradually consumed, and the dental nerve dries up.

Loosening of the teeth, the destruction of their roots, and suppuration of the integuments that cover them, are seldom confined to a single tooth. (Pl. XII. Figs. 7, 8.) These disorders may extend themselves to the neighbouring teeth, and very often cover the alveolar border of both jaws.

This disease which, as is perceptible, is local in its commencement, but makes great progress, and may even attack the whole dental arch. A prudent dentist will endeavour to save the patient· from these disorders, and prevail upon him to submit to the extraction of the tooth over which there is the greatest discharge from the gum, by urging, that, as the tooth is loosened, the disease is local, and can be easily cured. When, however, the affection of which we are speaking has spread itself over both jaws, we may still hope to arrest it, or at least we may greatly retard its progress, by extracting from each jaw two or three of the teeth that have become most loosened. To neglect such precautions would be to leave in jeopardy the greater number of the teeth. We can derive no advantage from internal treatment; but we can abate the intensity of the disease by the employment of tonics upon the gums, and still more by the application of the actual cautery upon the principal seat of the discharge.

Exostosis of the Teeth.—This disease is always difficult to discover before the extraction of the teeth. It affects only their roots in most cases; (Pl. XII. Figs. 16 to 21,) but sometimes only exists upon the side of the tooth. It presents a round and angular form, and under certain circumstances occupies the whole circumference and length of the root. (Pl. XII. Fig. 17.) Under other circumstances it only constitutes a morbid condition, and sometimes is accompanied by encysted decomposition. This disease, which is nearly always the result of engorgement and ossification of the dental periosteum, occurs particularly in subjects whose teeth have become painful, either in consequence of decay and denudation, or by the action of a gouty or rheumatic diathesis.

It is almost impossible to form a certain diagnosis of this disease. We may at most conjecture its existence from the heavy, dull pain that accompanies it, and the intensity of which is not always the same; from swelling of the alveoli; from the mobility of the diseased tooth, which is not met with in all cases; and from the affected tooth no longer being upon a level with the rest.*

The sole treatment to be adopted upon the first appearance of this disease, consists in subduing the pain by emollient and narcotic topical applications, by local depletions, and revulsives. If the pain still exist, and the tooth becomes loose, its extraction is necessary. Fox speaks of a young lady who was obliged to have all her teeth extracted because their roots were affected with exostosis.

Spina Ventosa.—This disease, which also attacks the roots of teeth, is very uncommon: it is analogous to exostosis, and presents similar symptoms and similar indications. The root is simply larger than usual; it is scooped out, its canal is very large, and its walls are very thin.

Necrosis of Teeth.—This affection differs but little from destruction of the roots. It generally supervenes after suppuration, destruction, or disorganization of the alveolo-dental membrane. Although it is oftener the result of a chronic or gangrenous inflammation of the soft parts which are in connexion with the root of the tooth, it may also be occasioned by exterior violence. Teeth affected with necrosis lose their natural colour; they become loose; sometimes they drop out; at other times

---

* This affection is supposed to be occasioned by an increased action of the vessels of the periosteum, and often occurs while the crown of the tooth is perfectly sound. "This disease," says Dr. C. A. Harris, "often continues for a long time without producing any inconvenience whatever. It usually first manifests itself by a slight soreness in the affected tooth, which increases as the fang becomes enlarged, until pain, either constant or periodical, and of a character more or less severe, is experienced."

If, from the dull heavy pain experienced in the tooth, we suppose its root to be affected with exostosis, we can but test it by tapping the side of the crown with a hard body. Severe pain at its root will indicate this affection.—S.

they remain in their sockets and occasion a fetid and purulent discharge from between their neck and the gums. After extraction, the root is seen to be reddish, yellowish, or blackish.

Inflammation of the alveolo-dental Membrane.—(*Periodontitis of Moderns.*) This affection may be acute or chronic. When chronic, it produces destruction of the root. (Pl. XII. Figs. 10 and 13.) Whenever it is acute, it is characterized by pain, at first dull, and after acute and pulsating, although the tooth appears otherwise sound. The gum inflames, becomes red and painful, and sometimes the swelling is communicated to the cheek. This disease may terminate in resolution, or in the formation of an abscess. It is to be subdued by emollient and narcotic gargles, and by the application of leeches above the angles of the jaws: by pediluvia, and tepid and emollient drinks.

When this disease passes to a chronic state, it is generally kept up by a constitutional cause, such as scrofulous, scorbutic, venereal, arthritic vices, &c. Then, as M. Marjolin remarks, it occasions between the teeth and the gums a fetid puriform discharge, which exposes the necks of the teeth and softens the gums. This affection is often very difficult to cure: the best local remedies, when the pain is slight or entirely absent, are bitter, astringent, stimulating, anti-scorbutic lotions, and frictions at least daily upon the gums and necks of the teeth, with a soft brush dipped in an astringent or bitter decoction. The application of leeches upon the tumefied gums, or scarifying them with the point of a lancet, will prove of advantage.

This treatment should necessarily vary according to the cause of the disease; and it is often necessary to assist it by the application of a cataplasm behind the ears or neck. We may also employ the same treatment that we recommended in the disease that we treated of under the head of destruction of roots.

Inflammation of the dental Pulp. (*Odontitis of Moderns.*)—This pain is generally more frequent among adults than children, and has its seat oftener in decayed than in sound teeth. It also happens more frequently when the decay approaches the dental cavity than when it has entirely exposed this cavity, and when the teeth commence to be denuded, than when denudation has considerably advanced.

This inflammation is particularly characterized by an acute pain, which increases when the sides of the tooth are struck; a pain which at first does not extend to the gums, nor to the jaw, but propagates itself there about the third day, if it does not gradually diminish. Then, all the nerves of the face participate in it. Sometimes, however, without assuming this character, it suddenly subsides, and the patient only feels a kind of numbness in the tooth. If, as it often happens, we are obliged to extract it, we will discover, by a careful examination, violent inflammation, suppuration, and gangrene of the pulp.

Although the causes of inflammation of the dental pulp are very numerous, we may say that it is most particularly occasioned by violent impressions of heat and cold, by the least shock upon decayed teeth, by the retention or decomposition of portions of aliment introduced into the decay of the tooth, and finally by every species of disease. It may be sudden, slow, acute or chronic, continued or intermittent, with regular or irregular intermissions.

The treatment of this disease is of that kind which is applicable to inflammatory affections, and should always have reference to the causes that occasion it. This is the reason, that, after having perfectly removed the decay, if any exist, we may advantageously employ narcotics, such as the extract of opium, incense, myrrh, or other resinous gum. The nitrate of silver, the sulphate of potash, in small quantities, and covered with a piece of cotton introduced within the cavity, the concentrated acids, ether, or essential oils, may produce the same results. A piece of cotton is to be saturated in these liquids, and after having been placed in the cavity, a piece of dry cotton should be placed on it.

The dental pulp is sometimes destroyed more promptly by cauterizing the decay with nitrate of silver or acids; but when the pulp of the incisores, cuspidati or bicuspides, is exposed, we can accomplish its destruction still better by means of a stylet heated to a red heat.

In cases where there exists violent inflammation, it may be reduced, either by frequent emollient lotions kept for a time

8*

in the mouth, or by the application of leeches behind the ear, or a large plaster of the extract of opium, or by keeping the head and face very warm. In all these cases we should prescribe pediluvia slightly stimulating.

As these various therapeutical means are not always sufficient to cure the disease, nor even to diminish the violent and insupportable pain, which, on this account, is called toothache, the only means left is the extraction of the tooth in which the disease is seated,

Fungus of the dental Pulp.—This affection can only take place when the orifice of the dental canal is dilated by disease, or when the canal is accidentally exposed. In the first case, the tumefied pulp becomes larger and redder, and its pedicle, which is continuous with the alveolo-dental membrane, enlarges; in the last case, the tumefied pulp has exteriorly the form of a little red tumour, circumscribed by the border of the aperture of the tooth. This tumour is usually very sensitive to the touch; in some subjects it hardens and disappears. The disease is remedied either by excising or cauterizing the fungus, or finally by the extraction of the tooth, when all other means have failed.—(*Marjolin.*)

Ossification of the dental Pulp.—This disease (says the author just quoted) presents two varieties. In a tooth affected by denudation, the pulp ossifies near the table of bone that still covers its canal. This ossification is a wise provision of nature, because it adheres to this table of bone, and increases its thickness. It often forms in decayed teeth a little osselet that rests suspended in the pulp, mentioned in our treatise on denudation of the teeth.

Such are the diseases capable of affecting the dental substance. We should here, perhaps, speak of some nervous affections of the teeth, and of odontalgia, properly so called; but this latter affection is generally the sequence of other diseases of the teeth, and they will be treated of separately, after having pointed out the various affections of contiguous parts.

SECTION III.

DISEASES OF THE TEETH RELATIVE TO THEIR CONNEXIONS.

Loosening of the Teeth.—Loosening of the teeth may be considered as an affection that depends more upon the condition of their own tissue than upon that of the parts with which they are in connexion. It may be produced by several causes; some are external, others internal. The external causes are blows or falls; artificial teeth badly constructed, or improperly attached by clasps or ligatures to the neighbouring teeth; using without precaution a tooth as a fulcrum; the accumulation of tartar upon the teeth, between the root and gums.

The internal causes are the various alterations of the gums, in becoming soft and spongy from a scorbutic diathesis, the use of mercury, a rheumatic or gouty affection, and severe sickness. Sometimes they spontaneously become loose in old age, especially if they be long.

Females, at their critical period, are often thus affected. I have under my care a woman, three or four of whose teeth became loose and dropped out together, at the period of cessation of the catamenia.

The means of re-establishing loosened teeth will be suggested by the cause of the affection. If the tooth has been accidentally loosened, the patient should be counselled to avoid using it in mastication, or disturbing it in any manner with his tongue or fingers. He should rinse his mouth several times daily with a tonic wash; and also brush the teeth gently with a soft brush, in order to keep free from unwholesome accumulations.

If the teeth have become loosened in consequence of the injudicious application of ligatures or clasps, it will suffice to discard the use of these. If they be loosened from the effect of tartar, it should be carefully but promptly removed; and, if the gums be not destroyed or much impaired, they will again adhere to the teeth, and render them firmly seated. The inci-

sores and cuspidati are more liable to loosen than are the molares, in consequence of their greater length, as they are thus
more seriously affected by their antagonists. In such cases,
filing is indicated, by means of which they should be shortened,
and thus their utility and beauty will be enhanced.

When the teeth become loosened from an internal or constitutional cause, the remedy is more difficult, and the treatment then is within the province of the physician. Tonic
lotions are here indicated ; but we should be very circumspect
in the use of such as are astringent, and when we have recourse
to them for the restoration of relaxed gums, it should not be
until after all inflammation has subsided.

Luxation of the Teeth.—This accident consists in the dis-
placement of a tooth, which may be inclined outwardly, inwardly, or laterally, and, at the same time, started more or less from
its socket. It may be simple, or attended with contusions,
wounds of the gums, fractures of the alveolar border, and even
of the maxilla itself. The extent of such injury is always
dependent upon the prior condition of the gums. Such luxations are sometimes designedly effected by the hands of the
dentist, as we shall have occasion to show in treating of operations upon the teeth; but they are more commonly the results of
falls, blows, &c. The incisores and cuspidati are more exposed
to them than are the molares and bicuspides, from their position, as well as because of their being held by a single root
each. Luxations may be complete or incomplete, and their
treatment should properly be much more simple than many
would suppose. It consists in replacing in its primitive position the luxated tooth, and there retaining it by means of a
ligature; but if, during the movements of the jaw, the tooth
thus replaced should be interfered with by its antagonists, we
should apply to the crown of one of the molares a platina or
gold plate to prevent the jaws from approximating and thus
again interfering with the injured tooth.

The patient should take no aliment which, in its mastication,
would do injury to the affected part. This precaution is of
importance; and by attention to it, and the foregoing, ten or

twelve days will suffice for the luxated tooth to resume all its functions.

This operation is very familiar to us, as we have often performed it in bringing into the dental arch irregular teeth that had grown inwardly or outwardly, or to retain decayed teeth that, having ached, were severed from their connexions, and replaced. Of a hundred facts, that are familiar to us, we will narrate but two having bearing upon this subject. The young Mazimbert, student at Dupras' institution, fourteen years of age, had in 1829 a central incisor that closed behind the inferior teeth, and which appeared so badly that he consented to have the deformity remedied. On account of the resistance of the alveolar border, our movements were necessarily slow and cautious; but one of his companions, hastening to witness the operation, gave our arm a sudden shove so as to cause us not only to break the external border of the alveolus, but also a greater part of the two adjoining alveoli. This tooth, as may be readily presumed, was thus thrown completely out of its socket.

This accident at first caused us some uneasiness, but our fears were soon dispelled upon inspection of the part. The tooth, adhering only to a portion of the fractured alveolus, was replaced, not in its primitive position, but in a range with its fellows, in such manner that the inferior incisores closed behind it. We employed no ligature to retain it in its new position. The patient was placed in the infirmary, and directed to use for several days a decoction of barley, and only such aliment as would be of easy mastication, and this in small quantities. We afterward substituted a healing and slightly stimulating lotion for the barley-water, and the patient eight days after returned to his duties, and scarcely had a month elapsed ere the tooth had become as firmly planted in its socket as any of its neighbours.

When we reflect that at the age of fourteen the orifices at the extremities of the roots of teeth are capacious enough to admit of a free communication of the nerves, arteries and veins, we can well comprehend why this tooth did not change in colour as do those that are luxated at a later period of life, and which usually assume a yellow or dark hue.*

---

* Luxation of the teeth is now recommended by no writer on dental sur-

The other case is that of a lady, aged forty-four, who had in the superior jaw only the two anterior molares. These served the purposes of mastication, and also to sustain artificial teeth, which she persisted in wearing notwithstanding the inconveniences they occasioned her. One of these teeth became decayed upon its crown, and occasioned severe pain, which none of the remedies applied during three days could subdue. We proposed the luxation of this tooth, to which the patient acceded; and after the operation had been effected, the artificial piece, sustained by means of these molares and a pivot, inserted into the fang of a central incisor, was replaced. We then plugged the decayed tooth. During the five years that have since elapsed, the patient has experienced no pain, and the artificial piece no longer inconveniences her.

Upon patients of indifferent constitution, and whose gums are turgid or continually engorged, luxating the teeth seldom results favourably. In such case recourse should be had to extraction of the tooth; particularly if it has been loosened and interferes with the movements of the jaw.

gery, and as Dr. C. A. Harris very justly remarks, is practised by none but the ignorant or inexperienced. Dr. H. states that "Mr. Fox was the first who endeavoured to cure odontalgia, by raising the tooth sufficiently in its socket to break the vessels and nerves that enter the extremities of the fangs, and then immediately pressing it down again to its former position. His hopes of success were, at first, very sanguine. He thought that, if he destroyed the nervous connexion between a tooth and the general system, the tooth would not be liable to ache. The result of his operations disappointed his expectations; he found that, although the paroxysms of pain were not so violent as before, yet the tooth soon became sore, and protruded from its socket. He, therefore, never afterward performed the operation, except under the most favourable circumstances.

"Subsequent experiments have not placed this operation in a more favourable light. The socket is generally much injured by the unnatural revulsion of the tooth, especially if it be one of the molares with its bifurcated fangs. An inflammation of the lining membrane and an effusion of the lymph follow, the membrane becomes thickened, and the tooth is in consequence protruded out of its socket, so that, at each occlusion of the jaw, it strikes its antagonist before the other teeth come together, and thus keeps up a constant irritation, and involves the adjacent parts in an unhealthy action.

"My own observation," Dr. H. continues, "has convinced me that the chances of success for this operation, even under the most favourable circumstances, are so uncertain that it ought never to be attempted." (Dental Art, p. 174.)—S.

Loosening of the Teeth.—The teeth may become loosened from various causes, as by blows, falls, and other accidents, by disease, the habit of working them with the fingers, and by old age. When loosened by any accident they soon become tight again; but if loosened by the effect of disease, they cannot be expected to adhere firmly again until health has been perfectly re-established. If loosened with the fingers, it will suffice to abstain from so pernicious a habit. The teeth of old men cannot be made firm in their places again, after becoming loose, without great difficulty. They frequently require to be shortened with a file that they may no longer be interfered with by those of the opposite jaw.

A loosened tooth should not be made fast to an adjoining tooth, for the purpose of restraining its motions, as that on which it may thus depend, will, in all probability, be injured in its position. It is better to carry the ligature to the second or third tooth from it.

Replacement of the Teeth in their Sockets.—This operation consists in replacing teeth that have been extracted, and presents chances of success more or less favourable, according to the health and age of the subject. It is also practised when a dentist unskilfully extracts one tooth for another, or when, by accident, the tooth has been knocked out. However simple this operation may appear, it requires precautions that cannot be too well attended to. Before attempting it, the mouth should be well examined. We annex a case in point.

M. Puydebat, of Auch, our friend of the Royal Court of Agen, when fifteen years old, in attempting to mount an unruly horse, received a violent kick, by which three of his incisores, and one cuspidatus of the superior jaw, and two incisores, and two bicuspides of the inferior, were forced into his mouth. Falling upon his back, he remained nearly two hours insensible. He lost much blood, and spat his teeth out upon the ground. Having recovered his consciousness, he returned to his farm, and, on the next day, was taken by his parents to a neighbouring town to receive such aid as could be procured. A physician, surgeon and dentist were consulted, the latter of whom demanded the teeth, which were soon brought to him;

he cleaned them, detached portions of the alveoli, still adhering to their roots, and replaced them in the mouth, in their respective places.   It may be easily concluded that portions of the fractured alveolar process still remained in the mouth; and it will not, therefore, be a matter of surprise when we add that violent inflammation succeeded this operation, and before the fractured portions were detached, suppuration had occurred. The obliteration of the sockets succeeded this loss of substance; and the patient, after so injudicious an operation, was obliged to adopt a severe regimen, and, for eight months after, could take nothing but liquids.   Two years later, as the teeth had not regained their primitive solidity, they were extracted, and his mouth was thus restored to perfect health.

We should, in such cases, have regard to the age of the subject especially, and, previous to replacing the teeth, their crowns should be shortened.   If as many as six or eight teeth have been knocked out, we should only replace four or five, choosing such as we think may be most likely to become firm again, permitting the alveoli of the others to become obliterated, that those that have been replaced may be the more firmly fixed.   Any splints that may be discovered previous to the operation should be extracted.   If they be sufficiently large to impair the walls of the alveoli, we should hesitate to replace the teeth, for they never can become firmly seated.

Dental Tartar.—Dental tartar is analogous to salivary concretions.   It varies in colour as much as in consistency, which sometimes resembles a granulous pulp, sometimes a hard, calcareous concretion, called coating or slime, according to its hardness.—Tartar may be yellow, gray, green, white, red, or entirely black in the mouths of persons who smoke tobacco. These varieties of colour depend, in a measure, upon the part of the tooth or gum that it occupies, the state of health of the subject, &c.   The texture of tartar is commonly granulous; it does not present a regular organization, and may be compared to the callus that unites the fractures of bones.   (Pl. XIII. Fig. 9.)

Tartar has been often analyzed by French and foreign chemists, but different results have always been obtained.   This might be accounted for by the fact of its having been taken from different subjects; but we believe that tartar may be different in different parts of the same mouth. Be this as it may, it is now well known that the basis of tartar of the teeth resembles that of bone, but that it differs from bone in the species of animal matter that unites its parts, and which is analogous to mucus. Such are the conclusions of M. Vauquelin and M. Laugier, published in an essay upon dental tartar, from which we extract the following :—

1. This matter, reduced to fine powder, loses seven hundredths of its weight of animal matter by desiccation.

2. Dissolved in muriatic acid, it leaves thirteen hundredths of its weight of animal matter of a yellowish white colour.

3. This animal matter, submitted to the action of boiling water for at least two hours, does not dissolve, and the decoction, reduced to the smallest quantity, does not give the slightest trace of gelatine. This result proves that the animal matter is not the same as that which exists in bones.

4. The phosphate of lime, precipitated by the ammoniac of its muriatic solution, becomes yellow after desiccation, which evinces the presence of a certain quantity of animal matter. This phosphate becomes black when heated in an enclosed crucible. In this state its weight equals that of seventy per centum of the tartar employed.

5. In the liquor in which the phosphate of lime had been separated, we put oxalate of ammonia. The precipitate thus produced, formed twelve per centum of the weight of the tartar used, and represented about nine per centum of the carbonate of lime.

6. The results obtained in the above operations did not represent the precise quantity of matter submitted to the analysis, and we evaporated the liquid in which the phosphate and carbonate of lime had been precipitated to discover if it contained any particles of animal matter. The muriate of ammonia, dried and heated slowly in a platina crucible, became black, and, being consumed, left a brown substance weighing three-fifths of a grain, which resembled the oxyde of iron, and

9

which was in fact composed of lime and phosphate of magnesia.

7. A fragment of tartar, exposed to a strong heat for about
one hour, became perfectly white, and lost 22.6 per centum.
Allowing seven per centum for the evaporation of moisture,
we will then have 15.6 of animal matter, presuming that the
carbonate of lime has not been decomposed in the operation.

8. A tooth covered with tartar, having been perfectly
cleaned, and afterward heated until it had become white, lost
33.2 per centum.   Thus, supposing that this tooth contained
the same quantity of water as the tartar, it possessed a greater
quantity of animal matter, since the tartar only contained 15.6
and the tooth 26.2.   This is without doubt the reason why
the teeth are harder, and have more consistency and elasticity
than the tartar which covers them.

9. Although the small quantity of tartar of the teeth upon
which we have experimented, has left us but little hope of
discovering in it the presence of the phosphate of magnesia,
we have analyzed 1.77 gr. of that substance by sulphuric acid
after the manner heretofore indicated, and we have obtained
fifteen milligrammes of phosphate of the ammoniac of magnesia, which represented 1.18 of the substance experimented
upon.

Desiring also to ascertain if tartar of the teeth contained *uric*
acid, or urate, we put a certain quantity of it into a solution of
potash; but discovered nothing of the kind.

By this analysis, one of the most perfect recorded, it is shown,
that this substance is composed, 1st, of animal matter, differing
from that which enters into the composition of bones; 2d, of
organic matter, 3d, of the phosphate and the carbonate of lime;
and, 4th, of a brown substance resembling the oxyde of iron,
and formed of iron and of phosphate of magnesia.

Authors do not agree upon the manner of the formation of
these various kinds of dental concretions.   Without recapitu-
lating hypotheses more or less ridiculous, I will state that the
opinion most generally received is, that it is produced in part
by a pathological secretion of the gums, and in part by a kind
of deposite of the saliva and other fluids that moisten the
mouth.

Every one knows with what facility tartar accumulates upon the teeth. It at first has a viscid and slimy appearance, and augments upon their crowns chiefly during sleep, forming itself into layers, which harden one after another, and adhere to the teeth like successive coats of mastic. It usually envelops the base of the teeth, accumulates in the intervening spaces, . fills their interstices, and penetrates as far as their roots in the alveolar cavity.

When only one side of the mouth is used in mastication, and the teeth are not carefully attended to, tartar will constantly accumulate upon the teeth thus thrown into disuse.

Among persons whose principal nourishment is easily masticated, the teeth soon become covered with tartar resembling very thick cement, in consequence of there being little friction in the process of mastication. But the most certain preventive is the constant use of the tooth-brush.

Tartar forms upon the teeth of all persons, but not uniformly. The quantity always depends upon the temperament, condition of health, or peculiar idiosyncrasy of the mouth. Upon the teeth of some persons its collection is very slow, while the utmost efforts of others will be necessary to prevent it. The teeth of individuals have been seen so completely incrusted with it as to have the appearance of one solid piece. (Pl. XIII. Fig. 9.) Examples of this kind are very common; but it is observed that persons whose teeth are most liable to such incrustations are of a pituitary, delicate and mucous constitution, whose mouths are constantly bathed with an abundance of viscid saliva, and whose gums are pale, soft, of a dull red, or livid and turgid aspect. Climate also influences this formation, and it is not so frequently met with upon the teeth of persons inhabiting warm or temperate climates as upon those who inhabit marshy and humid regions. It rarely exists upon the teeth of children of good health and constitution, and still more rarely upon the teeth of persons from twenty-five to thirty years old; but it is often met with in persons of advanced age whose teeth are apt to be so completely covered with this earthy concretion as to present a disagreeable and offensive appearance.

Next to the ravaging effects of caries of the teeth, tartar is

the chief agent in their destruction.   By increase of volume
and from its hardness, the cheeks, lips, and even the tongue,
are often irritated by the presence of tartar; it corrodes and
chafes the gums, and renders them liable to bleed upon the
slightest touch.   Fluxions, from which engorgements proceed,
with a purulent discharge, imparting to the breath an offensive
odour, may also be occasioned by the presence of this substance.
M. Duval asserts that he has seen these ulcers, when neglected,
pass into a state of gangrenous mortification, which, extending
itself over the gums, necrosed the subjacent maxillary bones.
He has also known tartar so to irritate the gums as to occasion
a gouty and rheumatic affection, and become the cause of pain,
loosening of the teeth, and their ultimate loss.

Independently of the disorders we have mentioned, and
which depend less upon the quantity of tartar accumulated than
upon the depth to which it penetrates into the alveoli, irritation
in the glands and salivary conduits, of a serious nature, may
proceed from its presence.   An abundant flow of saliva also
proceeds from this cause, and, being carried into the stomach,
gives rise to unpleasantness of feeling analogous to the symptoms of real disease, and tends to impede digestion.   These
symptoms disappear as soon as the foreign matter has been removed from the teeth.

From the evils described as attendant upon the presence of
tartar, it will readily be acknowledged that to prevent its accumulation, is a duty of no little importance.—This may be
effected by a proper regard to cleanliness.   Water, to which a
few drops of spirits may be added, is a good lotion.   It should
be applied with a brush and suitable dentifrice.   These means
will suffice unless the deposite has already become hardened,
in which case the aid of the dentist should always be sought,
as its removal will now require care and skill, of which we
shall have occasion to speak in describing the manner in which
this operation should be performed.   We need hardly remark
that the use of acids should not be resorted to in such a case.
They are always injurious, for the tartar cannot more readily
be affected by them than can the enamel or bony substance of
the tooth itself.

Our remarks upon the diseases of the teeth might here terminate, but that the subject of toothache has not hitherto been spoken of. This affection is allied to all of the preceding, but for the sake of perspicuity we deem it better to treat of it separately. In doing so we shall place ourselves under obligations to Dr. Mérat, whose excellent article in the thirty-seventh volume *du Dictionnaire des Sciences Médicales,* we shall make free with.

Odontalgia, or *Toothache,* is a peculiar pain, and may be regarded as one of the most frequent and distressing affections to which we are liable. It spares neither infancy nor age. Indeed, before their appearance above the gums, the teeth produce pain, and at the period of their protrusion, convulsions and even death, proceed from them. It would seem that bones so hard, and of a structure so well organized, might be preserved from pain; yet these, of all the bones of the human system, most frequently present this phenomenon; but, we again remark, there are few affections of the teeth that are not accompanied with pain, and this may be occasioned not only by the disease of the tooth itself, but also by affections of the adjacent parts, and by exterior causes.

Pain occasioned by Disease of the Tooth.—This is the most common description of toothache, and may proceed from a fracture or inflammation of the dental tissue, but more usually from decay of the organ.

Pain proceeding from Disease in the surrounding Parts.—This may derive its origin from all or any of the morbific conditions of the gums, alveolo-dental nerve, and even other parts of the mouth and face.

Inflammation, caries, and all other lesions of the alveoli, may determine it either by acting sympathetically upon the tooth through the medium of vessels and nerves, or by communicating to it the disease. As no external sign can be perceived, we are often ignorant of the source of pain, at least at its commencement, and it is not until after the extraction of the tooth, which is found to be in health, that we can ascertain the real cause of the affection.

9*

The dental nerves are sometimes subject to acute pain when there is no inflammation or alteration of the bony tissue; and this affection, which is called *dental neuralgia*, is very frequent. It differs from inflammatory odontalgia by the absence of pain and pulsation in the part, and is never followed by abscess.

Other parts of the mouth may also occasion toothache, by displacing the tooth, as in exostosis, abscess, polypi, &c., or by extending to them the disease of which they are the seat, as in cancer, caries, rachitis, &c.

Pain in the Teeth from exterior Causes.—This pain may proceed from affections of different parts of the organism, as rheumatic, gouty and erysipelatous vices affecting a portion of the dental arches; or it may result from an entire exterior cause, as the contact of very cold or hot air, or frequent mastication of acid or sweet aliment. In the first case the pain is not circumscribed, but may affect the entire jaw; in the second case we may experience less pain, but it is of a peculiar character, and has been denominated *setting on edge*.

We can cite numerous examples of periodical toothache, symptomatic of affections, of other and remote parts in which such affections have not in an immediate manner developed themselves. Hence an individual may often experience pain in one tooth while the cause exists in another; and thus the unaffected tooth has often been extracted. Indeed persons have been known to point out one jaw as the seat of pain while the malady existed in the other, and over the right instead of the left side. Sometimes, also, violent pain is felt where no decay whatever exists in the teeth; but this usually is in consequence of disease in the alveoli and periosteum. Hence it will be perceived how important it is that circumspection should be exercised in the application of remedies.

The Means of remedying Pain in the Teeth and surrounding Parts.

The remedies should be directed to the first cause of the disease. When, for example, it is occasioned by first dentition, we should, as far as possible, facilitate the dental eruption, first, by softening the gum and diminishing its thickness; secondly, by endeavouring to alleviate the local plethora by the means pointed out in our remarks upon first dentition. Vesicatory applications will also be of advantage in cases of sanguine turgescence.

When toothache is produced in adults by inflammation of the dental pulp or the alveolus, we should have recourse to the application of leeches, fumigation with a decoction of elder, emollient lotions, stimulating pediluvia, and cooked figs applied to the gums. If the pain be more especially experienced at night, it will be proper to foment the affected part of the head for about twenty minutes with hot flannels steeped in a decoction of camomile flowers, in which two or three poppy heads have been boiled. We should always endeavour to avoid the application of cataplasms upon the cheek, as, should an abscess form, that application will cause it to open exteriorly. Where, however, the judicious application of these several means proves unavailing, the tooth should be extracted, but not until the inflammation has disappeared.*

Dental neuralgia, of which we have spoken, should be treated with anti-spasmodic and sedative applications. The pain usually attends the course of the nerves, and violently affects the head and ears. It may be subdued by derivatives and emollients. Some surgeons have been successful by means of the application of moxa over the mental foramen, and by section of the nervous branch which ramifies to the teeth. We have sometimes relieved this affection by the application of small vesicatories or plasters, prepared with the extract of opium, to the temples, or behind the ears. These should be about half an inch in diameter.†

* It is improper to await the subsidence of the inflammation ere we extract the tooth. Its extraction is a means of producing this effect.—S.

† Mr. T. Bell, who, it seems, has paid much attention to this affection, says: " from the considerable attention paid to the different forms of the complaint, I have long since come to the conclusion that two distinct affections—distinct in their causes, and equally so in the effect which different remedies are found to exert upon them—have been confounded under these terms; the one constitutional in its cause, and curable by general remedies; the other local, which, though occasionally relieved to a certain degree by such treatment, can only be permanently cured by the removal of the local cause, which, unhappily, often lies too deep to be within the reach of any operation.

" It must be confessed that the symptoms of these two affections are so

Odontalgia most frequently results from caries of the teeth, and from portions of these organs being permitted to remain in their alveoli. If the pain be severe, and the decay has extended to the dental nerve, extraction is the proper remedy. If, on the contrary, the decay be small, we should have recourse to milder remedies, as the pain may in such case originate from the effects of heat and cold upon the general system, or upon the tooth itself.

Odontalgia, when merely indicative of rheumatic affections, the puerperal state, &c., falls more properly under the cognizance of the physician than that of the dentist.

similar as to be readily confounded, and perhaps it would be difficult to lay down any one character which should infallibly distinguish the one from the other. There are, however, some general diagnostic symptoms, which, after having seen many cases, will, I believe, enable the practicien to decide with considerable certainty in any well-marked case.

"In those which have a constitutional origin, periodical returns of the paroxysms are, if my view be correct, an invariable symptom. This may vary to a great extent, not only in the degree, but also in the regularity which may characterize the exacerbation of pain. In some cases the pain is incessant, and almost always equally severe; and it is only by careful attention that its periodical increase can be ascertained. In others, not the slightest painful sensation is perceived during the twenty-four hours, with the exception of a distinct and certain period, which never fails, and never varies, and during which, perhaps, the agony is intense.

"In the local disease, on the contrary, the pain is either continual, without any marked paroxysms of increased suffering; or the attacks are sudden, frequent, and interrupted by intervals of perfect ease, but recurring from time to time, and, in both cases, without any regular periods. This is the most obvious diagnostic character which has appeared to me to distinguish the two diseases. Farther observation may, perhaps, enable us to add other and more certain marks of distinction; but even this will, as I believe, be found generally sufficient to indicate the nature of the disease."

This disease is not confined to any one part of the body. The branches of the fifth pair of nerves are the most subject to it. After regulating the bowels, if requisite, with some mild purgative, the administration of the sulphate of quinine, and the arsenical solution alternately, will be found to effect a cure.

Local neuralgia is a disease, produced by local irritation, as exostosis of the roots of teeth, &c. On the extraction of such teeth, the affection immediately disappears. Mr. T. Bell says he has employed the following preparation with great success:

℞. Hydrarg. Oxymur. ʒi.
Unguent. Cetac. ʒi.
Misce, fiat linimentum.

The side of the face to be rubbed with this lotion.—S.

Although many substances have been discovered capable of mitigating the sufferings produced by toothache, or of curing it, we are nevertheless constrained to confess that there exists no specific for it. We may, however, produce momentary abatement by cauterizing the teeth, applying alcohol, sulphuric ether, essential oils, emollients, anodynes, and narcotics generally.

Very often the most severe pain will yield to the application of a little cotton saturated with essential oil, and introduced into the decayed cavity of the tooth. The annexed formula is the prescription of Dr. Handel, of Metz, and is an excellent antidote to toothache.

Opium, ...	½ drachm.
Oil of Henbane, ...	1 "
Extract of Belladonna, ...	} 6 grains each.
Extract of Camphor, ...	
Oil of Cajeput, ...	} 1 ounce and 6 grains each.
Tincture of Cantharides, ..	

An opiate of this kind is particularly applicable to odontalgia having its seat in the superior jaw, as it can be placed immediately to the seat of the disease, which could not be done were a liquid employed. Small pills, composed of opium and camphor, may also be advantageously employed; and we have used, with success, our *soothing pills*, composed of equal parts of the resinous extract of opium, camphor and incense.

The composition known as soothing drops, the formula of which we annex, is one of the most efficacious remedies we know of for toothache produced by caries of the teeth, or other affections of the mouth. It should be applied as follows: First, the cavity of the tooth should be cleansed with a piece of cotton, and then another piece, saturated with one or two drops of this liquid, should be introduced. If inflammation has proceeded from the affected tooth, cataplasms, composed of flour of flaxseed, and a few poppy heads, and from fifteen to twenty of these drops, should be applied to the cheek of the patient. This dressing should be removed every three hours. If the gums only are inflamed, a gargle should be used, composed of a table-spoon twice full of barley-water, and from six to eight of these drops, from which relief may be expected. It should be used several times a day, and retained in the mouth three or four minutes at each time.

SOOTHING DROPS.

Alcohol,	3 ounces.
Sulphuric Ether,	1 "
Tincture of Opium,	1 "
Turlington's Balsam,	3 drachms.
Essence of Cloves,	3 "

Misce.

This liquor should be kept in a vessel hermetically sealed.

The use of the magnet has also been proposed to relieve toothache. This remedy, though innocent, does not appear to merit the credit which the Abbots Lenoble and Lepelletier seemed anxious to attribute to it. We can hardly believe that the magnetic properties of any instrument, placed in contact with the teeth, can have any salutary effect upon a diseased nerve.

Electricity has also been recommended as a cure or pallia- tive in this affection, but our experience has not enabled us to offer an opinion upon its merits. We may, however, remark that this kind of treatment is at least of uncertain efficacy, and that it is but seldom used, since the pain it occasions is nearly as acute as that resulting from the extraction of a tooth.

The imagination of some individuals is sufficiently powerful to control the most distressing toothache. We have seen vio- lent mental emotion in persons of nervous susceptibility, pro- duce a similar effect. How can we, without attributing it to the imagination, account for the instantaneous cessation of toothache that many persons experience on approaching the door of the dentist; and also the effect of various charms, and certain prayers, the efficacy of which depends entirely upon the confidence reposed in them?

The following circumstance, which we witnessed in London, in 1825, will tend to show how far credulity may be taxed when a person is persuaded that certain means, no matter how ridi- culous, are sufficient to accomplish a cure. On passing one morning through one of the most populous streets of that city, (Newgate street,) we perceived in the midst of a crowd a gibbet, on which a man had, half an hour previously been hanged; and, to our great astonishment, we saw the hangman pass one of the hands of the corpse over the neck, stomach, back, and mouth of a young woman. On inquiring into the import of this, we were informed that she would thus be cured of pain in the breast and toothache. We should not have believed this report had we not seen the woman raise the hand of the dead man after the executioner had let it fall, and repeat the ceremony.

It will not be profitable to enlarge farther upon the means recommended for the cure of toothache. Their enumeration would occupy too much space. Every person can tell of some remedy, which, under some circumstance, has benefited him. We are, however, far from objecting to those means that have been called women's remedies; and, if they are not capable of injuring the teeth or gums, it is unwise to forbid them. If they be employed, time will thus be gained, and the affection will often subside of itself. The pretended specific will, of course, be accredited.

We have thus pointed out most of the diseases of the dental organs, and if we are limited in our enumeration of the various therapeutical, general, internal, and operative remedies called for, it is only to avoid fastidious repetition; our intention being hereafter to detail the various modes of preserving the teeth, the operations they require, and the different procedures to which the dentist has daily recourse to replace them.

The order adopted in this work places us under the necessity of treating of such of the parts of our organism as have any immediate connexion with the teeth; hence we shall speak of the gums and their principal morbid affections.

THE GUMS, AND THEIR VARIOUS MORBID AFFECTIONS.

The gums, firm and of a rosy white in a healthy state, polished and smooth in infancy, festooned in adolescence, hard and resisting in old age, are subjected to certain morbid affections which are peculiar to them, and which sensibly change their appearance. They inflame, tumefy, and even excoriate, under certain circumstances; and often become the seat of violent phlegmasiæ, aphthæ, pains, excoriations, fistules and ulcers. They may also waste away in such manner as to expose the alveolar borders; or they may be so engorged and swollen as to occasion fleshy excrescences which are often difficult to cure. Such are the different morbid conditions of the gums, and which we now purpose examining. They form, according to Dr. Aubry, three principal divisions, under the general terms, *inflammation, swelling, ulceration,* and *fungus* of the gums.

The first of these divisions embraces *aphthæ, inflammation* at the period of first dentition, *abscesses, phlegmons, dental fistules,* and *adhesion* of the gums to the cheeks.

The second shall include remarks upon *scorbutic affections, scurvy of the gums,* their *gangrene,* and the various alterations produced by scrofula, syphilitic virus, and the use of mercury.

In the third division we shall describe *epules* and other fungous tumours of the gums of the same class.

SECTION I.

INFLAMMATION OF THE GUMS.

Aphthæ.—This affection is characterized by a white, tuberculous eruption, superficial or confluent, which developes itself upon the interior of the mouth, and sometimes extends deeply into the œsophagus. It should not, properly, be classed with the diseases of the gums, as it only affects the buccal membrane which invests them. The pustules are so numerous as sometimes to impede respiration, mastication, and deglutition. Their presence often occasions an involuntary flow of saliva.

In adults, aphthæ generally have the appearance of small, white tubercles, superficial, round, of the size of a mustard seed, scattered in different pustules, or united in such manner as to form a thick crust. They may be transparent, opaque, or of a livid, black, or yellow colour. They seldom occasion disorder of the general system. In children, however, their appearance is regarded more seriously; they are often preceded by impaired digestion, anguish, heat, frequency of the pulse, sleeplessness, and convulsive agitation of the muscles of the face. These pustules have the appearance of small, distinct white buttons, separated by uninflamed intervals, and at first occupy that part of the gum through which the incisores are about protruding, and thence extend themselves to the commissures of the lips, the internal face of the cheeks, the tongue, and the palate. There is but little heat in the diseased part. At the end of a few days they become yellow, and drop off about the ninth or tenth day, but again appear, and sometimes are reproduced upon the internal membrane of the mouth. Such is the character which aphthæ sometimes present, but, unfortunately, they do not always exhibit so mild a nature.

When the pustules are confluent, the buccal inflammation is more intense; and they exfoliate only to be promptly reproduced. The mouth is burning, and can scarcely bear the impression of soothing liquids, so acute is the pain. The disease, under some circumstances, assumes a still more serious character; there is then difficulty in swallowing and breathing, the breast becomes heated, the voice hoarse, the mouth dry and interiorly covered closely with pustules. At other times a crust resembling coagulated milk is formed by the pustules. The volume of this crust rapidly increases and assumes a yellow or brown colour; an eschar is soon formed, the destruction of which exposes a brownish red ulcer, with a fetid sanies, which, when deep-seated, may terminate in gangrene, and sometimes in death.

This affection is always serious in young subjects, though not usually fatal. In adults it is less severe.

At all periods various opinions have been entertained as to the true cause of this disease. It has been observed to be most frequent in the latter part of autumn. Low and humid localities are favourable to its propagation; it is very common in Denmark, Holland, and Zealand. Individuals most subject to these eruptions are children and old men of lymphatic and feeble constitutions; and, also, persons subject to catarrhal affections, whose teeth are decayed, or covered with tartar, &c.

10

Habitual filthiness, use of bad aliment, defective lactation, inconsiderate use of mercurial preparations, very hard aliment, or asperities in the mouth occasioned by decayed or fractured teeth, are causes favouring the development of aphthæ. Under some circumstances, however, it assumes an epidemic character, especially in hospitals for infants.

The treatment of aphthæ, for which the dentist is frequently consulted, should entirely depend upon the cause originating it. Thus, in sparse aphthæ of children and adults, it will suffice to preserve them from morbific influences so that the eruptions may of themselves disappear. Soothing gargles, slightly acidulated, and emollient drinks, are the sole means indicated for adults; the milk of a healthy nurse is the best remedy for children.

If the aphthæ are confluent, the diseased parts should be touched with a brush dipped into a liquid containing sulphuric or hydro-chloric acid. The neck and head should be kept warm; lime-water and a decoction of bark should be used as a drink. When deglutition is difficult, we should substitute for these drinks gargles, injections, and medicated baths. If the eruptions depend upon asperities of the teeth, these should be promptly removed with a file.

Phlegmasia resulting from the Perforation of the Gums at the Period of Dentition.—We have already treated of plegmasia, in speaking of the phenomena that occur at the period of first dentition. We then witness inflammatory symptoms so intense as to involve the face and submaxillary glands, and which progress so far as to produce the most serious consequences. The maxillary bones themselves may be attacked, and the complete destruction of the gums of the permanent teeth may result therefrom.

The pain resulting from this buccal phlogosis may only be alleviated by the milk of the mother, which possesses a twofold advantage, by appeasing the thirst of the child and softening the tissues of the gum, and thereby removing in part the resistance presented to the approaching teeth. When this remedy may not be had, recourse should be had to mucilages of flaxseed, gum Arabic and marsh-mallow, to which should be added a little honey. This may also be applied to the gums by means of a brush made of a piece of the root of marsh-mallow. If the inflammation be very great, the above remedy should be persisted in, and, if possible, the milk of a healthy nurse should be procured.

When, however, the gum offers an obstinate resistance, we should, with the instrument represented in (Plate XIV. Fig. 4,) make an incision down to the tooth. The hemorrhage that may result from this should give no alarm, as it tends to allay the inflammatory symptoms. Should it, however, appear too copious, it may be arrested by oxycrate lotions or acidulated water.

The child that has escaped the evils of first dentition may yet be less fortunate in the process of second dentition. The tissue of the gums at this period, more firm and compact, presents greater resistance to the tooth that presses against it. The swelling is considerable, the part appears very red, and the pain becomes excessive. This especially occurs at the time of the eruption of the inferior permanent molares, and the inflammation may be so intense as to produce abscesses of a serious character, particularly should they be developed externally.

These evils may be most effectively remedied by scarification, or the removal of portions of the temporary teeth that may have occasioned them. The latter operation may be easily accomplished, as these teeth are at this time usually necrosed or partially absorbed.

Baths, stimulating pediluvia, diluent drinks and relaxing gargles, are generally indicated by such alarming symptoms, which often do not of themselves recede.

Phlegmon, or Abscess of the Gums.—It is not unfrequently that phlegmons or abscesses succeed severe inflammation of the gums, and these sometimes terminate in resolution, at other times in suppuration, but at times also they assume a more serious character. These inflammatory tumours have been called parules, or abscesses of the cheek, and are so often witnessed in practice as to be easily recognised. They may result from a peculiar constitutional vice, a rheumatic affection, inflammation of the tissue proper of the gums, and caries of

the teeth, maxillary bones, &c.   They may likewise arise from
an acute disease of the alveolo-periosteum, rupture of some of
its fibres, from contusions, blows and pressure upon the gums,
or from irritation of the dental nerves communicated to the
teeth.   They may also emanate from sudden impressions of
heat or cold, from the accumulation of tartar upon the teeth
and gums, the inconsiderate use of mechanical agents, elixirs
badly prepared, and many pretended specifics that are highly
extolled as means of re-establishing loosened teeth.   The improper manner of plugging teeth, and the insertion of several
artificial teeth at a time upon pivots, may also produce them.
These tumours are most commonly developed in the vicinity
of carious teeth, and more frequently near the anterior than
the posterior portion of the mouth.   The neighbourhood of
the superior incisores is especially exposed to them.   Sometimes the disease only consists of a pustule situated upon the
gum, and which developes itself in twenty-four hours; at
other times it consists of an enormous deposite disfiguring the
entire side of the face, and which suppurates at the expiration of
some weeks.

In all cases they are preceded by painful tension of the affected part, which gradually swells and reddens.   The opposite
jaw soon participates in this swelling, and extreme heat and
sensibility are manifested here, which are greatly augmented
by the movements of the jaw.   If this phlegmasia is very extensive, or if it be developed with rapidity, it soon occasions
general derangement; it produces cephalalgy, horripilations,
sleeplessness, acceleration of the pulse, and other symptoms of
fever.   The swelling extends itself to the head and ears; there
is difficulty in opening the mouth, impediment in speech and
mastication, and the saliva is secreted in greater abundance
than in a healthy condition.   After some days the inflammation may gradually disappear, especially if there be no continued cause, as the presence of a decayed tooth or root,
disorganization of the maxillary bone, &c.   It in this case terminates by resolution, particularly if, on its first appearance,
emollient topical applications have been made, together with
suitable revulsives, gargles composed of milk, or marsh-mallow
water, healing infusions slightly stimulating, &c.   By means of

these remedies the inflammatory symptoms abate, the functions of the mouth are restored, and the patient experiences entire repose.

Should the disease, on the contrary, tend to suppuration, the progress of the plegmasia through its course will be more precipitate. The inflammatory symptoms continuing to increase, we soon discover in the place primitively affected an augmentation of size and sensibility, accompanied by lancinating pains; a collection of pus may soon be detected by its fluctuations beneath the finger; the part soon becomes thinner and spontaneously ruptures to give exit to the purulent matter contained within.

This spontaneous opening of the abscess is usually internal, and occurs between the fifth and tenth days.

It will be perceived that in such cases it would be injudicious to limit ourselves to the use of local remedies; the source of the disease must be attacked, either by extracting a diseased tooth communicating with the part, or by effecting an opening into the phlegmon at an early period. This will be necessary, as the enlargement of the phlegmon may otherwise impede respiration and deglutition. It is often difficult to operate upon these affections when they are located in the posterior part of the mouth, and in order to do so without injuring the adjacent parts, the instrument described in Plate XIV. Fig. 4, should be selected. The abscess being opened the operator should be particular to incline the head of his patient in such manner that the pus may escape from his mouth and not descend into the stomach.

The opening of the abscess should be capacious, that it may not close prematurely, as a new collection of pus may otherwise be formed, and the retention of which may, by its communicating with sockets of the teeth, destroy their periosteum and occasion an ulceration that would soon assume a fistulous character.

Fistulous Ulcers of the Gums.—(*Dental Fistules of Moderns.*)—It often happens after the opening of abscesses of the gums that the succeeding ulcerations make no approach toward cure, although the most efficacious remedies be applied. We

10*

may in such cases infer the existence of undiscovered causes, as decay of a tooth or of the maxillary bone, or the presence of fractured particles of the alveolar processes.

These ulcers (which M. Duval has made the subject of a memoir) have their seat at the base of the inferior jaw, and sometimes near the mental apophysis of the maxillary bone. Their borders are callous and tumefied, their circumference is red, smooth or mammillated, and in general, slightly œdematous. Sometimes this ulcer presents only one orifice, and which is nearly concealed by the presence of a serous ichor which has been discharged from it and become congealed in the atmosphere. At other times we observe two or three of these orifices very close to each other. If the ulcer is exposed to the air, the dried serous matter will form a crust behind which fresh serum will accumulate, and becoming purulent, will constantly increase if care be not taken to evacuate it. Cases in which suppuration and necrosis of the bone have taken place, will exhibit one or two openings communicating outwardly, which give passage to a fetid, bloody pus. By means of a probe we can then discover that the bone is denuded. The pus forms for itself an issue into the mouth. The tooth involved is now no longer sensible and becomes loose, and we may with the fingers or the sound, remove the sequestra, which, with the tooth, should be taken away if too much resistance be not offered. The fistulous openings will then cicatrize.

The treatment of dental fistules is therefore limited to the extraction of the foreign substances, (including the diseased tooth,) which are the causes of them, and assisting the exfoliation of the necrosed bone by such remedies as art has discovered. To prevent these affections the extraction of all decayed and painful teeth is the only certain means. To prevent the pus from issuing externally, and thus disfiguring the face, a free incision should be made internally as soon as the affection manifests itself between the cheek and gum.

Adhesion of the Gum to the Cheek.—This adhesion, which is usually accidental, though sometimes congenital, may be occasioned by ulceration of the gum or cheek, and by the immoderate use of mercury. Phlegmons and fistules of the gums may occasion it. Adhesive inflammation of these parts may be partial or total, upon one or both sides.

The functions of the mouth are interfered with by these adhesions to a greater or less extent in proportion to the extent of the affection. They may generally be prevented by the use of mucilaginous gargles, and by frequently passing between the cheek and gum a brush dipped in this liquid. The adhesion may be destroyed with the fingers, if recent, and the separation being thus effected, we should endeavour to keep the parts from each other, that a new adhesion may not be formed.

SECTION II.

SWELLING AND VARIOUS ULCERATIONS OF THE GUMS.

Affections of the Gums in Scorbutus.

The gums, alveoli, and maxillary bones undergo great changes in scorbutus. Without giving a description of the disease, which would be altogether foreign to our subject, we shall point out the various alterations of the parts, and also the means customarily employed to subdue them.

In this disease the gums are generally first attacked. A troublesome itching is the earliest symptom; they soon tumefy, become red, and bleed on the slightest touch. Sometimes they will continue in this state; at other times the disease progresses. The gums then become fungous, of a livid red, and emit a fetid odour; they soon become swollen and ulcerate. This ulceration in some cases involves the whole dental arch. Hemorrhages frequently occur, and the teeth, which become black or brown, loosen and often fall out. The disease sometimes extends to the maxillary bones, upon which it produces extensive decay, and in this manner exposes the dental nerve, and thus occasions the most excruciating pains. Sometimes the gums become so black that one would suppose them to be gangrenous, if the odour, *sui generis*, indicated its presence. In scorbutic affections we often observe fungous excrescences which acquire a very large size. These excrescences are sometimes of a livid red, and sometimes of a sandy gray colour. Their forms are various, and, when they are not rough, upon large bases or straight pedicles, they are ragged as if torn. Sometimes these tumours have a firm consistency; but generally they are flabby and bloody.

There are remedies appropriate to these affections. When the gums commence to tumefy, and become spongy, and the teeth are becoming loose, and there exists no ulceration, it will be proper to have recourse to gargles, acidulated with the sulphate of alumine and sulphuric acid, which will also be useful in arresting the passive hemorrhages. If the fungous excrescences be very hard or firm, it will be well to excise them. In cases of simple ulceration, gargles of barley-water, honey of roses, muriatic acid, or even oxycrate lotions, will be proper. This treatment is generally successful with children. If the dental nerve be exposed, we should endeavour to fill the cavity of the tooth with cotton dipped in a tincture of opium. This means it will be necessary to adopt, as we cannot plug the tooth in this condition of the mouth, and the extraction of it might produce a hemorrhage difficult to check.

Such are the various means used to effect a cure of scorbutic affections of the gums. The treatment, it will be observed, is purely local; but entire success cannot be hoped for without resorting to general remedies, for which the physician must be applied to.

Scurvy of the Gums.—This affection, as its name indicates, is peculiar to the gums, and resembles, to some extent, the disease improperly called scurvy, which, at its commencement, is strictly local. Scurvy of the gums often incommodes but little the person affected, but, if neglected, may produce serious consequences. It is manifested by softness, lividity and swelling of the gums, which bleed upon the slightest touch. This swelling at first appears between the teeth, and there forms small fungi, whose surfaces become easily excoriated.

Sometimes inflammation attends these, and produces ulceration, which destroys a part of the gums, and thus denudes the roots of the teeth. Suppuration between the gums and alveoli is then brought on, and these parts are destroyed by means of a purulent, glutinous and fetid matter, which insinuates itself between the teeth and the walls of their alveoli. The teeth become loose, and, after a time, drop out. Sometimes the disease is confined to a part of the mouth; at other times it extends its ravages over both jaws. When it is partial, it may occasion but slight inconvenience to the patient; and it has been known to continue in this condition for years, resisting every remedy applied to it. The suppuration may be caused by filthiness of the teeth, and swelling of the gums and fulness of their vessels. This disease is observed in men from thirty-six to forty years of age; in women whose catamenial discharges are irregular, or have ceased; in subjects of a lymphatic, melancholic, pituitary temperament; persons inhabiting humid, marshy, and unhealthy localities; and such as have endured the suppression of some periodical discharge, or the repercussion of cutaneous diseases.

This morbid condition of the gums is cured by removing all foreign matter that may be found between the teeth, and by keeping the parts in a state of cleanliness.

The gums are often painful, and so much engorged as to rise above their natural level. In this case, they should be slightly brushed once or twice a day, and an emollient or narcotic decoction should be used in order to cause them to bleed, and thus to disgorge themselves. This mode of treatment is preferable to cutting, scarifying, or cauterizing them.* The general remedies capable of subduing scorbutic affections, properly so called, should not be neglected. The mouth of the

---

* Scarifying should not be condemned in these cases, as relief may often be the more speedily afforded by its means. It is recommended by Messrs. Hunter, Fox, and Bell. "The application of leeches," Dr. Harris remarks, "is also attended with the most decided advantage." "After the gums have begun to recover, amendment will be much accelerated, by washing the mouth with some tonic and astringent lotion."

Dr. Fitch recommends as a wash for the mouth a decoction of the inner bark of green white oak, which Dr. Harris asserts, he has prescribed and always found beneficial.—S.

patient should be kept strictly clean, and to accomplish this we should remove slime and all foreign substances that may have collected upon the gums, necks of the teeth and their interstices, and even in their decayed cavities.

The scorbutic affection being destroyed, the patient should pay the strictest regard to cleanliness, and substitute for the emollients or narcotics, tonics or absorbents.

Gangrene of the Gums.—This disease imperatively demands our attention. It has been called *putrefaction of the gums;* and is met with in adults, but more frequently in children, especially when collected in large numbers, as in hospitals, where the atmosphere is vicious, and the nourishment given of a bad quality. This singular affection is unseemly in its character and formidable in its effects. It progresses with frightful rapidity, and the loss of teeth occasioned by it is but a small part of the evil consequences attendant upon it. The children attacked by it have ordinarily swollen countenances and fulness of habit; the gums become tender, assume a purple colour, are painful and turgid, and the breath emits an odour highly fetid, offensive, and very warm; a species of gangrene supervenes, which is almost always fatal in very young subjects.

Strict cleanliness of the mouth, and hygienic remedies, aided by appropriate general treatment, will suffice to subdue this disease, the alarming symptoms of which we have often dispersed by recommending succulent and animal nourishment, wines, and the avoidance of all exposure to a moist and unwholesome atmosphere.

Affections of the Gums in Scrofula.—The gums in scrofulous subjects are generally pale and soft; but are sometimes tumefied, turgid and ulcerated. This morbid affection evidently arises from constitutional tendency. The appropriate treatment consists in the employment of internal remedies, which may be assisted by the use of such lotions as decoctions of bark, &c., frictions upon the diseased parts, with a small quantity of quinine and magnesia.

Affections of the Gums occasioned by Syphilitic Virus.—Upon the mucous membrane of the mouth this virus produces ulcers of a peculiar character, bearing no resemblance to other affections of these parts. Their treatment must necessarily coincide with that usual in syphilitic affections, but of which it is not our purpose here to treat.

Affections of the Gums caused by the use of Mercury.—These affections may be produced by the internal or external use of mercury. They present varied excoriations, which, on account of their cause, have been called mercurial excoriations. Persons who use this mineral as a medicine, and miners and others engaged in procuring and preparing it, are always exposed to these effects.

At the period of the formation of this affection, heat is experienced in the gums; these become engorged; small tubercles make their appearance, which imposthumate and leave ulcers, whose depth and extent are increased in proportion as the process of cicatrization is deferred. These ulcerations are generally more numerous than those produced by syphilitic virus. Their forms are various, their bottoms are gray, and sometimes bloody.

In cases in which the quantity of mercury absorbed is very large, the engorgement of the gums is excessive, the ulcerations are numerous, and not confined to the gums, but occupy the sides of the tongue and whole extent of the buccal membrane. The ptyalism is in proportion to the irritation, and the mouth of the patient emits an offensive odour. The precautions now taken in the administration of this medicine fortunately render these evils very uncommon.

When mercury has produced upon the gums or other parts of the mucous membrane which lines the mouth this description of ulceration, we should immediately suspend the use of it, and prescribe soothing gargles, or a mucilaginous decoction containing a few drops of laudanum. If the salivation be very abundant, we should endeavour to check it by the use of cold applications to the jaws, purgatives, and pediluvia.

Should the gums, after these various affections, remain soft, tumefied and turgid, it would be well to use the alcoholic tincture of rhatania, spirit of scurvy grass, or any other aromatic tincture.

SECTION III.

FUNGUS OF THE GUMS.

Fungous Tumours, or *Epules.*—These tumours, or fleshy
excrescences, generally soft and fungous, but sometimes hard
and cartilaginous, make their appearance upon the gums, or
gradually arise from the sockets of decayed teeth. At times
they are developed spontaneously, without any visible cause;
but at other times the cause is palpable. In the latter case,
they are the result of an abscess of the gums, which we have
named *parulis,* or they are dependent upon ulceration of the
gums, or decay of one or more teeth, (Pl. XIII. Fig. 8,) particularly when the roots are diseased. They may, sometimes,
be attributed to caries or necrosis of the alveoli, and even the
maxilla itself.

Five varieties of this disease are described, owing their classification to the several causes from which they spring. First,
simple epulis, unaccompanied by ulceration of the gums;
second, cartilaginous epulis; third, epulis proceeding from
parulis, occasioned by decay of one or more teeth; fourth,
epulis accompanied by decay of the maxilla; fifth, epulis produced by necrosis of the maxilla.*

* " Tumours and excrescences of these parts are very variable in their character and appearance. The surface of some is smooth; that of others is
rough, and sometimes covered with eroding ulcers: some are bulbous, and
have a broad base; others are attached to the gums by a mere peduncle:
some are soft, others are hard; the growth of some is astonishingly rapid;
that of others is so slow as to be scarcely perceptible: some are almost
destitute of blood vessels; others appear to be almost wholly composed of
sanguiferous capillaries: some are nearly destitute of sensibility; others are
so exquisitely sensitive that the slightest touch produces great pain, whence
they have been named *noli me tangere:* some are nearly white, others have
a grayish appearance: some retain the colour of the natural gum; others are
of a dark purple hue: finally, some exist for years, without being attended
with any very serious consequences, while others, in a very short time, bring
on a general constitutional derangement."—(*Harris' Dental Art,* p. 251.)—S.

Epulis generally appears under the form of a small tubercle, of a pale red, and having inequalities upon its surface. This tubercle is covered by a thin, smooth membrane, and has a pedicle more or less developed : it is slightly painful, gradually grows, and, after a time, assumes a volume of greater or less magnitude. The tumour may become sufficiently large to loosen the teeth, and incline them toward the cheek or tongue, in such manner as to produce pain. Tumours of this kind are, in general, soft throughout their whole course; but, at times, the opposite condition characterizes them. They have in them several perforations, from which is continually discharged a viscous bloody humour.

Their implantation upon the gums is not always the same. Sometimes they grow upon a simple pedicle, at other times upon a large base. In the former case they will grow without involving the gums, and hence their removal is not difficult; in the latter case they insinuate themselves between the interstices of the teeth, and occupy the opposite side of the alveolar border, in which case their removal is difficult.

From what we have said, these tumours will not be confounded with swelling of the gums, produced by a scorbutic diathesis or the use of mercury; for in these affections it is not a tumour which forms and grows upon the gums in the neighbourhood of diseased teeth, but it is tumefaction of the whole of the gums, which also become spongy and turgid. Nor should they be confounded with sarcoma of the maxilla, nor with phlegmons of the gums, the symptoms of which are altogether different from those that accompany epulis. Abscess of the gums is always accompanied by heat, redness and considerable swelling of the cheek; its progress is generally rapid, but it yields to antiphlogistics. The excrescences of which we are now speaking develope themselves slowly, are not accompanied by inflammatory symptoms, and do not yield to ordinary remedies. The characteristics we have described are palpable and distinct, and there can be no doubting the identity of these several affections.

Epules are not in general serious maladies, and may be easily cured, when not prolonged by some continued cause, and when pediculated. When caries or necrosis of the maxilla is the

11

cause, they will not yield until the affection of the bone has been cured. Their treatment will naturally be deduced from the causes from which they originated. The ligature, the knife, and actual cautery, are the means to be resorted to.

In case of simple epules, or cartilaginous epules upon a pedicle, the ligature or knife should be applied to the base of the pedicle. When hemorrhage succeeds this operation, it should be arrested with the actual cautery, which will also serve to destroy such portions of the tumour as may remain, and to repress it should it exhibit a tendency to be reproduced.*

If epulis be accompanied by caries of one or more of the teeth, the extraction of such tooth or teeth will serve to remove the cause of the tumour and to expose its pedicle. The knife should then be resorted to. After having with a bistoury extirpated as much as possible of the tumour, we should, as before directed, have recourse to the actual cautery. If the tumour be occasioned by caries of the maxilla, we should, having excised the former, change the caries into necrosis, also, by means of the actual cautery, and await the exfoliation of the necrosed parts. If the epulis be produced by necrosis, we should remove or destroy the fungous flesh, and wait until exfoliation takes place; a cure may then be effected.

Astringent powders and detersive gargles are the auxiliary means that should be applied during the whole course of the disease in the treatment of every variety of epules.

We here terminate our remarks upon the diseases of the dental organs proper, and some of the affections of the adjacent parts; and we shall now pass on to the second part of our work, in which we propose to examine the various general means employed for the preservation of the teeth, and the operations that appertain especially to the dental art.

---

* These tumours should always be removed by means of the ligature when possible, inasmuch as the hemorrhage succeeding excision should be dreaded. Arteries going to increased parts," Mr. Hunter remarks, "are themselves increased, and have not the contractile power of a sound artery." If the base of the tumour be broad, the mode that has been recommended of passing a needle through its whole breadth and carrying the ligature thence around either side, is advisable.—S.

PART II.

DENTAL HYGIENE AND THERAPEUTICS.

PART II.

DENTAL HYGIENE AND THERAPEUTICS.

GENERAL MEANS OF PRESERVING THE TEETH AND OTHER
PARTS OF THE MOUTH AT ALL PERIODS OF LIFE.

THE health and beauty of the teeth, and the wholesome
condition of the adjacent parts, may be impaired by so many
causes, that the means of protecting them from morbid affections have ever been objects of diligent research. These means
are generally simple, and are supplied by hygiene, and are
subject to general principles, which we shall indicate.

The teeth of first dentition require no particular attention,
at least when not affected by caries. When thus affected we
would recommend them to be brushed frequently to prevent
the progress of this disease. It is not until the age of seven
or eight years that the child should be required to brush his
teeth, and simply a brush and water should then be used.
This precaution will not only prevent caries, but will retard its
progress, and prevent the pain that may result from it. The
mouth will thus also be retained in a state of cleanliness and
agreeable freshness. We may also, without injury, detach, by
means of suitable instruments, the tartar that collects upon the
teeth of children at all ages.*

---

* The advice here given may lead to error, for it certainly is not in all
cases applicable. Indeed, we are of opinion that throughout the whole period
of life strict regard to cleanliness of the mouth should be had, and between
infancy and age there should be no distinction made except as relates to the
means used. Thus, although a brush, or any thing that could irritate the
gums of infants, should be avoided, the finger of the nurse may serve a good
purpose in keeping these parts free from accumulations of any substance,
and also in giving tone to them by the gentle friction thus applied.

From the age of fifteen to that of twenty years, we may, according to the condition of the mouth, employ powdered or liquid dentifrices. Persons upon whose teeth tartar easily accumulates, may add to the water applied a little brandy, or other spirituous liquors. The brush should be dipped into such liquid, the teeth and gums should be well rubbed with it, and it should be made, if possible, to penetrate the decayed cavities. A powdered dentifrice should also be applied three or four times a week, and should be rendered more or less tonic and active in its mechanical effects, according to the condition of the mouth and teeth.

At all ages the teeth should be well attended to, and experience proves that daily cleansing is their best preservative. It is proper to clean them after every meal, to remove particles of aliment that may adhere; if there be lodgments for such between the teeth, a toothpick will be proper. We should also endeavour to prevent the accumulation of a slimy substance, the layers of which, at first superficial, tend constantly to increase in thickness. The daily use of the brush will, however, suffice to prevent this. If the molar teeth of both sides be used constantly, the friction will in general prevent the accumulation of tartar, but still the habit of rinsing the mouth after eating should not be disregarded. We would here remark that a piece of linen, used by some persons in cleaning the teeth, is not adapted to the purpose, as thus the prominent parts only, which least require rubbing, are cleaned, while instead of cleansing the interstices the food is thus pressed more compactly into them.

The preceding advice is designed especially for delicate persons, and also for those who have good and handsome teeth, but are guilty of neglecting them. Persons who wear artificial teeth should be still more careful, especially, if they be manufactured from animal substances; otherwise such teeth will become covered with tartar and decompose, and be productive of an insupportable fetor.

Means of preserving the Gums.—Independent of the ordinary means of preserving the teeth in cleanliness, there are applications that become proper whenever the gums are not in perfectly good condition, and the importance of which we pointed out while speaking especially of the diseases of these organs. When the gums are soft, pale or turgid, the water used should be stimulated with spirituous liquors slightly aromatised; frictions applied with a soft brush will impart tone if the debility be merely local. If their sponginess, on the contrary, be produced by constitutional impairment, we should have recourse to constitutional treatment. Tonics are here indicated to give energy to the whole system.

Dentifrices, Powders, Opiates, Liquids, Elixirs, &c.—Although brushing the teeth, with the use of a few drops of spirits in water, will usually suffice to preserve them in cleanliness, there are persons who, from constitutional causes, or from previous neglect, are required to employ more energetic means. Hence many substances have been proposed for this purpose. These are called dentifrices, and are usually composed of several medicinal substances reduced to a fine powder. Among these powders some are innocent, such as charcoal, iris, soot, bark, salt. There are others, which are injurious to the teeth, such as acids. Others, again, are excellent agents in rendering the mouth clean and pleasant. These three classes of dentifrices we shall briefly review.

Charcoal holds the first place in our series of powders. Although this substance, finely pulverized, has been for a long time a popular dentifrice, because of its preservative qualities, its use is now almost entirely abandoned; the objections to it, however, do not result from any injurious effects to the enamel of the teeth, but from its insinuating itself between the necks of the teeth and the gums, it blackens them, and gives to them a gangrenous appearance. It may, however, be removed from this lodging by frequent washing and rubbing with a soft brush. Burnt crusts of bread, and all substances reduced to carbon, do not differ materially from each other.

Soot. The use of this article as a dentifrice has been long practised, and has been upheld by many who proved its excellence by the fact, that the teeth of chimney sweeps are always white. But this fact is not true. The teeth of these individuals appear so, contrasted with their skin. This substance, like the preceding, is troublesome and unpleasant, and it may readily be replaced by vegetable powders.

Bark, reduced to a fine powder, like other vegetable substances, can in no manner injure the enamel of the teeth, and on this account should hold a place in our first class of dentifrices; but its taste and colour, its tanning principle, which make the enamel yellow, and the fact that it contains no known useful property, all indicate its unfitness for this purpose. Powdered bark is, however, very beneficial in strengthening the gums when soft and spongy. What we have said of bark is equally applicable to tobacco.

Salt. (*Muriate of Soda.*) This article, recommended by many, is not at all injurious. It soon dissolves in the mouth, and can produce no other effect than that of causing an abundant flow of saliva, but by no means serves the purposes intended to be effected.

Alum.—*Alum, Cream of Tartar,* and *Oxalic Acid,* we place in our second series of powders. The former of these is a very strong stiptic, and should only be used in combination with an absorbent substance capable of destroying its acidity. Our third series furnishes an example of this, and among the powdered dentifrices which appear to belong to this class, we give the following formula.

DETERSIVE POWDER.

Magnesia,   ⎰
Cream of Tartar, ⎱ ....each one pound.
Sulphate of Quinine,..............five drachms.
Cochineal,.......................one ounce and a half.
Essential Oil of Peppermint,......four drachms.
Essential Oil of Cinnamon,........three drachms.
Essential Oil of Orange Flowers,...two drachms.
Spirits of Amber, Muskrose,.......one drachm.

Reduce each of these substances separately to a fine powder; grind the cream of tartar with the cochineal to colour it; place the essences with the magnesia in a vase, and when absorbed, mix with the first powder and pass the whole through a fine sieve.

This powder will clean the teeth perfectly without affecting the enamel: it strengthens the gums, gives them a rosy hue, and agreeably refreshens the mouth. The brush should not be very wet on being dipped into this powder, as some of its ingredients are soluble. It should be kept in a dry place.

We may rub the teeth with this two or three times a week,

and even daily, without inconvenience. For young people, from twelve to eighteen years of age, once a week will be often enough.

We here give the manner of preparing with charcoal and bark a detersive and tonic powder.

> Carbon of white wood, ...℥ viij.
> Bark,..℥ iv.
> White Ginger,................................℥ viij.
> Essential Oil of mint,........................℈ iv.
> Essential Oil of Cinnamon, ...℈ ij.
> Spirit of Amber, Muskrose,....................℈ ss.

Reduce to impalpable powder and mix.

An excellent dentifrice may be made of three or four hard substances selected with judgment. There is nothing that evinces so much charlatanism as the heterogeneous mixture of various powders, and to which an imposing name is given. Powders prepared according to the formula of an intelligent dentist, offer always a surer guarantee than those of the perfumers and others, who do not give the subject the requisite attention.

Acidulated dentifrices are only capable of imparting to the teeth a flattering whiteness; but we cannot be too circumspect in resorting to the use of them. They but produce upon the teeth the same effect that a drop of acid does upon polished marble. The calcareous phosphate composing the enamel is dissolved, and its polish is destroyed. The teeth in consequence retain more easily than before the species of slime which continually tend to accumulate upon them, and assume an indelible yellow hue. If such dentifrices be long continued, and if the acids which enter into their composition be very concentrated, it will expose the gelatinous substance of the teeth, which then become sensible to the slightest impressions, and finally decay.

Opiates and Mixtures.

The first quality of a dentifrice should be to render the teeth perfectly clean without injuring them. It should also be agreeable to the sight, the smell and the taste, and even tend to impart to the gums a rosy tinge to contrast with the whiteness of the teeth. A small quantity of cochineal, carmine, lack, &c. are usually added to powders and opiates for this purpose.

Opiates and Mixtures differ from powders by being composed in part of sirup or honey. These preparations are by some persons preferred to powders. There is, however, no good reason for this preference.

The following is the formula and mode of preparing a mixture which we recommend.

> Honey of the best quality, ...℔ ij.
> Alum calcined, ...℥ ij.
> Bark, extract of, ...℥ j.
> Essential Oil of Peppermint, ... ⎫ each ℥ss.
> Essential Oil of Cinnamon, ... ⎭
> Spirit of Amber, Muskrose, ...℥ ij.

Reduce the honey one-third, colour it with a piece of orchanet; mix the extract of bark into this, and strain it through a fine linen cloth. When it is nearly cold, incorporate into it the alum, and when quite cold add the essences.

This preparation has the same properties as the detersive powder, and may be used in like manner,

Liquors, Elixirs, and Tinctures, for the Mouth.

These various preparations are so many dentifrices used by dentists to maintain the cleanliness of the mouth, to relieve pains of the teeth, and to give tone to the gums. They should all have alcohol for their base; they are simple or compound, and are used instead of powders when the teeth have carious cavities, which are inaccessible to the brush, and when the gums are excessively sensitive. As those preparations are in general highly concentrated, a few drops should be put in a proper quantity of water, and the teeth and gums brushed with it. They are usually coloured with orchanet, cochineal, white moss, gum lack, saffron, &c., and aromatised with various essential oils. The following is a formula of one of these liquids, and may always be used with advantage.

> PHILODONTIC AND ANTI-SPASMODIC LIQUID.
> Alcohol, 38°.............................O iv.
> Essential Oil of Mint,.....................℥ j.
> Essence of Orange Flower, ...ʒ iv.
> Essence of Cinnamon, ...ʒ ij.
> Spirit of Amber, Muskrose,.................ʒ jss.
> Sulphuric Ether...........................ʒ ss.

After having coloured this liquor, filter it, and when put into a flask add the ether.

Persons who pay particular attention to the cleanliness of their teeth are very fond of using this preparation, as it leaves an agreeable perfume in the mouth. Eight or ten drops of this should be put into a tumbler of water, and the teeth and gums should be well rubbed with it by means of a suitable brush. It corrects the bad odour of the mouth, re-establishes and maintains the firmness of the gums, prevents caries of the teeth, and if properly used will arrest the progress of that disease.

This liquid will also be of advantage in subduing certain nervous affections, hemicrania, vomiting, indigestion, and in imparting tone to the stomach. For any of these purposes a tea-spoonful should be taken in half a tumbler of sweetened water; or a few drops of it may be put upon a lump of sugar, and retained in the mouth until the latter dissolves.

TONIC ELIXIR.

Root of Rhatania,.......................℥ viij.
Spirituous Vulneraria Water,............O viij.
Essential Oil of Mint,...................ℨ ij.
Essential Oil of Orange Peel,............ℨiij.

Bruise the rhatania root, steep it for about eight days in the vulneraria water, filter, and add the essences previously mixed with four ounces of alcohol.

This elixir possesses the property of curing several diseases of the mouth, as scorbutus in its incipient stage, aphthæ, swelling of the gums, which it also prevents bleeding. Fifteen or twenty drops should be put in the third of a tumbler of water, and retained in the mouth for a short time, and with a brush the teeth and gums should be well rubbed. If this lotion be used twice or thrice a day the ulcers will soon disgorge themselves and cicatrize, the swelling and discharge from the gums will cease, the bad odour from the mouth will be corrected and the teeth that may be slightly loosened will become firm again.

The inhabitants of the island of Molucca, and those of the southern parts of China, differing from us in their ideas of beauty in the dental organs, do not endeavour to preserve them in their whiteness, but tinge them a brick red with a preparation which they continually chew, and which is called betel, although the leaves of this vegetable do not form its principal ingredient. The natives of regions near the equator use this substance in a different manner. They spread slacked lime upon a betel leaf, and after having enveloped the fourth part of an areca nut with this, they roll it into a compact ball, and constantly retain it in the mouth. During their visits these people chew this substance; in saluting each other it is always presented in courtesy; and in taking leave on departure it is always presented enclosed in a little silk bag; they do not presume to speak to persons of rank without having it in their mouths. Betel does not corrode the dental substance, as many have supposed; it merely deposites upon the teeth a species of tartar which gives to them a red colour. We have been able to convince ourselves of this fact by carefully examining the teeth of a sailor whom we met at Gravesend in England. We also had occasion to make a similar examination upon the head of a Chinese, aged about thirty-six, which was presented to us by Dr. Busseuil of the Royal Navy. The teeth of this head, independent of their red colour, were also covered with a layer of tartar, at least one-fourth of a line in thickness. We detached some fragments of the tartar, and none of the teeth submitted to our research presented any traces of decay. The person above alluded to also had sound teeth. These two facts, with others we might add, appear to us more than sufficient to refute the following passage in the Dictionary of Medical Science, vol. II. p. 38:—"The betel, (*piper-betel*) is so irritating that it corrodes the dental substance, and persons in the habit of chewing it are deprived, at from twenty-five to thirty-five years of age, of the crowns of all their teeth; but this consequence does not prevent its general use throughout all the isles of the Indian Sea."

The inhabitants of the Philippines, instead of staining their teeth with the betel, continually rub them with the thin and smooth rind of the areca nut (*areca cathœu*.) This manner of cleaning the teeth has here become a habit.

The piece of skin destined for this use is usually from an inch and a half to two inches long. The common people use the rind as taken from the nut, but the wealthier bind a piece of ornamented silk around it.

It would have been easy for us in treating of dentifrices to multiply formulæ; but knowing that such enumeration would be of no advantage to the reader, we have preferred to merely give such as are of known efficacy. Tinctures, as elixirs, may be simple or compound, and may be extemporaneously composed. It is in this manner by macerating bark, myrrh, &c. in brandy, we obtain an excellent tincture for the teeth and gums.

Nothing need be added to what we have already said on the subject of dentifrices; but as their employment is of the highest importance, too much attention cannot be given to their selection and preparation. We therefore would in conclusion remark, as a summary of what we have said,

First, whatever may be the mode of preparing medicinal dentifrices, we should use no substance that is capable of decomposing the enamel, since the use of dentifrices should be to preserve the natural colour of the teeth by removing tartar that may have collected upon them.

Secondly, we should carefully watch their action upon the gums.

Thirdly, they should vary in form and composition to suit the parts to which they may be applied.

INSTRUMENTS AND MATERIALS USED FOR CLEANING THE TEETH.

Brushes.—In form and consistency these must vary according to circumstances. Thus small ones are proper for very young, and larger ones for grown persons, and a softer brush is proper for persons whose gums are peculiarly sensitive than for others. Judgment in each case is therefore necessary. But care should be taken to adapt them well, as thorough cleansing of the teeth and proper friction upon the gums are important; nor should the grinding surfaces and internal sides be less carefully attended to than their anterior surfaces. In brushing the molar teeth a slight rotary motion of the brush will prove serviceable in dislodging substances deposited between them.

Sponge or *Cotton,* attached to a handle or otherwise, has been unwisely recommended for these purposes. The same objections exist to them that we urged against the use of linen, namely, that it cleanses only the acclivities of the teeth, while it presses particles of food or other substances more compactly into the interstices.   Brushes made of the hair of the she-goat and badger have been made use of, but they are inferior to those made of the common bristles.   Their use, however, may be admitted when the teeth and gums are very sensitive.

Tooth-picks.—These are usually made of horn, quills, shells, fibres of flexible wood, ivory, bone, gold, silver and steel. Their name indicates their use, but they are only proper to remove foreign bodies that have insinuated themselves between the teeth, and which cannot be dislodged by the tongue or brush.   The teeth, and especially the gums, should be tormented as little as possible with these and similar instruments.

The best tooth-picks are those made of young goose quills, shells, flexible wood, &c.

Roots.—Sometimes the fibrous root of licorice, lucerne, the common rose, and marsh-mallow, are used for cleansing the teeth.   They are cut into pieces of four or five inches in length and boiled: when dried they are beaten into a kind of brush. They are then coloured red with a decoction of cochineal while heated, and perfumed with alcohol containing aromatic oil. These roots are, however, rarely used, and can in no respect be compared with the tooth-brush.

Coral Sticks.—Small sticks, composed of various calcareous powders, coloured red, and rendered partially soluble by the addition of a sufficient quantity of gum Arabic, have also been used for cleaning the teeth.   They are about the size of a crow-quill.   Their use has been abandoned, because they exercise too much friction upon the teeth, which, at the same time, they do not thoroughly clean, and they also chafe the gums.

GENERAL RULES FOR THE PRESERVATION OF THE TEETH.

Independent of the hygienic means that the gums and teeth require, there are also other precautions necessary for the beauty and health of these organs: these consist in avoiding whatever may be injurious to them. These indications may easily be fulfilled.

First, by refraining from washing the head in cold lotions; avoiding the use of repercussives, sometimes applied to destroy blotches of the face; also, pomatums, used to dye the hair, which are mostly composed of metallic, astringent and caustic substances.

Secondly, by avoiding the cracking of hard bodies with the teeth, or in any manner straining them by pressure, especially if they be long and weak.

Thirdly, by refraining from using the teeth to cut threads, &c. as women and children are in the practice of doing. By this habit the teeth are often fractured, and are hence subject to decay.

Fourthly, by not allowing particles of food or other substances to remain in the cavities of the teeth; by guarding against the use of improper dentifrices, such as coral, pumice stone, or waters, liquors, elixirs and tinctures too highly acidulated.

Fifthly, by protecting the teeth from sudden transitions of heat and cold, as in the alternate use of hot and cold drinks or aliment. After smoking, a current of air should be shunned. As it is not smoking that injures the teeth, but by the contact of cold air upon them, after being thus warmed, inflammation of their pulps is produced, which may result in caries, particularly in teeth, which, by their structure and position, have already a tendency to this disease.

Sixthly, by avoiding exposure to low and humid places. We have remarked that persons who reside in localities where the temperature changes frequently, have commonly indifferent teeth.

Seventhly, by refraining from drinking mineral waters in greater quantities than may be necessary; as their daily use, when special care is not taken with the teeth, will set these on edge, render them painful, and make them yellow, or cover them with a black slime; also, by abstaining from the free use of sweet-meats, and exposure to the effects of mercury, and other metallic substances, which, being reduced to vapour, may decay the teeth in a very remarkable manner. If we cannot wholly abstain from exposure to all or any of those deleterious causes, we may to an extent prevent decay of the teeth by brushing them two or three times a day with water.

These aphorisms might be extended, and much might be said of many habits that oppose the preservation of the dental organs; but such considerations would occupy too much space. We would therefore recommend to the reader, the more ample remarks upon this subject contained in works especially devoted to it.

THE VARIOUS OPERATIONS APPERTAINING ESPECIALLY TO THE DENTAL ART, AND THE DIFFERENT INSTRUMENTS PROPER IN THEIR PERFORMANCE.

Among the operations that appertain especially to the dental art, some are intended to facilitate the eruption and regular arrangement of the teeth; others consist in freeing those organs from all injurious influences, and remedying the various influences of which they are the seat, and which may occasion their destruction. We have already, in treating of the means by which we may remedy the evils of first dentition, indicated the procedures of this first class of operations; we shall now enter into the details that this important subject requires, after which we shall treat of operations of the second series. In our examination we shall endeavour to be as concise as possible.

Operations relating to the Teeth, and designed to facilitate their Eruption.

It has long been thought that the difficulty encountered by the teeth of first dentition, in rising from the alveoli, depended upon the resistance offered by the gums. Under this impression, after having tried various means to soften them, recourse was necessarily had to section of these parts, to give free issue to one or more of these teeth. This operation, seldom practised, because of the capability of nature to effect the desired object, consists in an incision made upon the gums with an instrument designed for this use. This incision should, in general, be deep, if we would hope for success. The evils that may result from this operation may be subdued by emollient lotions.

Manner of directing second Dentition.

Although the deciduous teeth usually assume a good direction, and arrange themselves properly upon the dental arch, as they are developed, this does not always happen with the permanent teeth, which tend to assume a defective position, either on account of the contracted space in the alveolar arch, or on account of its conformation. The permanent incisores and cuspidati are much larger than the teeth that precede them, and have, at their eruption, attained nearly their full size. It is thought by many that permanent teeth have attained their full size at the time of the protrusion of their crowns through the alveoli. This opinion I deem incorrect, and to demonstrate this we have drawn (Pl. XIII. Fig. 10,) two large inferior molares taken from the mouth of a child thirteen years old, one of which was extracted a year previous to the other. A comparison of these teeth exhibits a material difference in their size.* It is well known that at the period these teeth appear, the jaws have not attained their full size, especially near the alveolar border, which is at this time very narrow. It will, therefore, be perceived that the second teeth do not occupy precisely the same places that the deciduous teeth had, but often stand a little to one side of the place the deciduous occupied, in such manner that though the latter do not prevent the permanentes from appearing through the gums, they may cause them to take a mal-direction. The permanent teeth being larger than the deciduous, are necessarily more crowded, and arrange themselves with more difficulty.

---

* The opinion is entertained by some that the enamel is deposited by the membrane which invests it previous to eruption. Would not, therefore, the enlargement of the tooth after this necessarily destroy this covering?

The cases furnished by our author, though entitled to consideration, cannot be regarded as warranting the conclusions we are desired to infer. There is much danger of error in placing too much confidence in such. The disparity in size may have existed at the period at which the first of these teeth was removed; or, as frequently happens, the one may have been extracted previous to the complete eruption of the other.—S.

The first measure to be adopted at the time of the eruption
of the permanent teeth, is the removal of the deciduous ones.
These teeth may be easily extracted; the fingers alone will
often suffice to perform the operation, but forceps, adapted to
the purpose, may with propriety be applied. We should not
hesitate to extract such deciduous teeth whenever they may
occasion the mal-arrangement of the permanentes. Irregularities that may result from the presence of the deciduous teeth,
are always more difficult to correct than to prevent. But we
should not be too precipitate in removing the deciduous teeth;
first, because in their absence the jaws may contract, especially if the teeth of replacement be long in coming forward;
and, secondly, because these teeth have, in some rare instances,
been known to endure permanently. In these cases, however,
the teeth of first dentition retain their roots entire. These
teeth sometimes remain until old age. The deciduous teeth
are sometimes placed posterior, and sometimes anterior to the
permanentes, and at other times they range with them.

It often happens that the permanent teeth are developed
more rapidly than the maxilla. The teeth, then, not finding
sufficient space, present their lateral sides anteriorly, or are
forced within or without the dental arch. (Pl. XI. Figs. 1, 2, 7.)
In such cases the dentist should act with circumspection, and
on observing the maxillary bones to increase without facilitating the regular arrangement of the permanent teeth, he should
endeavour to correct their mal-position. Teeth, irregularly
arranged, are always unseemly to the view, do not admit of
being properly cleaned, and are more disposed to decay on this
account.

The best mode of correcting slight irregularities, is to extract
one or two to preserve the rest. In this manner, which may
at first appear harsh, the teeth being rendered less crowded
will be less liable to decay, and having thus plenty of room,
will naturally assume a regular arrangement. We may hasten
the approximation of the irregular teeth, if necessary, by passing silken ligatures around such of the teeth as should be
inclined toward each other. (Pl. XI. Figs. 1, 2, 7.)

As it is in general the anterior teeth that are badly arranged,
it might be supposed that one of these should be extracted;

but the approach of these toward each other would not autho-
rize such procedure for the sake of symmetry. In such cases,
according to the example of Garriot, the best practiciens extract one, two, three, or four bicuspides, according to the space
required in the anterior arch. We may also extract the cuspidati
to effect a handsome arrangement of the teeth, as it is known
that these teeth are often irregular. It is, however, not common for us to have recourse to this; first, because their presence is more essential to the symmetry of the mouth than that
of the bicuspides; and, secondly, because, having stronger
roots than the bicuspides, they serve as supporters of the anterior teeth.

If, on the contrary, we extract a bicuspid, there will still
remain one of the same class, and thus the mouth will not be
disfigured; its situation in the middle of each side also permits
the teeth to separate from each other with greater facility.

These procedures are always easy, only requiring judgment
and skill on the part of the dentist.

Mode of correcting Irregularities.

The mal-arrangement of the teeth arises from their inclination inwardly, outwardly, or laterally, or from disorder occasioned by their transposition. We should endeavour to remedy
these irregularities by all possible means. Success in such
cases will depend entirely upon the intelligence and ingenuity
of the practicien.

In general the means should act slowly, and be continued,
without occasioning pain; and, as the teeth that have taken a
bad direction, may always be removed with little effort, provided it be persevered in for a sufficient lapse of time, it suffices for accomplishing the desired purpose, to place a ligature
around the neck of the deviating tooth, and then attach this
ligature to a tooth at a proper distance from that to be removed.
(Pl. XI. Figs. 1, 2, 7.) If, for example, we are required to
remove a central incisor, situated anterior to the other teeth,
we should pass a ligature of proper size around the anterior
part of the neck, then bring it around the internal faces of the
two cuspidati, and tie around their anterior faces. If the ligature

be changed two or three times a day, and tightened at each time, the adjustment of the tooth can be effected in two weeks at most. The tooth should then be retained in its new position for some months by means of a ligature, or, which is better, with a thread of aloes, until the alveolar walls around the tooth shall have attained sufficient solidity to retain it in its place. We employ in this operation small crotchets or hooks, to prevent the ligatures from slipping down on the gums. (Pl. XI. Figs. 3 to 6.) This mode of regulating the teeth is simple and sure.

Gold or platina plates have also been used for this purpose, the manner of application of which was somewhat difficult; but this practice has grown into disuse, as it was not always practicable, and the results were not always as prompt and efficient as by the mode already described.[*]

When persons have been unwilling to endure the inconveniences arising from the use of the ligature or plate, an operation still more painful has been resorted to. This consists in luxating the tooth; but this operation should only be performed by an able dentist, since it is not unattended with inconveniences. The vitality of the tooth may not only be destroyed in the operation, the gums lacerated, the alveolo-periosteum injured, and the alveolar processes fractured, but

---

[*] Gold plates have been found to be very useful in the correction of irregularities of the teeth. Sometimes the incisores are situated so far back in the arch, that, at each occlusion of the jaws, they shut behind the inferior teeth. This is very difficult to remedy, and the best manner of effecting it is to adopt the plan recommended by Mr. Fox. It consists of a gold bar, about the sixteenth part of an inch wide, and of a proper thickness adapted to the curvature of the jaw, and fastened to the temporary molar on each side. The jaws are to be kept from coming entirely together by means of metallic caps placed upon the molares; two holes are then to be pierced in the gold bar opposite each deviating tooth, a silken ligature is now to be passed around each of these, and through the holes opposite to them, and tied. The ligatures should be renewed every two or three days until the teeth have been brought sufficiently far forward, to close anterior to the inferior teeth; the caps and gold bar may then be removed.

If only one of the incisores is placed too far back in the arch, a guttered plate may be adapted to the inferior arch, and upon it, opposite the irregular organ, an inclined plane should be soldered. M. Catalan, we believe, first recommended a fixture of this kind. It is simple, and will always ensure success when judiciously applied.—S.

the tooth itself may be broken; and it may happen that he will extract it in spite of every precaution.

Removal of Dental Tartar, and the Instruments proper in the Operation.

We have said, in another place, that simply a brush, impregnated with a suitable dentifrice, is commonly sufficient to preserve the cleanliness of the mouth; but means so simple are not always sufficient, especially when tartar accumulates between the teeth, where even the brush cannot penetrate, and when it accumulates, as it often does, upon the interior face of the anterior teeth of the inferior jaw. Instruments proper for its removal must then be had recourse to.

The removal of tartar requires address, care and precaution, but is not at all painful: it should be practised as often as this substance amasses itself upon the teeth.

The details into which I shall enter before pointing out the manner of removing this substance, will, no doubt, appear to some persons very minute; but they are essential to the dentist who wishes to obtain the confidence of the public.

Before commencing this operation, every thing that it is proper to use, should be in perfect readiness. The seat should be adjusted to a proper height. It will be well also to pay such regard to cleanliness, and neatness as to attract the approbation of the patient. The instruments to be used are for the most part shaped like gravers, hooks, &c. They should be very clean, well tempered, and have a fine edge. In this operation the dentist should also pay particular attention to the cleanliness of his hands; but it is by no means necessary that they should be dainty and white. The end of a towel should be folded around the hand he is about to place on the face of the patient. If the mouth he is required to operate on, be in a disagreeable condition, he should avoid spitting, or do it in such a manner that the patient should not perceive the motive.

In cases where the odour emitted from the mouth of the patient is highly offensive, it may be ameliorated by aromatizing the water, with which he should be directed to wash his mouth from time to time.

After having taken all the foregoing precautions, and placed
the patient in a proper position, and laid upon his shoulder a
towel intended to wipe the instruments, he may proceed to
remove the tartar in the following manner.

The dentist, standing upon the right of his patient, takes a
rugine, and holding it as he would a writing pen, commences to
clean the inferior central incisores. The mouth being open,
the index finger of the left hand serves to depress the lower
lip, and forms a support to the ring finger of the right hand;
the operator then insinuates the instrument beneath the tartar,
and detaches it in fragments from below upward. This process
is repeated upon the whole of the anterior sides of the inferior
teeth. To remove the tartar from the posterior surface of
these teeth, the patient's head should be inclined a little forward, and still depressing the lower lip with the index finger
of the left hand, the ring finger of the right hand, resting upon
the crown of one of the incisores, the tartar should be removed
as before described, but by means of a curved instrument.

To clean the teeth of the superior jaw, the left hand should
be passed around the neck of the patient, and the superior lip
should be elevated with the index finger. The ring finger of
the right hand should rest upon the crown of the tooth adjoining that to be cleaned, and with the instrument the tartar
should be detached from right to left, and *vice versa,* observing
the contour of the gum and avoiding to chafe it. The tartar
is easily detached from the molares with instruments of proper
shapes.

The posterior sides of the superior teeth, particularly the
incisores and cuspidati, rarely have tartar upon them, because
the continual action of the tongue upon them in mastication
and pronunciation prevents its accumulation. Notwithstanding
the greatest care in cleaning, the teeth of some individuals
will retain a yellow hue, which is in truth their natural colour.
It would be useless in such cases to endeavour to make these
appear white by scraping them. Should the instrument glide
over smooth and glassy concretions, these may be removed
by being rubbed with a piece of soft wood and finely powdered
pumice stone. There are other precautions necessary to be
observed to clean the teeth properly, but they are too minute

for description, but which will be learned from experience. We would merely add, that from time to time we should direct the patient to rinse his mouth, and thus relieve him for a brief time, and also cause him to expel portions of tartar that have been detached. We should, on concluding this operation, direct him to clean his teeth with a soft brush and a powdered dentifrice, reminding him of the advantage of giving to the brush a rotary motion in order to clean them thoroughly.

Manner of Filing Teeth.

The use of the file is necessary to remove superficial caries, and to equalize and separate teeth that are too long and too much crowded, and the disproportion of which will not allow of the exact adjustment of the jaws. It is also designed to remove asperities and inequalities produced by caries and fractures of the teeth, and the presence of which incommodes and injures the tongue, cheeks and lips. The file is also used to prepare the roots of teeth for artificial crowns. Files used for this purpose are half round, and sharp or blunt at their extremities. Those intended for separating the teeth have two cutting surfaces, and are of various shapes and sizes, according to the teeth to be filed. They are narrow, flat, and sometimes curved. The latter we frequently use to remove lateral caries from the incisores and cuspidati. By means of a file carrier, we are able to file the molares with as much facility as we can the incisores.

Whatever be the object for which teeth are filed, the patient should be properly seated and the operator should stand at his right. If, for example, we wish to remove superficial decay from the lateral side of a tooth, we should first examine if the contiguous side of the adjoining tooth be decayed also. If this be not the case we should use a safe-sided file, presenting its cutting side to the decayed tooth. If there be decay in both, we should use a file having two cutting sides. The action of the file should be gentle but firm in all cases. Should this instrument be caught between the teeth, becoming tightened, we should gently disengage it. If the decay be superficial, we should entirely remove it; but if it extend to the dental cavity, it should be separated sufficiently from the neighbouring tooth, that the disease may not be communicated to it. The soft parts of the decay should then be detached, and the cavity cauterized.* The tooth should then be plugged.

The curved form of our file enables us to remove a great portion of the posterior part of the teeth, which is the chief seat of decay in the incisores and cuspidati. To obtain the same result with a straight file we are obliged to make a large separation, and uselessly file away a portion of the anterior side of the tooth, and thus give it an unseemly appearance.

When a tooth is well filed there will remain no portion of the cavity, and a smooth surface should be left.

The manner of using a file upon the superior teeth is very simple. The operator should hold the instrument between the thumb and index finger of the right hand, and passing his left arm around the head of the patient, and raising the lip with the fingers of the left hand, he should proceed to file the tooth, supporting the right hand by resting the little finger upon the most convenient tooth in the inferior jaw. The file should be frequently dipped in water, which in cold weather should be warmed, in order to prevent the instrument from becoming choked up, and also to keep it at a uniform temperature, as its action will produce an injurious degree of heat. In filing the lateral surfaces of the teeth we should never omit leaving a shoulder near the gum, in order that the teeth may not approximate again, which, without this precaution, would generally happen.

In subjects of forty years of age the incisores and cuspidati are often above the level of the other teeth, and on this account become loose. We would recommend the filing of these teeth, as by being shortened they may be exempted from such injury. They generally become solid in their sockets after this operation. An example of this is furnished in the following case extracted from our *Manuel du Dentiste*.

We were applied to by a person fifty years of age, who had

---

* The whole of the decayed part should be removed. To prevent misapprehension, it may be proper here to refer to our objections to the cautery, in a previous part of this work. The reader will observe this in subsequent recommendations of this practice by the author.—S.

had for ten years a large accumulation of tartar upon the six anterior teeth of the inferior jaw, and which had deprived the teeth of their gums for at least five lines below their natural level, and so loosened them, that the least pressure with the finger would have been sufficient to occasion them to fall out. We illustrate (Pl. XIII. Fig. 9,) a case somewhat similar. Effects of like character often result from the immoderate use of antisyphilitic remedies. We commenced our treatment by first removing the tartar, and then temporarily securing those teeth to their neighbours by means of silken ligatures. We then made a horizontal groove at that point at which we designed to cut them, and afterward severed them by means of the excising forceps. The surfaces of these teeth were then smoothed off with a file, and a ligature was again applied. The patient was recommended to gently brush his teeth and gums several times a day with a healing liquid composed of equal parts of the tinctures of rhatania and bark, mixed with an adequate proportion of water. A month after, the gums and teeth of this person had become firm, and the latter have since continued firm in their places.

In this operation a narrow file is commonly used having but one cutting edge, and thus acting like a saw. We should, however, be very careful when we meet with teeth that are much longer than the rest. We should not in such cases rashly cut off as much of the tooth at one time as we wish to remove, as from its sensibility unpleasantness may be experienced. Some persons, in fact, experience an unaccountable irritation; others experience local pain, and a nervous agitation through the whole body. In such cases the operation should be deferred for some months, and again be resumed to be persevered in very slowly until the tooth has finally been reduced to its proper length. Using these precautions the object may always be accomplished, although it would be impossible to perform it at a single operation. By leaving an interval of three or four months between each attempt at reducing the tooth, the bony substance will lose its acuteness of sensibility, and thus admit of the renewed operation at each time. If, however, we are very anxious to effect the object at once, we

13

may possibly succeed by cauterizing it successively as the exposed part becomes sensitive.

Roots destined to receive artificial pieces are generally prepared with the half-round file. We also with this file remove osseous eminences and asperities that may injure the soft parts of the mouth; or we may first remove these asperities with the excising forceps, and afterward smooth them off with the half round file.

The use of the file has been condemned as a means of removing decayed portions of the teeth, and several noted practiciens have maintained that, from having portions of their enamel removed, the teeth become more susceptible of decay. We are far from concurring in this opinion, and if these practiciens had been careful and minute in their observations, they would have observed that teeth decay after filing only when they are permitted to grow together again; but this may be prevented by the mode of filing we have already indicated. A tooth may with safety be filed away as long as the patient can endure the operation, and until all particles of decay are removed, and no cavity is suffered to exist, provided that enough of its substance be still left to protect its internal part, or pulp; and as we thus remove the cause of the progressive disease, it is erroneous to suppose that the use of the file will tend to produce disease. We would assert, that where partial decay is thus removed, the teeth that are subject to this operation may be preserved in health as long as those that have never been affected.

Unfortunately, dentists do not make sufficiently free use of the file. This, no doubt, results in part from the difficulty of procuring good instruments, and such as can be applied with facility to the teeth in the posterior part of the mouth. There can be no danger from this operation, if the file be guided by a skilful hand. It is a precious instrument for the removal of decay. Its employment is even useful for the removal of decayed portions of the deciduous teeth, which should always, if possible, be preserved to the period of the natural molting. We cannot use it too often for the preservation of teeth, particularly at an advanced period of life, when so many different causes contribute to deteriorate them.

The permanent teeth should not, however, be filed previously to the thirteenth or fifteenth year, as from the thinness of their parietes, and the large size of the internal pulp, they are not capable of enduring the action of the file. If, as it happens with some children, the teeth manifest a disposition to decay at the time of cutting, which may be inferred from the thinness of their enamel, their bluish colour, mal-arrangement, &c., we should not then hesitate to use this instrument to effect their separation. To understand thoroughly the use of the file is not an easy matter. It does not consist in drawing the file backward and forward, or directing it to the various parts of the tooth, but we must also use it without jarring the organs, and cause it to cut in the desired direction. Hence, we can learn by practice only how to perform this operation well. We should endeavour so to direct the file as to cut in an angling direction upon the tooth, in order that a firmer hold may be taken, and the object thus more speedily effected. Files that are cut obliquely act more gently, though slower, than those that are cross-cut.

Teeth filed by a skilful dentist have the appearance of never having been touched with such an instrument. To give them this appearance, the corners, angles, and cutting extremities are rounded, and smoothed off with a very fine file.

Cauterizing the Teeth.*

The circumstances under which we are obliged to cauterize teeth to preserve them are numerous. It is resorted to to destroy the dental nerve when it has become painful, and to arrest or dry deep-seated or superficial caries. Fire and caustics are the means of cauterization to which the dentist generally has recourse; the actual cautery is that most used.

* * For our opinion of the suitableness of the actual cautery for the purpose of destroying the nerves of teeth, the reader is referred to our remarks at page 67. Those remarks have regard to the means of merely obtunding the sensibility of a tooth for the purpose of plugging, as well as for the purpose of destroying the nerve.

The author, however, prefers the actual cautery to the use of the concentrated acids. In this we agree with him; but neither can be too strongly deprecated. The only application of this agent in which we can concur with the author in his recommendations as above is for the suppression of obstinate hemorrhage after the extraction of teeth, in cases in which no other means will apply.—S.

We would, however, remark that the application of fire is insufficient; it has been known to augment instead of relieving the pain, and it has been also remarked, that when the decay is far advanced this means will render the affected tooth brittle and less capable of preservation. Some nervous persons prefer having the diseased organs extracted to submitting to this operation, as the pain attendant upon it is very acute. We are far, however, from disapproving of the actual cautery. We think that from its energetic action the happiest results may be obtained. It may suddenly subdue violent pain, and arrest superficial decay, and is of the highest utility in arresting hemorrhage. This mode of cauterizing is very useful in the incisores and cuspidati, which are sometimes so extensively decayed that we are unable to remove the decay, lest the tooth be rendered too weak. Such teeth may be cauterized from time to time to arrest the progress of the affection.

When we wish to destroy the dental nerve with the actual cautery, we should employ a platina stylet three inches long, adapted to a handle, and having at about eight lines from its extremity an ovoid enlargement, in order to retain the necessary heat to effect the desiccation of the nerve. This bulb should be moveable, that the point of the instrument may be lengthened. When we wish to use it, we should heat the stylet and its bulb, and in this condition insert it promptly into the dental canal, giving it a slight rotary motion, and then immediately withdraw it. We have pursued this plan for fifteen years with uniform success. It is seldom that a second application is necessary, but we at all times entirely destroy the nerve. The actual cautery is particularly applicable to the roots of the incisores, cuspidati and bicuspides. If water be taken in the mouth, and no pain be occasioned by it, we may be sure that the operation has been successful. We should then remove the cauterized parts of the tooth, and fill the cavity with cotton saturated with spirituous liquor; and after drying the interior of the cavity it may be plugged. In cases in which we do not wish to apply the actual cautery for this purpose, we sometimes resort to another mode. This consists in the extraction of the nerve. To accomplish this, we take two or three pieces of fine gold or platina wire, and attach them to a handle. These wires should then be insinuated to the extremity of the root, and by a slight rotary movement we are, in the first attempt, often enabled to extract the nerve. We do not by this method disorganize the soft parts of the dental cavity, and the tooth is in readiness to be plugged. This latter practice is the most effective means of wholly alleviating the pain. It is particularly advantageous in preparing a root to receive an artificial crown.

Before cauterizing a tooth that is much decayed, we should endeavour to remove with a file the greater portion of the diseased part, and by means of an excavator the soft parts within the cavity should also be taken away; the cavity should then be well cleaned and dried with a lock of cotton, and the cautery should be applied to the affected part with great care, and should be repeated several times, according to the extent of the decay. If, after these precautions, the disease still progresses, we should again resort to the cautery, and afterward the tooth may be plugged with advantage.

The instruments employed in cauterizing are of various forms according to the different parts to be operated on. That most commonly used is a flat or round hook. It is necessary, when operating, to always have several in readiness, in order to change them if necessary. This, however, should be avoided as much as possible, that the fears of the patient may not be excited. The flame of a wax candle or spirit lamp is sufficient to give it a proper degree of heat. These instruments are generally affixed to a metal handle by means of a spring or catch. When it is proper to heat them to a high temperature a cork handle will be of service, as this is a bad conductor of heat.

Many persons cannot endure a heated iron applied to their teeth; and recourse must in such cases be had to the second mode of cauterizing, which is by the use of caustics. Liquid ammonia, and sulphuric or nitric acid, are the substances employed for this purpose. The manner of using these is very simple. A piece of cotton of the size of a pin's head, saturated in one of these ingredients, and placed in the cavity of a tooth, will effect this purpose. Another piece of cotton should then be placed upon this, and the whole should be covered finally with some soft bees-wax. We should use much caution

13*

in the use of these liquids.   They have disadvantages, as they tend to soften the osseous substance of the teeth.   If negligently dropped upon the adjacent teeth or soft parts of the mouth, they will occasion the patient inconvenience and produce injury.   The inflammation of the alveolo-periosteum, may also be increased by the use of the acids as well as by the actual cautery when used at a very high temperature.   Hence, we repeat, they should be resorted to as seldom as possible; for, although they may give rise to less terror than the actual cautery, this advantage does not compensate for the injury that may be inflicted.   What we have said of acids will equally apply to the nitrate of silver.

If the extraction of the nerve, or cautery by fire or the acids, be impracticable, we must then obtund the nervous sensibility by means less violent.   The means we would recommend appear to act upon the principle of escharotics.   These substances are *myrrh, incense, extract of opium, ether, essence of cinnamon, cloves* and *mint,* and other *essential oils* and *highly concentrated tinctures.*

Any of the substances here enumerated will tend to contract and obtund the nerve, and if not sufficiently energetic to destroy it wholly, the irritation produced by them will alleviate and sometimes remove the pain.   If this method do not succeed, no harm at least will result from it, and in hopes of success its trial will always be advisable.

Manner of Plugging Teeth.

When, by the means we have already indicated, we have deprived the dental nerve of its extreme sensibility, we must use some means to arrest the progress of decay.   The dental art furnishes us with a method of doing this, which we daily practise.   It consists in introducing into the cavity formed in the tooth leaves of metal or other substances until it be compactly filled.

This operation is called plugging the teeth.   Lead was formerly exclusively used for this purpose.   It is an operation of great importance, and we shall treat of it in detail.

A tooth may be plugged when decayed, if there be no discharge of matter from the dental canal, and if the presence of heat and cold, the contact of an instrument, or the retention of particles of food in the cavity, do not produce pain. Before operating, we should always inform ourselves whether the tooth presents such condition. If it do not, we may occasion pain so acute as to render the tooth incapable of being preserved by this mode.

The sound or excavator is an instrument proper for examining the cavity of a decayed tooth. We, in general, use the double spiral excavator, because its various curves enable us to introduce it into a cavity upon any part of the tooth. It is particularly useful to reach the lateral surfaces of the molar teeth. This sound or probe, is very simple, consisting of a piece of wire having its two extremities terminating in a semi-circle, one inclining to the right and the other to the left. When the operator is convinced, from examination, that there is no sensibility in the cavity of the tooth, and that it is larger internally than externally, he may then proceed to plug the tooth. The material used may be lead, tin, gold, or platina leaf, or fused mastic; sometimes wax, mastic, or *compositions* capable of resisting the action of the saliva. These various materials are introduced into the cavity of the tooth, and rendered so compact as to effectually exclude the air and saliva. If the operation be well performed, in good time, with metallic substances, the teeth may be preserved for a number of years, and even through life. Lead, of all the substances which we have enumerated, is most generally used for plugging teeth; but as this metal oxydizes and becomes black as soon as applied, we prefer the use of tin foil, as it is prepared by the goldbeaters. Gold and platina are still better, but these metals should have a certain degree of malleability. As regards wax and other compositions that are used for this purpose, they are not sufficiently solid to be retained for any length of time, and their use is now rejected. There are some cases, however, where their application becomes indispensable, particularly when we wish to conceal upon the anterior teeth a cavity which the presence of metal would expose. When this mode of preservation is employed with discernment, we may hope to obtain success, and for this purpose we may advantageously use the fusible metal of Darcet, used for the first time by our confrère, M. Regnart, who has improved it by adding a tenth part of mercury.   This composition consists of

Bismuth, ... 8 parts,
Lead, ... 5 "
Tin, ... 3 "

It is fusible at the temperature of boiling water.   It is used in the following manner:—

After having excavated the tooth, and cleaned, dried and prepared the cavity for plugging, a piece of the composition of adequate size is to be introduced, and a probe, or plugger, is to be made hot enough to cause this to melt.   With this instrument the amalgam should be pressed compactly into the tooth, and, when hardened, its surface should be smoothed off.   This amalgam becomes very hard and solid.   We would, in certain cases, prefer it to lead, as it accommodates itself better to the shape of the cavity.   Many dentists use this article exclusively, the advantage of which we have made known to many of our confrères.   We are much indebted to M. Regnart for this discovery.*

When we have discovered that the tooth is in proper condition to be plugged, we should commence with an excavator to remove particles of food or other foreign bodies, and all the soft and decayed portions of the tooth, and to form little notches and irregularities within the cavity that the metal may be more easily retained.   A piece of cotton saturated with alcoholic liquor or essential oil should be then introduced into the

* For this operation, gold is the only substance known that can be permanently relied on; although there are cases in which tin and even lead may be of temporary advantage when employed with skill and judgment.   I regard cements (paste) fusible metals, amalgams, succedaneums, and all other substitutes for the above named metals, as impositions on the public, never having seen a single operation, in which these substances were employed, which would not have been more permanent if even lead, the poorest of the above named metals, had been used; because it is less subject to decomposition and oxydation, to say nothing of the poisonous qualities of the mercury which most of the others contain.   I have never known a perfect master of the art of stopping teeth, either to employ or recommend the substances which I here condemn; and I believe the use of them is almost wholly confined to those persons who are unacquainted with this nice and difficult art.   E. Parmly.—S.

cavity, and afterward a piece of dry cotton should be introduced in order to absorb the moisture. After having in this manner perfectly dried the cavity, the metal or other substance may be inserted. A sufficient quantity of the metal used should be formed into a tube and urged into the tooth by means of a suitable instrument. We should then press it firmly and condense it by means of a plugger. When the cavity has thus been made completely full, we should remove whatever little excrescent parts there may be, and burnish the surface well. In filling cavities situated upon the crowns of teeth, the metal should not be cut off even with the tooth, as it will become more firmly condensed in the process of mastication. It will be found that this operation is difficult, and often impracticable, particularly if the disease be situated upon the lateral surfaces of teeth that are crowded, or upon the posterior surfaces of the molares. If the teeth themselves be very sensitive, we should fill their cavities with cotton dipt in essential oil. This should be renewed every day. This will protect the nerve from the impressions of the atmosphere, and by absorbing the pus that may be discharged from the dental canal, it will prevent the tooth from being offensive.

Notwithstanding the utmost precaution that may be taken in this operation, it is not uncommonly followed by severe pain, and sometimes considerable inflammation, which may terminate in abscess. If this pain continue, we should remove the plug and allay the irritation by the means commonly indicated. If there be no discharge from the dental canal, we may again plug the tooth. When the tooth is sensitive to the contact with a foreign body, we should in some manner accustom it to support its presence, which may be done by performing the operation at various times. We should not at first press the metal sufficient to exclude the air and moisture. We may some weeks after press it again, and when we discover that in this manner the tooth has lost its sensibility, we may remove the plug thus coaxed in, and insert a plug well at one sitting. This operation is generally very delicate, and requires patience and perseverance.

Manner of Luxating Teeth.

When the patient is desirous of preserving a tooth which

is the occasion of pain, we sometimes have recourse to luxation, and afterward replace it in its primitive position. The pain may in this manner be often relieved, but success will not always attend such operation; nor should it be practised under all circumstances. We may, however, attempt the luxation of a tooth if it be painful, and if it be sufficiently solid to be in no danger of breaking by the operation, or when it has taken an improper direction. This operation should in general be only practised upon young and healthy persons, and whose gums are in a healthy condition. It is also necessary, before performing this operation, to acquaint ourselves with the constitution of the subject, as luxation will not be of use when practised upon persons of weak constitution, whose gums are soft or turgid. The tooth, under such circumstances, would never become firm in its socket, and its extraction would soon become necessary. It should be practised only upon certain teeth and at a certain age. (1.) The incisores, cuspidati and anterior bicuspides are the teeth that may be luxated. (2.) The most favourable periods of life appear to be from thirteen to thirty years of age. It is more difficult to luxate than to extract a tooth, because the movements during the operation should be very moderate, that the vessels and nerves distributed to the part may be lacerated as little as possible, and that the alveolar border may not be fractured. It is well known that a luxated tooth cannot regain its primitive solidity in the socket after having been entirely removed; for, if once extracted and replaced in its socket, there is little probability of its resuming its functions of life. We shall comment on this subject when treating of transplanting teeth.

The manner of luxating a tooth differs but little from that of extracting; it is simply to rupture the dental nerves, and by the guidance of the hands to cause it to take the required direction. The operation being performed, we are sometimes obliged to retain the tooth in its new position by attaching it to an adjoining tooth until it becomes firmly fixed in its socket. The patient should be directed not to masticate solid aliment, and to make use of tonic gargles. Luxation, though practicable upon the anterior teeth, should not be attempted upon the molares; it may occasion bloody effusions in their sockets, and deposites which will necessarily require the extraction of the tooth. These teeth not regaining their attachment, will often occasion fistulous openings, and should they remain after the operation, it will only be for a few years. Evils of this kind are more than sufficient to cause us to abandon a practice that holds forth so little prospect of success. We sometimes, however, luxate a decayed bicuspid, and shortly thereafter plug it. The only inconvenience resulting from this is a slight sensibility at the roots.

Of accidental luxations produced by external violence, we need only remark that the mode of treatment is the same as in the preceding cases. When it happens that several teeth are thus luxated, it will be sufficient to replace them and maintain them properly in their positions in order that they may regain their attachment.*

Manner of Extracting Teeth.

As soon as the dentist concludes that a tooth cannot be preserved by any of the foregoing means, he should propose extraction without hesitation, and should perform no other operation to prolong its retention. He should, however, apprize his patient that, no matter what may be the skill of the operator, or the excellence of the instruments used, this operation is always attended with pain. There are few persons who attain to advanced age without having at some time to submit to it. Unfortunately it appears to the vulgar eye to be of easy performance, as it is daily executed by the most illiterate dentists, and by empirics who sometimes have discretion enough to shun cases that may be attended with difficulty. But the evulsion of teeth requires practice and manual dexterity, and in many cases the utmost

---

* It will be perceived that the author's recommendations of this practice are qualified; but it is still proper that we should remark that it is now universally condemned by scientific dentists. When a front tooth has been accidentally loosened in its socket the application of ligatures to hold it firmly in its place, and the use of antiphlogistic remedies to the gums, if called for, should be resorted to. But even in this case, if the alveolus should be found much injured, or if the luxation of the tooth be sufficient to sever the nerves and vessels entering at the apex of its root, its extraction would be the more judicious step. We say this, too, with a knowledge of the many cases that have been narrated of the replacement of teeth in their sockets, that had been completely withdrawn.—S.

prudence and discretion will require the aid of an accurate knowledge of the diseases of the teeth and of the anatomy of the mouth.

When the decay has penetrated to the dental canal, when the tooth is sensitive to the impressions of heat and cold, and when it occasions pain in mastication, it is customary to perform the operation of extraction. As the loss of one or more of the teeth, however, cannot be regarded with indifference, we cannot be too circumspect when we are desired to perform this operation. The dentist will, indeed, be frequently led into error if he pays regard to the representations of his patients at all times, and extracts all the teeth that may be pointed out to him as the causes of pain. The patient is very often wholly deceived on this point, and will point out, as the seat of pain, a tooth in the superior jaw when suffering, in fact, from one in the inferior; and a sound tooth is as likely to be pointed out as one that is decayed. Sometimes, indeed, the pain appears so general that the patient believes all his teeth to be affected.

The dentist who has regard for his reputation, should, in such cases, act very prudently, in order not to be deceived into a serious error: he should carefully examine all of the teeth supposed to be affected, making use of a dental mirror. Each suspected tooth should be tested by being shaken with the finger, and if the seat of greatest sensibility be not thus ascertained, let the teeth be tapped severally with the plugger or other hard body; should this not lead to the discovery, let the patient then be directed to take cold water in his mouth. When convinced of the existence of disease, and having, by some such means as are herein described, identified the individual tooth that occasions the pain, the practicien may proceed to extraction, but not till then, by means of instruments intended for this purpose, and which we shall describe after having pointed out certain general rules for their application.

Whatever may be the method adopted to extract a tooth or root, there are certain precautions that cannot be too strictly observed in order to ensure success. Having taken a proper hold with the instrument, we should proceed slowly and cautiously, depending more on skill than force; thus we may avoid fracturing the tooth or alveolar process, bruising the gums, or loosening the adjacent teeth. The movements in extracting should generally be moderate, but firm, and continued. Most dental authors direct us to apply the force required in the direction of the roots of the tooth to be removed; thus it may be drawn obliquely, or turned upon its transverse axis by depressing the crown, and at the same time elevating the root. We may even take a tooth out of its socket laterally by applying sufficient force; but whatever may be the class of teeth we wish to extract, luxation must always precede extraction. Thus the tooth should be grasped firmly by the neck, as low down as possible, and, by being inclined inwardly or outwardly, its connexion should be severed. It is better, however, to luxate and extract the tooth from within outwardly; the form of most instruments requires this, except of the improved key, which will act in either way with equal advantage, particularly in the extraction of the molar teeth. It is difficult with the old key to extract these teeth, and when we attempt it, we may occasion extensive fracture of the alveolar process, from which sometimes proceeds a hemorrhage difficult to arrest. The last molares of the inferior jaw are sometimes so situated that the base of the coronoid apophysis forms, opposite their roots, a sharp, yet firm ridge, which will expose us to such accident, should we attempt to remove the tooth inwardly.

The modifications which we have made upon the key of Garengeot, are such that we may often with this instrument extract the last molar outwardly when this tooth is hidden in the base of the coronoid apophysis. These teeth may also be extracted in the opposite direction with the same key. If the operation be well performed we need hardly fracture the alveolus; this accident is serious, however, only when the maxillary artery is ruptured by it, which, fortunately, scarcely ever happens. A skilful dentist will, at first sight, perceive if a tooth be difficult to extract, and, in such case, he will acquaint his patient of it, but in such manner as not to alarm him; and should the operation not prove as successful as desired, the operator will not then be censured. Such intimation should particularly be given when the crown of the tooth is so much decayed as to present a frail hold for the instrument. On ex-

14

tracting teeth which will be likely to produce much pain from the divergence of their roots, as is usually the case when the crowns are very low, the difficulty of the case should also be revealed to the patient. In performing this operation we may, it is true, remove a portion of the alveolar process, but this accident is not of serious import.

We have here, in a general manner, pointed out the mode of extracting teeth. We shall now examine the instruments used for this purpose, and the manner of their application.

INSTRUMENTS FOR THE EXTRACTION OF TEETH.

Of all operations in dental surgery, the extraction of teeth may be supposed to require the greatest variety of instruments. We have, however, found that inconvenience resulted from an excessive number of these, and have endeavoured to reduce it. Five or six will in general suffice. It is only necessary to know the use of these, and to learn, by practice, the skilful application of them. A good practicien seldom, indeed, makes use of more than two or three, and these being familiar, he is dexterous in the exercise of them. Those generally used are the following:—1. The *Key of Garengeot,* modified; 2. *The straight forceps;* 3. The *curved forceps;* 4. The *curved hawk's-bill forceps;* 5. The *straight hawk's-bill forceps;* 6. The *lever and hook;* 7. The *elevator.* Some dentists also use the *pelican, fish-tongue, stag-foot,* and *excising forceps.* The use of these last instruments is now abandoned.

Garengeot's Key, and the Manner of using it.

Of all instruments intended for the extraction of teeth this is the most ingenious. It consists of a handle of adequate size, of a shaft forming nearly a right angle and terminating in an enlargement, into which are made two slits, and through which passes a screw or pin designed to form an axis for a hook to revolve upon. This hook is to be applied to the crown of the tooth to be removed, and the enlarged part of the shaft, into which its opposite end is inserted, forms the fulcrum upon which the whole instrument revolves in the process of extraction. This instrument is particularly useful in the extraction of the molares, the crowns of which are capable of enduring the force necessary to be applied.

Having placed the patient in a suitable position, the hook of this key is applied to the neck of the tooth in such manner as to lodge the crown in its concavity. The fulcrum is fixed on the opposite side a little above the extremity of the root. Being thus placed, the fulcrum is a little lower than the hook, the resistance upon the crown of the tooth, and the support upon the opposite side of the alveoli. The power is in the handle of the instrument. When all these precautions have been taken, and a piece of soft leather has been placed in such manner as to protect the gum from injury, with a rotary motion of the key, we extract the tooth either inwardly or outwardly, as we may have previously determined upon. The tooth is often extracted with this instrument alone; but sometimes, after having luxated it, it is prudent to suspend the effort, lest we break away the alveolar process and lacerate the gums. The operation in such cases should be completed by means of straight or curved forceps. A rotary movement should now also be adopted so as not to remove the portion of the alveolar process that may have been fractured, nor to tear away the lacerated gum. It is important that the operator should not be too precipitate, nor apply too much force with this instrument, as the evils described may also be produced with it.

Although Garengeot's key is the best instrument for the extraction of the molares, it may be perceived, from what we have already said, that it has its inconveniences, which it is proper should be remedied. Jourdain, Bourdet, Come, Anguermann of Leipsic, Messrs. Laforgue and Duval, and many other dentists and surgeons, have modified it and made many ingenious improvements. We have improved this instrument, and called it *Garengeot's Key Improved*. This, from its construction, may be applied to in the extraction of decayed teeth that present the greatest difficulties. It differs from all the modifications and corrections of that instrument up to the present day: first, by its handle being moveable; secondly, by the curvature of its shaft; thirdly, by the facility with which we may make a fulcrum of the tooth adjoining the one we wish to extract; fourthly, by its hook, which nearly describes a right angle. We shall describe this new instrument, and analyze its parts, and endeavour to point out the advantages which it possesses.

Garengeot's Key Improved.

The moveable Handle.—This handle is larger than others, and the shaft is retained in it by means of a strong spring in such manner, that the operator can in a measure contract the instrument by means of pressure upon this spring. The force of the key is in this manner greatly increased.

The curved Shaft.—The curvature of the shaft forms nearly a right angle, and thus we are enabled to witness the action of the hook during the process of extraction, and readily discover if it slides from the neck of the tooth. This hook should be well adapted in size. When it is too large, the fulcrum of the key will glide upward to the neck of the tooth and fracture it; and if too small, the same accident is liable to occur. Should the fulcrum not descend sufficiently low upon the maxilla, we are also liable to take hold, with the hook, of the gum and alveolar process of the opposite side, and inflict injury and pain upon them. The curvature of the shaft presents another advantage, in enabling us to convey the tooth inwardly by placing the fulcrum upon the palatine side of the arch. This we are under some circumstances obliged to do, especially if the inner side of the tooth be destroyed by decay. The hook is then to be reversed, and the fulcrum placed upon the external side of the maxilla, for the removal of a tooth that does not require this mode of procedure. This key is particularly useful for extracting the dentes sapientiæ, the alveolar border of which does not offer sufficient surface exteriorly for the support of the fulcrum of an instrument. It is essential that the hook should not be too large, lest the fulcrum should descend below the eminence formed by the oblique ridges of the maxillary bones, as these would yield sooner than the tooth could be drawn.

Point of Support.—This should be directly anterior to the tooth to be removed. This is particularly essential in removing the dentes sapientiæ of the superior, as well as inferior jaw.

Hooks describing nearly right Angles.—These hooks embrace and seize the tooth better than those that describe a semicircle, as these latter are liable to slip toward the crown of the tooth; and they require more space than the former, and consequently oblige the patient to open his mouth widely, which is very fatiguing, especially to persons whose mouths are so small, that we can with difficulty introduce this instrument as far as to the second molar.

The straight Forceps.—These instruments should be six or eight inches long, their beaks should not be more than seven or eight lines in length, and their angles should be rounded. The beaks may be made of various sizes, and so constructed that their points will almost touch each other. The inner surfaces of these beaks, instead of being denticulated as they usually are, should be hollowed out and adapted to the crown of the tooth.

These forceps are in general used for the extraction of the incisores, cuspidati, and bicuspides. Their handles should be straight, and fluted that they may not slip from the hand of the operator.

In using these forceps we raise with the index finger of the left hand the lip, placing the thumb upon the crowns of the teeth. With the forceps in the right hand we take hold of the tooth as far beneath the gum as possible, and pressing sufficiently hard to be sure that the instrument will not slip, but not hard enough to crush the tooth, we should by a semirotary movement luxate the tooth, and then draw it perpendicularly and a little outwardly.* In certain cases, particularly with children, we may make use of a pair of forceps of small size with advantage.

* It is erroneous to advise the luxation of the bicuspides by means of a rotary motion. The movement should be outward, inward, and perpendicular.—S.

The curved Forceps.—These forceps differ from the preceding in having their beaks slightly curved. The curvature requires that the handles should be longer, and also slightly curved, but in an opposite direction from the inclination of the beaks. We use these instruments in general to remove from the lower jaw teeth that have already been partially extracted, and which offer but slight resistance. In extracting the teeth of children a smaller pair of the same shape are used.

In imitation of some English dentists we sometimes use large straight and curved forceps for the removal of the incisores, cuspidati, bicuspides and molares, however firm they may be in their sockets. This requires the instruments to be large; but the performance of such an operation with these instruments requires much skill and practice.

The curved Hawks-beak Forceps.—These resemble the straight forceps, but have their beaks arched in a direction with their handles. The superior beak is six or seven lines in length, while the inferior is only five or six. The extremities of the beaks should only be a line or a line and a half in thickness. This gives them the appearance of a parrot's or hawk's-beak. The superior handle is curved in the direction of the beaks as is also the inferior, but it is a few lines shorter. The whole length of the instrument is about four or five inches.

These are generally used for the extraction of the incisores, cuspidati, and bicuspides, of the inferior jaw. They are used in the following manner:—

The superior beak of the instrument is placed upon the internal side of the neck of the tooth, and the inferior upon the external side of the neck. Thus adjusted, we should gently press the instrument, then work the tooth outward and inward, and at the same time endeavour to raise it from its socket.

The hawks-bill forceps, however, are not very sure in the hands of persons unaccustomed to their use; for, if the tooth be firmly fixed in its socket, it may be fractured. This will not be surprising when we reflect that by embracing the teeth posteriorly and anteriorly with these forceps, the action and point of support are upon the same line, and the alveolar walls may present resistance equal to the force applied.

These forceps are used for the extraction of the teeth of children and loosened adult teeth, particularly such as have become so from luxation or disease of the alveolar membrane.

The straight Hawks-bill Forceps.—The model of this instrument was presented to us by Mr. Nasmyth of London. Its use is for the extraction of the anterior teeth of both jaws, and it is applied in like manner as the straight forceps. Its larger beak should rest upon that side of the tooth toward which we wish to luxate it.

The simple Elevator.—This is nothing more than a shaft nearly straight and rounded, but having a flat and cutting end. (Pl. XIV. Fig. 2.)

In using this instrument we should insert it as far as possible into the lateral part of the alveolus, and then endeavour to elevate the root in the direction of the socket. It may be applied in many ways, however, and for the luxation and removal of certain teeth, as well as for the former purpose.

The Fish Tongue.—Some dentists use an instrument called by this name for the removal of the wisdom teeth. (Pl. XIV. Fig. 1.) Its name and reference to the plate will sufficiently indicate its form.

The extraction of a tooth is a painful operation, and many persons would prefer enduring the pain of toothache for a long time to submitting to this operation. It is, however, the only sure means of relief; yet we will state that it is sometimes attended with serious results. The extraction of one or more teeth deprives the adjacent ones of a part of their support; the alveolar border flattens down; mastication and pronunciation become more difficult, especially in subjects of advanced age; and the cheeks fall in, giving to the physiognomy an appearance of decrepitude. These inconveniences are sufficient to induce the dentist to avoid performing this operation, whenever other means can be resorted to of giving efficient relief. The other means are those we have already described, as cauterizing or extracting the dental nerve, luxating the tooth, removing the decayed portions with the file, or by the complete

excision of the crown after the manner of the American dentists, who, it is said, were the first to substitute this practice
for extraction.

Excising Forceps.

Excision of the teeth, which Mr. Fay, American dentist
resident in London, now practises, consists in cutting off the
crown of a tooth with a pair of strong forceps. These forceps
may be curved or straight, and their beaks have a cutting edge.
With these instruments we can excise the largest teeth without danger of splitting them. Pl. XV. Figs. 1, 2, represents
two pairs of these forceps after Mr. Fay's patent. Fig. 3 exhibits a pair of curved forceps seizing a large molar and excising
it in the direction indicated upon the tooth. Figs. 4 and 5
represent the tooth excised. We observe upon the internal
part of the crown the cavity that contained the dental pulp.
The surface of the remaining portion of the tooth will not
present a sufficient cavity to allow of the continuation of the
decay, and it will be so flat that saliva and particles of food
will not be retained here any more than upon the crowns of
any of the teeth. This operation has been approved of, by
several intelligent English surgeons, who expressed their approbation of this mode of treatment in the London journals
in 1826.

" Mr. Fay in such cases, has recourse to excision. We have
had occasion to examine his improved forceps, and we are convinced that this operation can be performed *without pain.* The
basis upon which we found this assertion is, that in a thousand
cases we meet with nine hundred and ninety-nine, in which
disease has not its seat in the roots of the teeth, but in their
crowns. It is therefore only necessary to remove the diseased
part in order to give immediate relief. Daily experience con-
firms this truth. A new bony deposition takes place and protects the tooth from external injury. The cheeks do not sink in
as after the extraction of the teeth, and the roots which remain
will serve as a base for artificial pieces. Mr. Fay's mode
simply consists in removing with the excising forceps the
crown of the diseased tooth. No evil consequences will result
from this; whereas, were the tooth filed, as many dentists

would do, it would always occasion acute inflammation and other evils not less serious. We may add that, were the root of a tooth found to be diseased, Mr. Fay by his ingenious mode would excise it with as much facility as he does the crown. (Extracted from the Globe and the Traveller.)

A higher encomium upon Mr. Fay's mode of operating could hardly be given than the foregoing; but it is not enough that it should be eulogized by the journals; it should receive the approbation of the dental profession. It has not obtained this, however. Most of the reputable dentists of London disapprove of it, because, as they assert, the dental nerve not being entirely destroyed in the operation, the least heat or cold suffices to produce acute pain. They even pretend that Mr. Fay himself, in excising teeth, has often occasioned injuries; and they not only allege that the operation is extremely difficult to perform when we desire to excise the tooth at the commencement of its roots, but they regard it in all cases as being oftener injurious than useful.

We do not agree altogether with the English dentists on this subject. We think, on the contrary, that it is a good means of avoiding the extraction of teeth. Of twenty cases that may appear to require this last operation, at least one half of that number will admit of the former practice without danger, provided that it be not performed upon subjects under the age of twenty; as after this period of life the dental canal has so contracted as to leave but a small opening after excision. This may be seen in Plate IV. Fig. 4, which represents a tooth of a child twelve years old. We here perceive a cavity, very large and deep, in which the dental nerve existed. By the side of this, (Figure 7,) may be seen the drawing of a tooth taken from a subject forty years old. Its cavity is almost obliterated. In the latter case the practice here inculcated might have been pursued with success, while none could have been hoped for in the former. We have performed the operation several times, and always with success; but we only attempt it upon such persons as confide in us, and who know the advantage to be derived from such practice.

Before terminating this chapter, we will speak of another

method of avoiding the extraction of the teeth, and which has been proposed by M. L. Fattori, which is found in the *Revue Médicale.* "This method is based upon the following principle, namely, that whatever be the cause of pain, it will cease when we divide the nerve that supplies the part with sensibility, or by any other means suspend its functions. Hence to destroy toothache we should discover means by which we may sever the dental nerve at the point where it enters the root of the tooth. This is what M. L. Fattori has succeeded in doing by means of a trepan, with the point of which he cuts the dental nerve. This surgeon, having for a long time given this subject his whole attention, and having examined a great number of teeth, became competent to determine in a majority of cases the precise location of each dental ramification; and by means of needles of various lengths and sizes, adapted to his trepan, he cuts the nerve after having perforated very speedily and without pain the diseased tooth, which, by this operation, becomes insensible.

If it should chance to happen that the pain is not relieved by this operation, on account of the needle not coming in contact with the nerve, which it is known often varies its direction, he then has recourse to a second operation, in which he always succeeds."

The idea of dividing the dental nerve at the point where it enters the tooth, is certainly very ingenious, and we congratulate M. Fattori on pointing out so novel a method of curing odontalgia. This operation, however, appears to us difficult to be put in practice; but if we add to this plan all of the modifications of which it is susceptible, it will, we doubt not, supplant the operation proposed by Mr. Fay. We may indeed not be far from a period when extraction of the teeth, like many other operations, will be but seldom resorted to.

Our remarks upon the various instruments used for extracting teeth, and the proposed substitutes for this operation, here close. It would have been easy for us to diminish the number of these instruments, as experience shows that with our improved key we can, under all circumstances, perform this operation. But, as in many cases, the other instruments spoken of, are more easily applied, we have thought it proper to describe them.*

* We would here remark—

First, that the key is less used at the present time than it was at the period when this work was written; indeed there are many dentists of high reputation who have discarded its use altogether.

Secondly, that the improvements made in the construction of the various kinds of forceps used are such, as in our opinion, to enable the dentist to perform all operations with them, that the key would enable him to do, with greater certainty, and less likelihood of the occurrence of unpleasant accidents.

Thirdly, that the practice of excision, recommended in the text, is at all times unsafe, and will, in many instances, if pursued, be attended with painful, and even fatal consequences. There are cases, it is true, where a tooth has been accidentally broken off, in which we would permit the root to remain as a support for the adjacent teeth; but these cases are so rare, that we would regard the wilful excision of the crown of a tooth as a barbarous operation, unless it be a superior incisor or cuspidatus on which it is designed to place a crown by means of a pivot.

These remarks will apply to the author's entire treatise on the instruments used for extracting teeth. We would here add a description of some of the forceps most generally approved of, but that they are so various, and in many instances their differences are so minute, that our prescribed limits will not admit of it.

For the extraction of the superior molares, however, we think the forceps recommended by Mr. Snell are certainly superior to any in use. We will give a description of them in his own words. " For the upper molares, a strong pair of forceps is required, just sufficiently curved to keep the handle free from the lower teeth. The practicien should be provided with two pairs, one for each side; the termination of the inner chop should be in a flat groove, similar to the shape of the tooth on that side, which, it will be remembered, is the side where the single large fang is situated. The outer chop should terminate in two grooves, with a fine point in the centre, which point should be carefully introduced, as nearly as possible, between the two fangs, which are situated on the outer side. The convenience of two pairs of forceps is evident, as each pair would be especially adapted to one side. The tooth having been firmly grasped with a pair of these forceps placed sufficiently high, and having been pressed firmly outwards and inwards, may be removed with the greatest facility."

" The molares of the lower jaw require two pairs of forceps, one for each side, on account of the hook to turn around the little finger, which, it will be evident, must be on opposite sides of the instrument, for the opposite sides of the mouth. These forceps should be strong, with beaks short, and terminated by a double groove, with a fine point in the centre of each, so situated that as the lower molar teeth have two fangs only, the two points may be introduced between them." The handles of the lower molar forceps have been so constructed as to obviate the necessity of having two pairs.—S.

PRECAUTIONS AFTER THE EXTRACTION OF TEETH.

Whatever instrument may be used in the extraction of a tooth, there are certain precautions proper to be observed after the operation. The dentist should, for example, before permitting his patient to rinse his mouth, allow the blood to run for a few moments, or favour the discharge of blood by the use of tepid water; and only advise tonic and acidulated lotions when it continues to flow several hours after.

It is not necessary to approximate the gum with the fingers unless we think that it has been widely lacerated, or that a portion of the alveolar process has been splintered. In the latter case, the splinters should be removed with the fingers, or with a small pair of dressing forceps.

The patient should be advised to cover his mouth, or to avoid exposure to the cool air for several days. A healing lotion may be used with propriety during this period. The patient should also be cautioned against sucking the gum, as this may occasion a second hemorrhage. By paying strict attention to this advice, complete success will always attend us in our operations.

THE ACCIDENTS THAT MAY RESULT FROM THE EXTRACTION OF TEETH.

In spite of the utmost skill and care on the part of the dentist, serious accidents will sometimes occur in the extraction of teeth; but these may generally be remedied.

They affect the general organization at times, either before or after the operation, producing pain, convulsions, &c.; and at other times lesions of the adjacent parts are occasioned, as— 1. rupture or laceration of the gum; 2. fracture of the alveolar process; 3. hemorrhages arising from lesions of the part; 4. luxation and fracture of the jaw; 5. fracture of the tooth to be extracted, or some of the neighbouring teeth; 6. loosening of the adjacent teeth; 7. complete extraction of these last. The affections first alluded to here, affecting the general organization, are altogether beyond the control of the operator's will; but those of the second class are, in most cases, the result of defective instruments, or the unskilfulness of the dentist. We shall examine some of these accidents in particular, and ascertain in what manner they may be repaired.

Pain of the Teeth after Extraction, and attendant Evils.

The pain produced by extraction of the teeth is usually very acute, but it is of brief duration. We sometimes, however, see persons who experience pain for a long time after this operation; and, as we have already observed, derangement of the whole physical economy is attendant upon it. Some indeed faint away after the operation; and others, especially women, whose nervous systems are feeble, experience universal trepidation, and attacks of epilepsy, as we have had occasion to witness in the course of our practice. A species of tetanus is sometimes, though rarely, produced. Involuntary weeping is also produced. This resulting from a shock imparted to the eye by the rupture of the dental nerve, which also communicates to that organ. We have even known suppression of the catamenial discharges, and miscarriage, to proceed from the extraction of a tooth when performed without the full concurrence of the patient.

We are far from pretending that it is in the power of the dentist to avert all the disasters we have enumerated. This is impossible. But, by his address, he may ameliorate their severity. He should be an adequate physiognomist to perceive, at a glance, the physical and moral condition of his patient; and he should be prudent enough to avoid proceeding with the operation, unless convinced that he can effect it without injury. Bland and persuasive manners are also worthy of being cultivated by the dental practicien.

Contusions and Lacerations of the Gums.

Contusion of the gums is generally produced by pressure upon them with the key, or some instrument used in like manner. Laceration of the gums is generally produced by

15

fracture of the alveolar process. It seldom occasions serious consequences; but has at times been known to give rise to inflammation of a very alarming character, which all possible means should be resorted to in order to subdue. Considerable hemorrhage may also be produced by this accident, but can be generally checked by the use of acidulated and spirituous gargles, which should be persevered in as long as the case may require.

Fracture of the alveolar Process.

It often happens, when a tooth is unskilfully extracted, that a portion of the alveolar process is brought away with it. The danger of the occurrence of this accident also depends upon several circumstances, as the adhesion of the tooth to its socket by its periosteum, the thickness of the parietes, the length, number, curvature and divergence of the roots, &c. When, however, such accident has occurred, we should endeavour to detach the splinters that may adhere to the tooth before showing it to the patient, as no good can result from such exhibition, but alarm or disapprobation may be excited. If this cannot be done, it will be well to apprize the patient of the accident, and by means of pressure we should arrest whatever hemorrhage may ensue. By means of emollients, the inflammation that may occur may then be remedied; and the same means will also cause the inflammation to terminate in resolution.

Hemorrhage.

Hemorrhage is one of the most serious accidents that may result from the extraction of teeth. It usually occurs in consequence of the accidents we have already mentioned. It may also, unavoidably, result from the size, situation, and peculiar form of the tooth, the tendency of the vessels of the part, the habit that many persons have of sucking the gum, exhaustion after extraction of the tooth, scorbutic diathesis, &c.

This result does not always manifest itself at the moment of the operation, but hours, and even days after. It then occurs

in consequence of the disturbance of the coagulum in the alveolus, or because of irritation by means of some mechanical agent,
ere the mouths of the vessels have adhered.

When a tooth is properly extracted, the discharge of blood
that takes place is usually spontaneously arrested. It may
even be imprudent to suppress it, as it contributes to prevent
inflammation. It may, however, happen that hemorrhage, very
slight in appearance, may continue so long, or be so often repeated, as to become dangerous. We should then hasten to
relieve it by the customary remedies; but these sometimes
fail.

In simple cases, the discharge from the gums may be arrested
by the use of gargles slightly acidulated, pediluvia, and by
a mild regimen.

If the hemorrhage be obstinate, and resist the remedies above
indicated, after having removed the splints adhering to the
gums, we should apply to the wound a piece of white or yellow
wax, softened, and direct the patient to close his jaws forcibly,
and maintain it in this position for a number of hours. A
bandage carried beneath the inferior jaw, and upward over the
head, will here be of advantage to prevent the mouth from
opening involuntarily. Some practiciens use at times, to arrest
these hemorrhages, pledgets of cotton saturated with acidulated
water; at other times pieces of tinder or powdered agaric,
resin or gum Arabic powdered finely.

We may, in extreme cases, resort to either the potential or
actual cautery; but these means require much circumspection,
are productive of pain, do not always effect the desired object,
and always alarm the patient. We would prefer the application of the wax, as above indicated.*

---

* "Excessive hemorrhage from the extraction of a tooth does not appear to
be dependent upon the manner in which a tooth is extracted, but seems
rather to be attributable to constitutional temperament. Hence, whenever a
tendency to it exhibits itself in one member of a family it is usually
found to exist in all." (Harris's *Dental Art.*) Dr. Harris uses for the suppression of such hemorrhage pledgets of cotton or sponge saturated with the
tincture of gall nuts; but, he remarks, "pressure, after all, is the only thing
on which we can rely." If it be so applied as to act directly on the mouths of
the bleeding vessels, it will be found to be more efficacious than the most
powerful stiptic, or any other remedy to which we can resort.—S.

Before dismissing this subject, we would remark upon hemorrhage occurring after the extraction of a tooth in a subject of a scorbutic diathesis. It is a fearful affection, and frequent returns of it may well be apprehended. In defiance of the most efficient means that are known, it may terminate fatally. Under such circumstances, as in the preceding cases, we should fill up the cavity, and keep the jaws of the patient closed by means of a bandage.

Rupture of the maxillary Sinus, Fracture of the alveolar Arches, and Luxation of the Jaw.

Surgeons and dentists have been known to fracture the walls of the maxillary sinus, to bring away a part of one or both of the alveolar arches, fracture the jaw, and sometimes occasion its luxation, by pressing the instrument too firmly upon the inferior jaw. These accidents, fortunately, are very unfrequent. M. Duval relates several examples of this kind. When we were in Calais, in 1815, we treated a case of this kind. The patient was a labouring man, and had the inferior jaw fractured by means of a key having a straight shaft. It was in consequence of observing this accident, and from having seen a short time previous in the possession of Mr. Fox of London a key of this kind somewhat varied in its construction, that we were induced to make some alteration in the key of Garengeot. The tooth in the case we speak of had been extracted with the fulcrum of the instrument upon the palatine side of the arch, and the surgeon, on account of the construction of the shaft of the instrument, had to rest an angle of this fulcrum upon a neighbouring tooth, and in consequence the tooth was broken and the jaw fractured. The accident had occurred nine months previously to our seeing the patient, whose condition, on examination, we considered very alarming. We discovered a considerable fracture of the inferior maxilla on the right side. This fracture had necessarily been occasioned at the time of the extraction of the tooth. A portion of bone, extending from the angle of the jaw to the cuspidatus tooth, and to which several teeth were still adhering, was necrosed, and, acting as a foreign body, it occasioned a continual mechanical irritation.

This increased the fistulous openings, which were numerous, and exhibited several splints. A piece of bone, terminating in a point, and about one inch and three lines in length, and eight lines in width, (Pl. XIII. Fig. 1,) rested upon the external part of the cuspidatus.

Such was the situation of the patient when we proposed the removal of this bone. He willingly acceded to it, and after we had cautiously detached from the principal sequester a large part that was adhering to it, we with some difficulty removed it.

The remaining portion of this bone, about an inch and nine lines in length, and about eight lines in width, and occupying, like the first part, the right side of the jaw, and from which the teeth had been detached, was in a few days after removed, with greater facility than the first.

The irritation and inflammation ceased from that time; the fistules cicatrized in from fifteen to twenty days; mastication becoming easier, digestion was re-established; and in about three weeks the patient was entirely cured.

At the time of our last journey to England, we had occasion to see the person who was the subject of this operation; he was but slightly disfigured, although he had lost a greater portion of the right side of the maxillary bone, and although the cuspidatus antagonized with the superior second molar of that side. We took an exact impression of both jaws of this person, and formed articulating moulds from them.

It should not be concluded from this particular case, that it is always proper to remove the portion of bone fractured from the jaw. Such conduct, under circumstances differing from those that we have related, might be improper. If the fracture in this case had been recent, it would have been better to endeavour to effect a reunion, and only have recourse to the removal of the osseous fragments when our efforts had failed. Cases of this kind, however, are seldom met with in practice.

Luxation of the Jaw is not always owing to imprudence on the part of the operator: it may arise from a peculiar disposition of the articulating surfaces. But, whatever may be the cause, it should be immediately reduced, and the consecutive injuries should be relieved by all possible means.

In order to reduce a luxation of the jaw, the thumb, enveloped in a piece of linen, should be placed within the mouth, and with the fingers under the chin, we seize the jaw. Pressing near the condyle with the thumb, and raising the chin at the same moment, we bring it into its place. The other hand is at the same time pressed upon the forehead.

Loosening, Fracture, and complete Extraction of the Teeth.

Loosening of the Teeth.—The loosening of the teeth adjoining that we are about to extract may be occasioned as often from the confusion that the patient causes, by his alarm at the apparition of the instrument, and thus occasioning its derangement after it has been properly applied, as from the improper manner in which it is used.

Under such circumstances we should allow the loosened teeth to remain, redress those that have been luxated, and maintain them in their places by ligatures as we would a single luxated tooth.

Fracture of the Teeth.—The molares are sometimes so solidly implanted in their sockets, and adhere to them so strongly, that it often happens that we break them in the attempt to extract them. The instrument is sometimes broken, though this is uncommon. This accident is not always occasioned by the sudden motion of the hand, as is usually supposed: it may be occasioned by various other causes. Fracture of a tooth may sometimes be unavoidable from its extreme brittleness, or from its being extensively decayed; sometimes from the disposition of its roots, which may be strong, crooked, divergent, convergent, or nearly united at some point to the socket; and sometimes, as in the loosening of teeth, by the patient grasping the hand of the operator.

If the fractured portion is not deep in the socket, and we can yet seize it, we should attempt its extraction; or should it not be loosened, by destroying its asperities with a pair of forceps, and smoothing its surface with a file, it may be suffered to remain. If it be very deep in the socket, we should not disturb it, as its extraction may cause the patient pain, and its presence may not prove inconvenient. It is even well to preserve them; for the dental nerve and pulp being destroyed, there is no sensibility in them, and they will continue to maintain the neighbouring teeth in their sockets, and in old age they will prove useful in mastication.

We deem it proper here to remark, that before operating upon teeth that present prominent points upon the alveolar border, and the crowns of which are short and thick, too much care cannot be taken by the practicien, as such teeth are often removed with great difficulty.

Accidental Extraction of one or more Teeth.—Sometimes in attempting to extract one tooth, we extract two which are found to be united. (Pl. VIII. Figs. 4, 7.) An accident of this kind cannot be ascribed to the unskilfulness nor awkwardness of the operator: but to extract a sound tooth through mistake or a permanent for a deciduous tooth, is indicative of the grossest ignorance.*

The only means of repairing so gross an error is immediately to replace the tooth or teeth thus extracted, and to resort to the use of ligatures. We can furnish numerous examples that have occurred in our practice of teeth that, having been removed either by a blow or fall, or by the awkwardness of a dentist, and that were again placed in their sockets, and became as firm as ever. This operation is somewhat analogous to that of transplanting teeth, of which we shall now speak.

Transplanting Teeth.—This operation, practised in Paris

* We cannot refrain from remarking here, that of the many accidents described by our author but few could occur from the use of properly constructed forceps. A review of them indeed will not be without profit to one who would listen to evidence in deciding upon the description of instruments he would adopt the use of in practice. For ourselves there is but one consideration that induces us to pay any degree of deference to the recommendations of the *extracting key:* it is that there are some dentists of eminence who still use it, and who contend that it is not only a good and safe instrument, but that it is superior to the instruments of more recent invention. We would, however, suggest, and with deference, whether the ease and certainty in its application, acquired by years of familiar practice be not in reality the grounds of such preferences.' Mr. Snell remarks on this subject that "considerable differences of opinion exist, and probably will continue to exist as to which are the best instruments; each operator feeling a preference for that with which he has been accustomed to operate successfully."—S.

about two centuries ago by a surgeon, consists in extracting a tooth from the mouth of a young and healthy person to be inserted in the freshly opened alveolus of another person, who has been obliged to submit to the extraction of a tooth of the same class.

This dental prothesis, which still unfortunately enjoys some reputation in England and Germany, is almost entirely abandoned in this country. It is a cruel practice, disapproved of by every sentiment of humanity, and should be discarded from French surgery. In 1812, while young in the practice of dental surgery, we performed this operation in two cases, the subjects being about eighteen or twenty years of age. We transcribe verbatim, two letters, written to us since that period. The details they contain will give us a correct idea of the advantages we may hope to obtain from this operation of transplanting teeth.

Vie, October 15, 1825.

MONSIEUR:

I have received your letter addressed to Mademoiselle de C * * *, now my wife, and I hasten to reply to it in conformity to your wish.

The tooth that you inserted for her in 1812 never became firm, and eight or ten months after that time she removed it. It did not retain its colour. You will doubtless recollect that you were obliged to file its root two or three times, and its never having become solid may perhaps be attributable to this. It occasioned no inflammation.   With respect, yours,   R * * *.

Vie, December 20, 1826.

MONSIEUR:

In conformity with your desire I hasten to inform you that the tooth you inserted for me in 1812 still remains in its socket, but has never been firmly seated, and I think it will finally fall out. The part of the gum that covered its root began to recede three or four years since. At present the root is entirely exposed. The tooth has not preserved its colour.

I have the honour, &c.   S. L * * *.

P. S. I omitted to inform you that this tooth has never been the occasion of pain.

PART III.

MECHANICAL DENTISTRY.

PART III.

General Considerations upon artificial Teeth.

In the preceding chapters we indicated the resources presented by the dental art to remedy the diseases of the teeth,
and pointed out the various means of extracting them when
their preservation becomes impracticable. It now remains for
us to examine the various means of replacing teeth that have
been lost, and the materials of which these are manufactured.
This part of our art has been called *dental prothesis.*

We shall not here enter into a detail of the antiquity and
origin of this prothesis; but will recommend the reader for
this to the learned pamphlet of M. Duval which bears the
following title: *Conseils des Poètes Anciens sur la Conservation
des Dents.* We will merely say, that the polished people of
antiquity paid particular attention at all times to their teeth,
and endeavoured to repair their loss by mechanical means.

We see, indeed, by the writings of travellers, that the Chinese, Indians, certain colonies of America, Africa, Asia, &c.,
in compliance with ideas more or less capricious, cut their
teeth in various ways with flints. It is also known that the
people of the colonies inhabiting New Zealand and New
Holland shape their teeth in such a perfect manner that they
appear to have been operated upon with a file. We have made
(Pl. XVI. Figs. 3, 4, 5, 6,) several drawings from the natural pieces and designs furnished us by Dr. Busseuil.

Whatever may be the origin of odontotechny, it is certain
that this branch is carried to a greater degree of excellence at

the present day than it ever attained in former times, particularly in our country, where this department of dentistry has
become so good and so general as to be considered as an art,
the many advantages of which all classes of society have felt.

It was Fauchard, our tutor, who first, in 1728, gave a treatise
upon the *Moyens de Remplacer les Dents et de Remédier aux
Vices de Conformation de la Voûte Palatine.* Several French
and foreign works have appeared since that time, and although
incomplete, they furnish valuable information upon the subject now before us. They appear to us to be susceptible of
important additions, and if we cannot flatter ourselves that
we can furnish a perfect treatise upon this part of the science,
we at least hope to point out the various improvements that
have been recently introduced, not only in dental prothesis,
but also in the various ways of applying incorruptible teeth.

ARTIFICIAL TEETH.

We designate as *artificial teeth,* teeth destined to replace such
as have been lost by some cause. When these teeth are properly constructed, and when rightly adjusted and maintained
in the mouth, they possess all the advantages of the natural
teeth, as well as ornaments of the mouth, as for the purposes
of pronunciation or mastication. They completely remedy
the great inconvenience resulting from the discharge of a part
of the saliva from the anterior part of the mouth, occasioned
by the loss of the anterior teeth.

When artificial teeth are well adjusted, they often contribute
to the solidity of the dental arch, particularly in the mouths
of persons whose teeth are long, and whose gums are liable to
be chafed by them. In this case a support is afforded them
which ensures their solidity; but there are certain conditions
a compliance with which is required, that these may fulfil the
end desired.

They should as nearly as possible resemble in form and colour the lost teeth. Their retention should not depend upon
the adjacent teeth in such manner as to impair them.

It is important that artificial teeth should be preserved in perfect cleanliness; they should be cleaned as often, or oftener, than the natural teeth require to be.

The materials that have been used in constructing artificial teeth are the bones and the teeth of oxen, horse, sheep, stag, and several other animals; ivory, mother-of-pearl, teeth of the hippopotamus or sea-horse, of the whale, human teeth, *incorruptible* teeth made of mineral paste. Persons who have been deprived of their front teeth, have, for a long time, replaced them with artificial teeth made of white wax.

We shall briefly examine these various substances, the number of which have been greatly reduced. We would, however, here remark, that the teeth of the hippopotamus, the human, and the incorruptible teeth, are most generally used at the present time.

Bones of the Ox.—These bones, being entirely destitute of enamel, bear but little resemblance to the natural teeth, and are very porous: they become yellow, and decompose very soon. They have, however, for a long time been used for fabricating supports or bases resembling the gums. For this purpose the femor has been used, after having been cleansed in clay and exposed to the dew to whiten.

Teeth of Oxen, Horses, &c.—As we cannot give these the shape of the human teeth by means of the file, it is easy to detect them otherwise than by the absence of the enamel, which does not cover the surface of these teeth. Their colour does not resemble that of the human teeth. If, however, we are obliged to use them from the want of human teeth, we should choose those of animals advanced in age, because of their central cavity being smaller than at a younger period of life; they are hence more solid, and better adapted for the reception of pivots, by which they are to be attached to the artificial base.

Ivory.—Sometimes parts of sets, and sometimes complete dentures, are manufactured of this substance; but, like the preceding, it is not a good imitation of the natural organ. Ivory, being void of enamel, becomes yellow very soon in the mouth, and the saliva and mucus decompose it, after a time, in spite of the care that may be taken. (Pl. XVII. Fig. 21.)

16

In case we cannot procure a substance more resisting, as the tooth of the sea-horse, we should prefer the ivory of young elephants, and the central part of the tooth near the point. The grain at this point is more compact, and the ivory usually lasts longer than that of any other part of the tooth. Green ivory, that is, ivory taken from the teeth of animals that have been recently killed, is preferable.

Mother of Pearl.—We need merely name this material. It is unfit to be used for this purpose, and has been seldom employed.

Hippopotamus.—The use of the tooth of the hippopotamus in manufacturing teeth, is of recent date, as ivory was, for a time, almost exclusively used; but the inconveniences of the latter, already named, and the superiority of the sea-horse tooth, have induced dentists to abandon the use of ivory. At the present day the tooth of the hippopotamus is much used, both with and without the enamel.

These teeth are obtained in commerce from Africa, and the most distant parts of Asia. Such as are least hollowed out are considered best, as their ivory is more compact than those that are hollow. These teeth vary much in size, colour, form and enamel.

The incisores of the hippopotamus are short, semi-cylindrical anteriorly, contain a deep furrow, and are enveloped with enamel, the colour of which, when polished, resembles that of the human teeth. Their semi-circular form enables us to carve from the same piece several teeth having enamel upon them. They sometimes contain deep furrows, by which we are enabled to carve six or eight teeth thus shielded with this substance.

The tusks of this animal are larger and longer than the incisores, and are curved like those of the wild boar. Their least weight is two pounds and a half. They sometimes weigh nine pounds, but this is uncommon. The teeth are flattened posteriorly, and convex anteriorly, and are covered with enamel only on the latter side. Their size enables us to form complete dentures of them, not enamelled, or bases upon which enamelled teeth are afterward to be attached.

We should make use of such as have their internal substance compact, white and smooth. The best are white, round, enamelled at their smallest part, and have not large ridges or deep depressions, and are not cracked in the direction of their curvature. To preserve them they should be kept in a humid place. When using them or working them, we should be careful not to expose them to the sun, fire, or current of air, as such exposure will tend to crack them, especially in such places as are not protected by the enamel.

If we cut a hippopotamus' tooth transversely through its middle, we will perceive a furrow, whose depth depends entirely upon the age of the animal. We should as much as possible avoid this furrow in manufacturing pieces. If its use cannot be avoided, the piece should be so constructed that this defect may not be perceptible, as this part is yellow, and more easily acted upon by the secretions of the mouth.

However perfect and beautiful may be the piece of this material used, its extreme whiteness, which at first pleases the eye, sooner or later is lost, and a bluish or yellow hue is assumed.

Artificial bases are generally made of the tooth of the sea-horse, and human teeth are inserted into this; and when these bases are neatly carved and polished, they present a very good appearance.

The incisores of the inferior jaw of the hippopotamus are called, improperly, in commerce, the teeth of the sea-cow. These teeth are round, and have no enamel, and when they are of a proper size, complete dentures are manufactured out of a single piece by its being cut lengthwise.

Teeth of the Whale.—These teeth are sometimes in commerce mixed with those of the sea-horse. They are as strong as the latter, but differ very much from them in form, and in their durability. They may, however, be used in the manufacture of the bases when we cannot procure a substance more compact.

Human Teeth.—Of the various articles used in replacing the lost organs, the human teeth, without doubt, merit the preference, since they are such as were given us by nature. We shall indicate the manner in which they should be chosen, and the various preparations they should undergo before insertion.

These teeth are generally obtained from the mouths of persons who die in hospitals, and whose bodies are brought into the amphitheatre for dissection. The best are such as are not decayed or cracked, and have been taken from subjects between the ages of eighteen and forty years. The teeth at this time of life are firm and of the most desirable consistency, and are capable, for a long time, of resisting the destructive agents to which they are constantly exposed. The teeth of younger subjects are too tender, their canal is too large, and they are incapable of resisting deleterious influences. Those of old men are hard, but yellow and much worn, and crack very easily. We should prefer the teeth of adults which have been recently taken from the subjects. We should reject all such as are not entirely sound, or the cavities of which are red or black, as they very soon become black in the mouth and decay. It is true, that if a cavity be found upon the side of a tooth used for this purpose, we may drill the decay out, and insert a plug made of the tooth of the hippopotamus; but these should not be used if sound ones can be procured.

The teeth being chosen, we should preserve them in such manner as to be able to use them at any moment. They should be extracted from the subject with care, and portions of the alveolar process, periosteum, gum, or tartar, that may adhere to them, should be removed. The extremities of their roots should be pierced, and they should be strung in the order in which they had been placed in the mouth. They should then be steeped for seven or eight days in water, which should be changed every twenty-four hours. At the expiration of this time, they should be again cleaned by being rubbed with a piece of soft wood, as willow or fir, wet and dipped in powdered pumice stone. In this manner we can remove all foreign bodies from the teeth. If there should remain any stain or spot, it should be removed with the file or grindstone. They are next to be washed with soap and water, and the process of cleaning is to be concluded by immersing them in alcohol.

We generally use the eight superior teeth, viz: four incisores, two cuspidati and two anterior bicuspides. It will be well, however, to procure the eight corresponding inferior teeth, as they are sometimes required.

The teeth, being thus cleansed and assorted, should be placed in a vase and covered with sand, bran, fine grain, saw-dust, or any thing capable of excluding the air, heat, and cold.

Some dentists preserve them in water or diluted alcohol. This is a bad practice, as they become yellow and crack afterward when exposed to the air. Others preserve them in equal parts of wax, chalk and oil; but this is inferior to the simple mode we have already recommended. When we cannot procure the eight teeth from the same individual, care should be taken to select such as harmonize well together. We should be cautious in using teeth that have been procured from cemeteries; for, after having remained in the earth for a time, their enamel is apt to be dull. Their bony substance, also, is likely to be yellow, or of a brown hue, which is the result of decomposition. While preparing teeth of this kind, they often break very easily, and when inserted soon become black and decay.

When we wish to insert two or three of these teeth, we adjust them upon a platina or gold plate, if the alveolar border be not too much absorbed. If this be the case they should be mounted upon a sea-horse base, and secured to it by means of platina rivets.

Animal substances of which artificial teeth are made possess the inconvenience of being liable to a speedy softening and decomposition; and they tarnish and emit a disagreeable odour. We are therefore obliged to renew them frequently. To obviate this inconvenience, it has been proposed to manufacture artificial teeth of earth, capable of being hardened by means of heat, and enamelled like porcelain. These teeth are called incorruptible.

Incorruptible Teeth.—M. Duchâteau, apothecary at St. Germaine, in Laye, in 1774, first imagined the construction of porcelain teeth resembling those of ivory that he wore, and from which he had experienced much inconvenience; and for this purpose applied to the porcelain manufacturers of Guerhard in Paris. But the first attempts made by these were unavailing,

on account of the contraction of the material in the process of
baking.   This difficulty induced M. Duchâteau to use fine
porcelain, which vitrifies in a heat of from thirty to thirty-five
degrees, according to the pyrometer of Wedgwood. (The hard
porcelain now used must be submitted to a heat of one hundred
and thirty to one hundred and forty degrees, according to the
same pyrometer.)   In order to obtain complete success in the
trial of the pastes, and in the mode of application of the teeth,
he consulted several distinguished artists, and also M. de Chemant, at that time dentist in Paris.   These artists gave advice
relating to the mode of manufacturing porcelain teeth; and
M. de Chemant directed their mode of application.   To the
paste first used was now added colouring earths, which rendered
it more fusible, and susceptible of being baked in a simple
muffle.   After several unsuccessful attempts he at length completed a piece of a grayish white colour, and which had shrunk
very little.   These he adapted to the alveolar border.   Satisfied with his experiment, M. Duchâteau attempted to execute similar dentures for persons of quality; but, being wholly
unskilled in the dental art, he did not succeed in his enter-
prise.   In 1776 he communicated this discovery to the Royal
Academy of Surgeons in Paris, and in return received the
thanks of the Academy and the honour of membership.

M. de Chemant, having improved this composition by the
addition of Fontainbleau sand and Alicante soda, chalk, oxyde
of red iron, and cobalt, manufactured similar teeth.   He inserted several of them, and twelve years after obtained from
Louis XVI. a patent for the invention.   Duchâteau and others
disputed the title to this discovery, and entered a protest; but
they failed of success, as their title was not legal.   Hence it
is to M. Chemant that it is to be attributed, as, but for him, it
would still be unknown.

This important discovery has since that time been greatly
improved, and incorruptible teeth are in general use at the
present time.

We have spoken in detail, in the second edition of our
Manuel du Dentiste, of the perfection to which M. Fonzi has
brought these teeth.   M. *Pernet Desforges,* and several other dentists, have laboured with great success, and we ourselves have

for the last ten years contributed to their general reputation, by inculcating the mode of making and applying them, and by selling them to our professional brethren at prime cost. The incorruptible teeth now manufactured in Paris resemble very closely the natural teeth. Some old practiciens, a number of them of reputation, yet universally use human teeth and those of the sea-horse; but we can easily comprehend their motive in this: they are already advanced too far in their career to deviate: they do not study new discoveries, and the use of the new teeth requires great practical knowledge, which they will not acquire.

Wax.—Some persons often remedy the loss of teeth, by filling up with a piece of white wax the space that these organs had occupied. There can, however, result little advantage from this practice, first, because persons who apply this material are obliged to renew it often; secondly, they cannot make it so secure as not to be in danger of being lost either in speaking or eating. These inconveniences are sufficient to cause them to abandon its use. Yet we must confess that we have known persons who wore such teeth for many years.

Upon a review of what we have already said of the various kinds of artificial teeth, we will observe—

1. That we should totally renounce the use of teeth manufactured from mother of pearl, the bones of oxen, ivory and wax;

2. That under certain circumstances we may employ the teeth of oxen, sheep, hind, and some other animals, and also the enamelled part of the tooth of the hippopotamus;

3. That the tooth of the hippopotamus is superior to all these substances when several teeth are to be made;

4. That the human teeth, as they are such as are given us by nature, are daily used with great success;

5. That the improved incorruptible teeth leave us nothing to desire, as regards the close imitation of nature, their hardness, and their applicability under all circumstances.

To be sure of our work, it is important in this, as in every thing else, that we should perform it ourselves, and to succeed we should know the materials used, and be familiar with the

use of proper tools.   Application and some aptness in mechanism are therefore essential.

Before proceeding to the exposition of the various means by
which artificial teeth are retained in their proper places, we
shall examine the foundation of the objections that have been
urged to their use.

It is said that artificial teeth cannot be made to perform the
principal functions of the natural teeth, which are those of
mastication, because the various movements of the inferior
jaw in the comminution of food, by acting against the artificial teeth, occasions the loosening of the natural teeth, or the
roots upon which the artificial teeth are sustained.

We cannot indeed hope for a substitute for the natural teeth
as good and complete in all respects as themselves; but if the
losses we are unfortunately afflicted with may thus be partially
restored, we should be gratified.   Should we therefore deny
the utility of dental prothesis, because we cannot equal nature
in the beauty and excellence of her mechanism?   Artificial
teeth well executed and applied are, however, of great utility,
nor need we apprehend the results thus anticipated.

The objection made to the use of animal artificial teeth, that
they impart an unpleasant odour to the mouth, is only valid in
cases in which they are inaccurately applied, or in which the
persons wearing them are neglectful in regard to cleanliness,
or fail to renew them when decayed.   If, however, incorruptible teeth be used, no more care is necessary than is required
by sound natural teeth.

It is also said that teeth artificially inserted occasion pain,
and often require to be removed some days after being applied.
These inconveniences never occur when they are prepared by
a skilful dentist, and when the gums and roots are in health
at the time of their insertion.   Such condition of these parts
is a subject requiring close attention.

It is also said that artificial teeth become loose and fall out
spontaneously.   This is true; but such inconvenience only
takes place in teeth of bone that have been for a long time
worn, and when the saliva has entirely destroyed the parts
surrounding the pivots by which they are retained.   The falling out of an incorruptible tooth can only occur from an acci-

dent that may break it or detach it from the solder; such an accident may also occasion the loss of a natural tooth.

It is also erroneous to suppose it necessary to take out the artificial teeth every night. On the contrary this should never be done, for this will wear away the roots, if the teeth be implanted upon them, and hasten the destruction of the natural teeth if these be used for supports, as already described.

In refuting the objections urged to artificial teeth we have in some manner already pointed out the advantages resulting from their use, and which will be more perceptible if we reflect that these teeth are intended less to masticate solid aliment than to remedy a deformity, and an impediment to pronunciation resulting from the loss of teeth. These inconveniences may be wholly overcome by the use of artificial teeth such as are used at the present day.

We confess, however, that persons who have several artificial teeth will at first experience embarrassment in moving the tongue in the articulation of sound. In a few days, however, becoming accustomed to their presence, pronunciation will become easier, and less unpleasantness will be felt.

Before indicating the manner of replacing lost organs, and retaining them in their positions, we deem it necessary to point out the manner of taking an impression of the part of the mouth that they are to occupy, and the manner of making plaster, sulphur, wax or composition moulds, and also brass moulds with mated parts. Whenever natural teeth have been lost, artificial teeth may be inserted, and the number required is never an obstacle to dental prothesis.

THE VARIOUS MODES OF TAKING IMPRESSIONS, MAKING MOULDS, STAMPING PLATES, &c. &c.

The place to which artificial teeth are to be attached must first be prepared, and an impression of the mouth taken, before the artificial piece can be made; thus these teeth can then be properly adjusted with reference to those that are in the mouth. For the purpose of taking such casts, some dentists use modelling wax composed of ten parts of wax and one part of turpentine.

This wax, however, softens too easily, and, notwithstanding the care taken in withdrawing the impression, there is danger of having it injured in such manner that the moulds made from it will be larger than the natural parts.

Some practiciens use the white wax, others prefer the yellow, as they are obtained in commerce. These are generally preferred to the modelling wax, as they are much firmer. We, however, believe that none of these are hard enough, and require great care to prevent the accident we have spoken of. This has induced us to use a composition of twelve parts of white wax, one part of white lead, and half a part of oil. This may be coloured with cochineal, orchanet, or white moss. The wax should be slowly melted, the oil then added, and in order that the white lead, which is very heavy, may be well incorporated with it, the mixture should be well stirred, until congealed.

When we wish to make use of this preparation, we cut it into small pieces and place it in warm water, and, when very soft, place it in a linen cloth to press out the moisture and render it solid. Having attained a proper consistency, it is then placed into a tin or silver frame used for the purpose, and the impression of the mouth is then taken.

After having taken the impression, it should be immersed in cold water to harden; it may then be placed upon a level plane, and surrounded with a border of mastic, an inch in height, and adjusted so that the plaster may not escape. A sufficient quantity of fine plaster should then be put into a vessel, and water added thereto until it be brought to such a consistency as will admit of its running freely. Pieces of fine wire should then be inserted into the depressions of the wax, that the teeth may not be liable to break from the plaster on being withdrawn: a small quantity of the liquid plaster should then be poured into the mould, and a slight tap with the frame should be made upon the table, that the air bubbles may escape. The remainder of the plaster may then be poured in. When it has become sufficiently hard the mastic may be removed, and a few hours later the wax may also be removed, being first softened in warm water; care, however, being taken not to wet the plaster if it can be avoided. But this may also be removed by means of a knife, or by melting before a fire, care being taken not to cut the plaster in the former operation, nor to calcine it in the latter.

Manner of preparing a Mould of Wax.—After having obtained an impression as we have directed, we melt common wax, and when this is on the point of congealing a small quantity at a time should be poured into the impression, which should have been previously oiled. It will be perceived that this wax should not be poured in hot nor in too great quantities; for we would thus be liable to melt a portion of the impression. We may then withdraw the mould before it becomes entirely cold, and after having oiled it, as well as the impression, they may be placed one into the other.

Manner of preparing a Sulphur Mould.—This does not differ from the foregoing.

By means of these procedures we may obtain several moulds from the same impressions, and finally from one of plaster. But as these moulds are not hard enough to enable us to stamp up a plate, we are obliged to make one of a composition, of eight parts of bismuth, five of lead, and three of tin, or of brass. The following is the mode of obtaining these last.

Manner of obtaining a Metal Mould.—Into a box twelve or eighteen inches square, and four inches high, put potter's earth moistened, and into this carefully introduce the plaster, wax, or sulphur mould, and in order that the impression may be exact, we should render the earth compact around the mould, and then let this be carefully withdrawn in order not to enlarge the impression. The metal, when on the point of congealing, should then be poured into the sand.

The manner of making brass moulds is similar to the mode practised by founders in casting this metal into the various shapes desired. Founder's earth or sand is pressed upon all the sides of the model; an exact impression being thus obtained, a conduit should be made through which to pour the fused metal. The sand, however, should be partially dried, that the passage of this may be facilitated. But these moulds cannot in general be made with as much facility as the foregoing, and they require to be repaired with care after they have been cast. They should be scoured in nitric acid diluted, to remove the impurities that may adhere to them; and with fine sand rubbed on by means of a piece of soft wood their surface should be rendered smooth.

To stamp a plate we should place it between two hard, resisting bodies, which may be pressed against each other by means of a hammer or vice. The counter mould should be somewhat softer than the mould, and of all metals lead should be preferred for this purpose.

The manner of forming counter moulds is simple. A small quantity of sand or potter's earth should be placed in a box of proper dimensions; the mould should then be pressed into this, with the back downward, four or five lines deep; this should then be surrounded with a piece of sheet iron or pasteboard, leaving a space of a few lines between this wall and the mould. The metal may then be poured upon the mould until it is covered to the depth of an inch. The same result may be obtained by making in potter's earth an oval or round hole larger than the mould. The lead being poured into this hole, and when on the point of congealing, we may force into it that part of the mould that is to be used in stamping the plate; and when both have become cold, they may be separated with a hammer.

Manner of stamping Plates.

A rough pattern of paper or sheet-lead having been cut out, it may be placed between the moulds and slightly stamped. It may then be withdrawn and fashioned into the shape that it is designed the plate should have. The pattern thus obtained should then be placed upon the metal plate to be used, which should then be scribed and cut out by it. In this manner there will be less waste of the metal than if a previous pattern had not been made.

The metal plate should be well annealed to render it pliable, and adapted to the male mould as neatly as possible by means of a pair of round pliers. The corresponding mould should now be fitted upon it, and force applied, as before mentioned, but it would be well to place a piece of iron upon the mould to equalize the force applied.

The plate being properly stamped, it should be reduced with a file in all parts that are superfluous, and when thus finished it will accurately fit the mouth as designed. (Pl. XVIII. Fig. 2.)

Manner of inserting artificial Teeth.

The loss of one, two, three or four teeth, or a complete denture, may be remedied by means of artificial teeth; and to such perfection have we arrived in adjusting these, that they, in a great measure, perform well all the functions of the natural organs.

Artificial teeth are inserted upon pivots, upon metallic plates, and upon the sea-horse base, and are sustained by means of ligatures, clasps or springs; and the choice of one or other of these various attachments depends upon the nature of the case.

A person having lost a superior incisor, cuspidatus or bicuspis, or even an inferior cuspidatus, or bicuspis, the root of any of which may remain in health, we may insert an artificial tooth by means of a pivot. If, on the contrary, the root be nearly or wholly destroyed, we will then have to insert a tooth upon a plate.

Preparation of a Root previous to the Attachment of an artificial Crown.

It is not often that the root of a tooth is injured by any accident that may fracture the crown. To remove any portion of the latter, however, that may remain, a file will usually answer; but if there be any considerable portion of it, recourse should be had to a small saw that turns upon a pivot, and by means of which we may cut around a tooth. Having removed the crown, we should then file the neck off below the free edge of the gum, so that the joint of union between the crown and root may be concealed. The canal of the root should then be prepared. If the nerve be sensible, its sensibility should

17

be destroyed by means of some of the remedies which we have already indicated.

When the root has thus been prepared, we should have un-tempered drills of different sizes in readiness, and, commencing with the smallest, the dental canal should be gradually enlarged. The drill should, from time to time, be withdrawn, and dipped into water to prevent its being choked up. Without this pre-caution we are in danger of breaking the drill. When a hole of sufficient depth has been made with a small drill in this manner, we should apply a larger one, and so on, until the ca-pacity of the canal is sufficient. This opening should then be cleansed by injecting water into it; and by means of a slender probe, with a piece of cotton attached to the end of it, and saturated with alcohol or some stiptic liquid, we may remove particles of bone that may be left in the cavity, which should then be completely dried.

Pivot Teeth, and the manner of inserting them.

We designate as pivot teeth such teeth as are adapted to the purpose of pivoting, by having their roots cut off and their crowns hollowed out in such manner as to receive a pivot, as already described in regard to the roots. These pivots are made of platina or gold, but we have seen wooden pivots in the teeth of persons coming from America. We are unable to discover what species of wood they make use of for this pur-pose, but we have known many such pivots to endure longer than the teeth in which they had been used. Eight months ago we inserted for a friend of ours a human tooth, by means of a pivot made of box-wood. This tooth remains very solid. Teeth made of the tooth of the sea-horse may be pivoted in this manner. When incorruptible teeth are used, the pivots are to be soldered to their clamps.

A pivot tooth should correspond in form, size, colour, and all particulars, to the teeth beside which it is to be placed. After having sawed it off at its neck, the root upon which it is to be placed should be coloured, so that, in placing the crown upon it, we may immediately discover the points at which it should be filed to cause it to fit closely. A piece of wax may then be placed between the crown and root, and upon pressing it we may discover the exact position that the pivot should occupy in the crown. The pivot may then be screwed or riveted into the crown. (Pl. XVII. Figs. 7, 12.)

We next, with a probe, measure the depth of the root, in order to ascertain the length that we should make the pivot, which, being cut to its proper length, should be filed down to the size of the drill last used in drilling the root. Notches should then be cut in the pivot. (Pl. XVII. Fig. 2.) It should then be wrapped around with cotton, thread, silk, or, which is better, the white skin that covers the birch tree, (*Betula Alba*, Lɪɴ.) This kind of skin, composed almost entirely of resin, resists for a long time maceration. It is very thin, and may be detached very easily from the tree, particularly when green. It is better than cork, filaments of asbestos, &c., and does not possess the inconvenience of thread, silk and cotton, which become decayed and emit a fetid odour. For the last ten months we have constantly used this article, and the advantages it possesses have been daily exhibited. It serves well to maintain the pivot tooth solidly upon the root. We make with this pellicle a small strip about a line in width, and having dipped it into varnish, as we do all substances used for this purpose, we wrap it closely around the pivot, and having dried the canal in the root which is to receive it, we put the tooth in its place.

What we have here said of pivoting teeth is only applicable in cases in which the canals of the roots are not much injured by decay. A tooth inserted in this manner is very solid, and cannot be easily detected. But, unfortunately, we cannot always have recourse to a mode of replacement so simple. We are sometimes obliged to insert a pivot tooth upon a diseased root. Under such circumstances we must proceed as follows:—

All the soft parts that can be detached should be carefully removed from the root, and one or two little pieces of wood, having been previously dipped into varnish, should be placed in the cavity in such manner that the pivot of the artificial tooth may be inserted with these without doing injury to the parietes of the root. Little metal tubes may also be used under such circumstances. (Pl. XVII. Fig. 11.) But, if the root be so much impaired as not to admit of these auxiliary means, we may then have recourse to *plates, ligatures,* and *clasps,* which we shall describe after relating the accidents sometimes attendant upon the insertion of pivot teeth.

These evils may be produced by a pivot that is too large or too long, or by its breaking in the root. In the first case, it may touch the remaining portion of the dental nerve, and thus pain, inflammation, abscess, fistules, or a puriform discharge occasioned by a cyst at the root, may be produced. (Pl. IV. Fig. 3.) In the second case, the broken pivot may remain deep in the root, particularly if brittle metal be used; but this accident is of unfrequent occurrence. To remedy it, however, is, sometimes difficult. Should the fragment of the pivot be too deep to be grasped with forceps of proper construction, a drill may be introduced on opposite sides to admit of the insertion of a suitable instrument.

We may also use for this purpose an instrument constructed by M. Miel, and which, having modified, we have used during fifteen years. It is made of soft steel, and is cylindrical in shape; its diameter is about three or four lines; its extremity is denticulated; it is open for the distance of about six lines from this extremity, and the edges thus approximating are thin and elastic, and capable of passing each other upon pressure being made externally upon the tube. This instrument may be fitted to a socket handle capable of receiving such of different sizes. (Pl. XIV. Fig. 5.)

When this instrument is to be used, the distance between the branches should be regulated and adapted to the size of the pivot to be withdrawn. By giving to this a rotary movement on insertion into the root, it penetrates with facility, as the terminal saw not only destroys the little inequalities, but also the intermediate substance between the root and the pivot. Loosened in this manner, the pivot may be withdrawn by means of narrow beaked forceps.

We have already remarked, that in inserting a pivot tooth regard must be had to the condition of the root; hence it would be imprudent to insert one upon a root that has been impaired through the whole length of its canal. The puriform discharge that exists in such cases, particularly if the subject be young, being suddenly suppressed, would occasion evils similar to those produced by pivots of too great length. If, however, we are obliged to insert a pivot tooth upon a root much diseased, we should merely render it firm enough not to drop out, and thus let it remain until the discharge has ceased or obtained another passage, when the pivot may be rendered firm.*

These evils may also be alleviated by the application of leeches over the diseased root. Pediluvia, soothing gargles, emollient and narcotic lotions made of marsh-mallow root, barley, figs, honey, and a poppy-head; and when the inflammation has subsided we may substitute for these remedies, tonic lotions, prepared with some alcoholic liquid, which should be used twice or thrice daily until the part has been restored to health. We should not, as is often done, merely wash the teeth with these lotions, but they should be retained in the mouth for a time, and the diseased gums should be slightly rubbed with a brush saturated with them.

LIGATURES, PLATES AND CLASPS USED TO RETAIN ARTIFICIAL TEETH.

If any of the modes of retaining teeth could be applied under all circumstances, there would be no occasion for the variety of methods named. Attaching teeth by pivots is certainly the best means; but as there are certain conditions essential in this operation which we do not always meet with, it is necessary to resort to other means. Ligatures, metallic plates and clasps are therefore used.

---

* We would here express our decided disapprobation of the practice of inserting teeth upon roots in the condition described. Health should first be restored to the part; or, if this be impracticable, the root should be extracted, and in due time the tooth should be inserted upon a gold or platina plate. There are cases, however, in which, without pain, a discharge slightly ichorous is for some time emitted. In such cases, a recent invention of Dr. W. H. Elliot, will apply very aptly. It consists of a small gold tube passed through the pivot, and having an opening continuous with it through the artificial crown.

To permit the discharge to find "another passage," (i. e. through the alveoli and gums, we suppose,) is a recommendation that hardly needs a comment to make apparent its absurdity.—S.

Ligatures.—Ligatures used to retain teeth in their places are made of raw silk, an article known in commerce by the name of Chinese root, aloes, platina or fine gold.

Some discretion must be exercised by the dentist in regard to the proportions of the ligature to be applied, as this will depend upon the exigencies of each particular case.

Raw Silk.—This must be wrought into what is called *twisted raw silk.* In this state it is very strong. It does not decompose in the mouth so soon as ligatures made of ordinary silk, hemp, or flax; but, like these last, it possesses the inconvenience of being seen, and of swelling more or less according to its degree of tension. The more tightly these ligatures are drawn, the greater their liability to approach the gums and inflict injury upon them.

China Root.—This article is nothing else than raw silk, twisted very hard, stretched, and immersed into copal varnish. This ligature will not contract nor become injured by the juices of the mouth, so soon as the others we have enumerated; although it is not wholly impervious to these fluids.

Thread of Aloes.—This is taken from the silk worms at the time they are going to spin. It is dipped into vinegar, and afterward stretched into pieces two feet in length; it is then extended upon a plank with its ends secured that it may not contract, and suffered to dry in this situation. This ligature is stronger than the former, and is scarcely perceptible upon the teeth. Its only inconvenience is its tendency to stretch on becoming wet; but this may be remedied by steeping it in warm water for half an hour before applying it.

Metallic Ligatures.—Gold and platina are the only metals used for this purpose. They are more durable than other ligaments, but are difficult to conceal. They wear away the teeth sooner than other ligatures, are inelastic, and require to be rendered malleable before being used.

Plates, Clasps and Springs.

Plates.—These are always made of gold or platina when artificial teeth are to be inserted upon them. They should accurately fit the part they are to occupy, sometimes extending a few lines on the inner side of the alveolar border. The pressure upon the gums should not be too strong, as the neighbouring teeth may thus be loosened.

Clasps.—Small branches of gold or platina, round, half round, or flat, are thus denoted. They are soldered or riveted to the artificial piece, and their extremities serve to secure such piece to the adjacent teeth. Their form varies according to each particular case. (Pl. XVIII. Fig. 9.)

Springs.—These differ from clasps in being made of gold less pure than the former, and in being longer, that they may be applied to teeth remote from the artificial piece. (Pl. XVIII. Figs. 5, 11.)

ARTIFICIAL TEETH, THEIR FABRICATION, AND MODE OF ATTACHMENT.

Dentists have given the name of *blocks* or *pieces* to several teeth united and retained in the mouth by means of ligatures, plates, clasps, or springs. These pieces or parts of sets are sometimes carved out of a single piece of the tooth of the sea-horse; sometimes they consist of human or incorruptible teeth mounted upon a sea-horse base. Whatever may be the plan adopted, the part to be occupied must first be prepared, and an impression taken in the manner heretofore indicated.

Teeth, carved from the Sea-horse Tooth.

In order to adapt the base of these to the mouth, a plaster, wax, or sulphur mould is preferable even to metal. We should be provided with two of these; by one the piece may be cut out roughly, and it may be finished by the other. The piece of sea-horse tooth used should be always larger than the space to be filled. It should be enamelled anteriorly, that the three or four anterior teeth may be furnished with enamel. To give the form of the teeth, it is only necessary to scribe out the form of the teeth and carve them superficially.

If a plaster mould be used, we should first cut away one or two lines from the sides of the teeth adjoining the space to be filled, that the piece may be too large, rather than too small. The cast should then be covered with black or red paint slightly gummy; the piece applied to this will exhibit upon its prominent parts marks indicating the points at which it should be reduced. The rasp may be used upon the block of sea-horse until it be partially adjusted, when the flat graver should be resorted to. As we carve the piece slight portions only should be removed at a time. This precaution should be observed until a perfect fit has been made.

The repeated application of the piece upon the mould may wear the latter away. The second mould may then be used, by which it may be completed. The base being thus adjusted, the teeth may be carved out upon it, and reduced to a proper length. It may then be applied to the mouth for which it was intended.

These general rules are applicable to one or more teeth carved out of the sea-horse tooth.

Natural Teeth mounted upon the Sea-horse Tooth Base.

The first thing to be done here is to adjust the base as described in the preceding remarks. The teeth being selected, their roots should be sawed off at a proper place, and they should then be placed upon the base in their right positions, and secured by means of sealing-wax. This being done, a hole should be drilled through the base and into the tooth, and a rivet temporarily inserted. (Pl. XVII. Fig. 16.) These should then be withdrawn, and larger pins or a screw inserted. (Pl. XVII. Fig. 17.) The teeth having been thus attached, and the base coloured so as to imitate as nearly as possible the gums, it should be rubbed with *shave-grass*, and polished with the same material and a little powdered pumice stone. With a brush and water we may then remove all particles of foreign matter.

A rose colour may be imparted to the sea-horse, by putting muriatic acid adulterated upon it. It should then be dipped into common water, and having been dried, we may imitate the gums by spreading upon it a coat of *vinaigre rouge de maille,* which ladies generally use in their toilet.

Half-round files are made use of to clean the teeth thus inserted, and they may be polished also with a piece of soft wood and pumice stone, and afterward with a little Spanish white.

Incorruptible Teeth mounted upon a Sea-horse Tooth Base.

These are mounted in much the same manner that the natural teeth are. They require some variation in their mode of application in consequence of a groove with which they are provided. It is necessary that we should ascertain the precise spot upon the base that is to correspond with this groove. This may be done by the use of a piece of wax with which the tooth is temporarily attached to the base. When the tooth is detached an impression will be made upon the wax by the fissure, which will indicate the place that should be drilled to receive the pivot of the incorruptible tooth. This pivot is afterward to be riveted to the base.

Human Teeth mounted upon a metallic Plate.

Having stamped and prepared a plate as we have indicated, it should be placed upon a plaster cast with a piece of wax. The teeth to be inserted should then be sawed in such manner as to be of full length. Their extremities should be then dipped in red colouring matter, and placed upon the plate. When withdrawn, the place left coloured by them will indicate the situations they should occupy.

A small hole in the heel of the tooth and a corresponding one in the plate being made, and a pin being passed through these, the teeth may be retained in their places. (Pl. XVII. Fig. 13.)

All the teeth being thus properly adjusted, pivots of proper size should be soldered upon the plate; the holes made in the teeth should then be enlarged to suit these pivots, and the teeth adapted to the plate: by means of these pivots, which are riveted at the posterior sides of the teeth, these are retained. Screws are sometimes used for this purpose. These are to be screwed into the teeth with a piece of the inner skin of the birch tree dipped in varnish. Many English dentists employ no other means to secure artificial teeth to the plates. This mode is preferable to riveting the pivots; they can be more readily adjusted in this manner, and we can remove the tooth without breaking it or diminishing the length of the pivot.

Teeth are sometimes fastened by means of several pins passed through the plates and into their bases; but this mode is inferior to that of securing with a single attachment.

INCORRUPTIBLE TEETH.

Mode of Application.—These are furnished with three little clamps, (Pl. XVII. Fig. 9,) which are inserted into them previous to their being baked. A little metal stud is to be embraced by these clamps, and soldered to them to retain the teeth upon the plate.

The incorruptible teeth are generally made without a heel; thus constructed, they do not touch the teeth in the opposite jaw, are more easily adjusted to the plate, and occupy less room in the mouth. Sometimes, however, a heel is made of metal, and is soldered to the pin with the tooth. (Pl. XVII. Fig. 8.) These heels are not so thick as those made of the substance of the artificial tooth, are stronger, and are more easily adjusted to the base.

Manner of adapting the shape of artificial Teeth.—A hard grind-stone, from twelve to twenty inches in diameter, is used for this purpose. This grind-stone, the sides and surface of which should be well dressed, should turn vertically, and dip into a trough containing water. A suitable contrivance should also be made to prevent the water from flying from this when revolving, and to catch a tooth as it falls from the hands of the person holding it, an accident likely to happen to one not practised in this operation.

A grind-stone, similar to those used by glass-cutters, is also necessary; others of softer texture may also be required. These should be about six inches in diameter, and ten lines in thickness. They should be wet whenever used. Wheels of iron and steel are also used in the process of shaping these teeth.

Incorruptible teeth may be modified in shape in all parts except upon their enamelled surfaces. If, however, they be too brilliant, a duller hue can be given them by rubbing them with moistened pumice stone. If they be too convex, this may be reduced by grinding; and they may be again polished by means of a wooden wheel, having finely powdered pumice stone applied to them damp: to complete this operation, dry pumice stone of a still finer texture may be used.*

Manner of Soldering a Pivot to an Incorruptible Tooth.— There is, as we have described, a perpendicular groove in these teeth, and clamps are inserted into them, previously to their being baked or hardened, at the sides of this groove. A stud being fitted into this, and these small platina clamps secured upon it, we solder them to it. A pivot adapted to the root, to which this is to be applied, may now be attached to this stud, or the pivot and stud may be constructed of an entire piece, and adapted previous to the attachment of the tooth.

To solder well is not difficult, but requires certain precautions which we shall point out.

The teeth to which we would attach a metallic stud, should at first be gradually heated, as the sudden application of heat would cause them to crack. While heated, the enamel should not be suffered to come in contact with any hard body, as it may thus become tarnished. The flame applied to melt the solder should be concentrated, and removed the moment this

* The teeth spoken of by our author are the French manufacture, it will be remembered, and which require to be shaped and adapted by the hands of the dentist. The superior mode of manufacturing teeth in this country, and perhaps in France too, at present, render unnecessary the author's minuteness of description as to the manner of grinding them.—S.

object is effected, as its continuance would diffuse the solder and render the attachment weak. If, as sometimes happens, the teeth appear smoked and dingy, we may restore their primitive colour by exposing them to a pure fire, and afterward immersing them in water, to which a small quantity of nitric acid has been added.

In attaching incorruptible teeth to a plate, (Pl. XVIII. Fig. 4,) the adaptation of this being first completed, the teeth should one by one be adjusted to their places and retained by means of wax. With vermilion or other colouring, the situation of the groove in the tooth is marked upon the plate. The teeth are then removed, and at each point thus marked a pivot is to be attached so as to exactly correspond to the groove of the tooth when replaced. (Pl. XVIII. Fig. 3.) The teeth, thus arranged, may now be soldered. These attachments being completed, the work should now be smoothed off with a file, and afterward with pumice stone, &c., and finally by means of a burnisher.

Artificial teeth thus prepared may last a long time. Should any accident, however, occur to them, it may readily be remedied. To do this the plate and teeth should first be well cleaned. The manner of doing this is as follows: First, brush them well with soap and water, and dry them slowly before the fire. When the metal has become red in this situation, the piece should be slowly cooled, scoured, and boiled in pure water. The piece will now exhibit its former brilliancy, and may be proceeded with as when new.

COMPLETE SETS, AND THE MEANS OF THEIR ATTACHMENT.

The loss of the teeth of one or both jaws may be supplied by means of artificial teeth constructed into what are termed complete dentures or sets, which are secured in the mouth by means which will be described hereafter.

The form, size, mode of attachment, &c., of dentures are various as the cases to which they are applied. As regards the materials of which they are constructed, they are the same as in the partial sets already spoken of.

In preparing to construct these, our first measure should be to remove all such teeth or roots as offer impediment; or, should there be roots remaining in a healthy condition, they should be filed even with the gum, that they may not interfere with the plate. The presence of these is indeed desirable, as they prevent the absorption of the gum, and thus preserve the form of the mouth and alveolus, and facilitate the adaptation of the artificial piece.* When the mouth has been thus rightly prepared, we may proceed to construct the plate, and to adjust the teeth to it.

Complete Sets made of the Sea-horse Tooth.

An impression of each jaw should be first taken, and afterward an impression of both jaws at once. This latter is called an articulating cast. The plaster moulds having been made from these, pieces of sea-horse tooth of adequate size should be shaped and adjusted, and the desired form given to them. The internal and external contour of the denture should also be roughly formed. These should then be tried in the mouth of the person for whom they are intended singly, and if adapted to it, they should be withdrawn and a piece of wax placed between them, that they may adhere, and then returned to the mouth again; or without this being properly antagonized, they may be united in the mouth by means of sealing-wax applied to the cuspidatus teeth, which are the more prominent. When thus removed together, an articulating mould may be made from them.

It is only after this mould has been made that we can judge of the relation that these teeth will have with each other; and it is by this that we are to determine the shape of the dentures anteriorly and posteriorly.

Having ascertained that in all these particulars our work is well adjusted, nothing will remain but to proceed to carve out

* This is incorrect. There are cases in which a healthy root may be made use of to sustain a plate, but even this should not be done where other advantageous means of support can be had; in no other case is it proper to place a plate over a root. Its presence will work evil: sooner or later it must be removed and the patient will thus be subjected to a repetition of the trouble and expense incurred in having the artificial tooth or teeth inserted.—S.

18

the teeth. These should be first made a little longer than we
desire ultimately to have them: if we wish them to close directly upon each other, the cutting edges of those first formed
should be marked with vermilion, and the traces left by these
upon their antagonists will indicate the manner in which they
are to be carved.

When we wish that all these teeth should be covered with
enamel, it will be necessary to attach several pieces together
by means of rivets, in order that an enamelled front may be
presented.

Complete Dentures of human and incorruptible Teeth upon a Base of Sea-horse Tooth.

These dentures only differ from the preceding in having
sixteen or twenty natural or incorruptible teeth riveted to bases
of sea-horse tooth. All that we have said relative to the
adaptation of complete dentures of sea-horse teeth is applicable
to these: eight or ten human or incorruptible teeth, for each jaw,
should be selected for this purpose with much judgment. Two
molar teeth should be carved at each extremity of the bases to
which these teeth are attached. (Pl. XVII. Fig. 15.)

Complete Sets of human Teeth upon Gold or Sea-horse Tooth Bases.

The directions already given in regard to the preparation of
partial sets of these teeth, in connexion with the foregoing
remarks upon complete sets, render minute description of this
operation unnecessary. The mode of taking a cast of the
mouth, and of making plaster and other moulds therefrom, in
the former, and the manner of articulating described in the
latter, is here applicable.

Superior Dentures maintained by means of a metallic Plate adapted to the inferior Jaw.

The superior teeth being lost, and the inferior, or a greater
portion of them being preserved, artificial teeth may be sus-

tained in the superior jaw by means of spiral springs. To procure means of attaching these springs, a metallic band should be adjusted along the inferior jaw, to which studs should be connected for the attachment of the springs. This band should not exceed four lines in width; otherwise it would extend to the fraenum of the tongue, and a pressure would then be exercised upon the teeth which would cause them to incline anteriorly. This plate should conform to the contour of the dental arch. It should be of sufficient thickness to have teeth attached to it by means of an extension over such parts as have been deprived of these organs. This band may be rendered more solid by adjusting upon a bicuspid of each side of the mouth a cap which should accurately fit it. (Pl. XX. Fig. 3.)

MANNER OF ATTACHING DENTURES IN THE MOUTH BY MEANS OF SPIRAL SPRINGS.

The means by which we attach double sets in the mouth differ materially from the mode of inserting partial sets. Springs of simple construction, called spiral springs, are used for this purpose. (Pl. XX. Figs. 2, 3.) These are attached by the anterior bicuspid by means of a stud inserted horizontally into the plate to serve as a pivot or axis for the spring.

Manner of making spiral Springs.

Spiral springs are made of gold wire of eighteen carats. This wire should be prepared by being passed three or four times through a drawing plate to reduce it to a proper size. It should then be annealed, and again passed through the plate in order to condense it well. It may now be cleaned by being boiled in diluted nitric acid, and afterward rubbed with pumice stone by means of a piece of soft leather. The operation of polishing may be completed with rouge. It should then be wound into a spiral form upon a lathe, or by means of a vice; the adaptation of apparata for this purpose will depend much upon the invention of the operator, as many modes are used by different dentists.

Spring Carrier.—We call by this name a little structure proceeding from the artificial piece to which the spiral springs are to be attached. (Pl. XX. Fig. 5.) It consists of a pin rising perpendicular to the piece, from which a projection again issues horizontally at a proper height, say from five to eight lines. Upon this last process the end of the spring is to be attached, and made to revolve between two rings or small plates made to confine it and to protect the cheek from being affected by its action.

To the ends of the springs are attached gold or platina pieces shaped into eyelets which are to revolve upon the spring carriers already described. (Pl. XX. Fig. 4.)

Spiral springs present two advantages that render them superior to all others: First, the facility with which they may be executed; secondly, the firm manner in which they act, and their durability.

A precaution necessary to be observed in applying these springs, is, that the point of attachment, by means of the spring carrier, should be accurately ascertained, as the least deviation, backward or forward, will render them unavailable.

So well adapted are these springs to the purposes for which they are designed, that, occupying little space in the mouth, the patient soon becomes unconscious of their presence; and whatever annoyance may be experienced, will arise from the presence of the teeth themselves. This, however, should be endured for a few days, as in that time use will remedy it.

OBTURATORS, OR THE MEANS OF REMEDYING LESIONS OF THE PALATINE ARCH.

Unnatural communications between the mouth and nasal fossæ, not only proceed from accidental diseases, but are sometimes congenital. The separation of the palate bones, and of the soft palate, sometimes accompany hare-lip. For this separation, art has as yet only effected a palliative remedy. M. Roux, however, one of the most celebrated surgeons of Paris, several years since attempted to perform upon the soft palate an operation similar to that by means of which we remedy hare-lip. Complete success favoured the happy idea of this learned professor, who, since that time, has had occasion to perform this operation several times. He has given to it the name of *Staphyloraphy*.

Congenital lesions of these parts come properly under the cognizance of the surgeon; we will, therefore, content ourselves with pointing out the causes of accidental communication between the buccal and nasal cavities.

Various accidents, but especially fire arms, may occasion a wound in the palatine arch, with such loss of substance and destruction of the bone, as to render it impossible to effect a perfect cicatrization of the parts. Venereal ulcers do not always limit their ravages to the mucous membrane of the palate and palatine roof, but are often extended to the bones themselves, which, becoming necrosed, (Pl. XIX. Fig. 5,) a perforation or loss of substance is the result. There are cases in which the soft palate is divided. (Pl. XX. Fig. 8.) This constitutes one of the most serious evils. Particles of aliment, no longer confined by this part, pass into the nasal fossæ and trachea, and occasion suffocation, always very annoying, and sometimes dangerous. Pronunciation is imperfect, and sometimes unintelligible. To remedy these inconveniences various means have been contrived, called obturators, which are intended to obliterate the accidental opening.

The obturators first used were very simple. They were made of sponge, cotton, wax, mastic, or other substance capable of closing up the opening in the palate. But these were found insufficient, and metallic obturators sustained by sponge, metallic clasps, a button, or bolt, obturators with moveable wings, obturators attached to a plate to which teeth were also attached, &c. were used. We shall describe these several kinds.

Obturators sustained by Sponge.

This obturator, which was introduced by Ambrose Paré, is composed of a metallic plate adapted to the concavity of the part to which it is to be applied, and larger than the opening by one or two lines in circumference: a little metallic rim, higher than the thickness of the walls of the part, is to be attached to the convex side of this plate. (Pl. XX. Fig. 9.) In this latter circle or rim several holes are pierced to pass a metallic or silken ligature to which a piece of sponge of proper size is attached, and introduced through the opening into the nasal fossæ. The sponge, once introduced into the nasal fossæ, becomes saturated with mucus, swells, and by resting upon the floor of the nasal fossæ, retains the plate firmly in its position.

It will be perceived that an obturator of this kind, though of easy application, possesses disadvantages. In the first place the expansion of the sponge from moisture, dilates the hole, instead of facilitating its contraction; secondly, its long retention in the mouth occasions a fetid odour.

Obturators sustained by Clasps.

The opening in the palatine roof may cicatrize in time, provided no foreign body should prevent it. Obturators sustained by a sponge were on this account discarded, and a plate substituted. This plate is simply placed over the opening and sustained by means of ligatures or clasps attached to the teeth. (Pl. XX. Fig. 1.)

Obturators sustained by a Button.

This kind of obturator consists of a metallic plate like the preceding; upon the convex side of which is soldered a circular eminence extending as high up as the walls of the wound; upon this is adapted a kind of oval button, which is about half a line larger than the wound. (Pl. XX. Fig. 10.) It is necessary to use some force in introducing this button; but being inserted as far as its neck, it will then hold the plate immediately in contact with the palatine roof, and prevent the air from entering the nasal fossæ.

Obturators sustained by a Bolt, and *Obturators with moveable Wings.*—[These obturators are ingenious and complicated in their construction, but of no practical utility; and as they can-

not be intelligibly explained without the aid of minute drawings, the translator has deemed it justifiable to omit them.]

Obturators connected with Dentures.

These only differ from obturators connected to the teeth by
means of ligatures and clasps in the length of the plate which
extends over the alveolar border, and to which artificial teeth
are attached. We may insert four, six, ten and even twelve
teeth upon these extended plates. To the ends of such plate
clasps should be attached to secure it to such of the natural
teeth as will afford it support. Plate XX. Fig. 11, represents an
obturator of this kind, furnished with twelve teeth, which we
made several years ago for a woman thirty-four years of age. This
woman was under antisyphilitic treatment from her fifteenth
year. The plate of this obturator is constructed so as to close
hermetically two large openings in the palatine roof; and one
of its borders closes a third opening which communicates with
the maxillary sinus. This woman appears to enjoy good health;
she is large and fleshy. At times, however, she experiences
violent headache from which she suffers much, even for a week
continually.

It will be difficult to point out precisely the particular circumstances under which each of these obturators should be
applied. The choice should always depend upon the nature of
the disorder to be remedied.

THE CARE NECESSARY FOR THE PRESERVATION OF ARTIFICIAL TEETH.

Persons who wear artificial teeth cannot take too much care
to preserve them in a condition of perfect cleanliness. We
have already spoken of the necessity of having a second set
to replace those worn, should they be injured. It is well to be
thus prepared for such accidents, since even sound natural teeth
are not wholly exempted from them. It will be well also to
lay aside for a few days, from time to time, teeth made of ani-

mal substance, as they may thus be preserved longer. They should be cleaned with a hard brush and soap and water, and with a weak solution of soda or bi-chloride of lime. Having been well dried and enveloped in a piece of linen, they should be put in a dry warm place. A piece thus preserved loses the moisture it may have absorbed, and the bad odour with which it may have been impregnated. These precautions are also necessary to prevent the piece and teeth from cracking.

If pivot teeth, well adjusted and secured to sound roots, require no particular care, it is not the same with animal artificial teeth retained by means of ligatures, springs and clasps. These require great care, because resting upon the soft parts, the viscid secretions of the mouth are deposited between these soft parts and the artificial pieces where they are not well adjusted. We should not wait for pieces sustained by ligatures, especially animal or vegetable, to become loosened before renewing their attachment. We should, on the contrary, replace them by attachments more durable. The larger an artificial piece is, the more care it will require.

Artificial teeth composed of sea-horse teeth require more care than those composed of human teeth, and if neglected will become very unpleasant; but the necessity of cleansing all of them daily is apparent.

ARTIFICIAL GUMS.

When the loss of the substance of the alveolar border is very great, it should be repaired. The manner of doing this is by carving an imitation of the gums upon artificial pieces; these pieces should be first well adapted to the part, that, after the gums have been carved out, they may not require to be retouched.

A TREATISE ON MECHANICAL DENTISTRY.*

CHAPTER I.

1. It is no part of the design of this series of articles, written at the repeated solicitation of many of my professional brethren, either to demonstrate the general utility of artificial teeth, or to persuade the community to procure them. The wants of the student in dentistry will be consulted and met, as far as practicable, in the following treatise; and no pains will be spared by the author, in his efforts to collect and communicate in the plainest terms, all the practical instruction which the present condition of our art can supply.

2. Each section of this treatise will be numbered for the sake of convenient reference, and as many explanatory cuts will be given as the nature of the subject may demand. If, in attempting to make the details of the art perfectly intelligible to the student, the author should seem to the older members of the profession to be too minute in his illustrations, they will, no doubt, on a moment's reflection, admit the validity of his excuse.

3. By MECHANICAL DENTISTRY is understood the art of constructing sets and parts of sets of artificial teeth; of inserting single teeth on roots or fangs; and of constructing artificial palates in cases where the natural organ is deficient.

A description of the method of proceeding in every supposable case will be the object of this series of papers.

4. The implements proper to the mechanical dentist will be

* The first three chapters of this treatise are part of Dr. Solyman Brown's excellent article, published in the American Journal of Dental Science. For the fourth chapter we are indebted to Professor C. A. Harris.—S,

minutely described as they become necessary in the progress
of the work; it being premised that a bench, hammers of various
kinds, an anvil, vice, files, &c. must be understood to be essential.

5. It being the opinion of the author, founded on a settled
conviction resulting from observation and experience, that the
necessity of using human teeth, blocks of ivory, or other
animal substance, is wholly superseded by the great improvements which have been recently made in the manufacture of
incorruptible, mineral teeth; the directions given in this essay
will relate exclusively to the latter, which he hopes every ho-
nourable practitioner will endeavour to introduce into his practice, to the exclusion of all substances which are liable to be
decomposed by the fluids of the mouth, lose their beauty, and
infect the breath with loathsome poison.

Of the Insertion of a single Tooth on the natural Root.

6. As broken parts of the crown often remain attached to
the root, a pair of excising forceps becomes necessary. This
instrument should be about five inches in length, having the
cutting edges one-tenth of an inch in breadth.

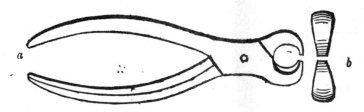

In this wood cut (*a*) represents the forceps, and (*b*) the
breadth and shape of the cutting edges. These forceps should
be of sufficient strength and material not to bend or spring
under the pressure of the hands, and should be used with such
gentleness as not to strain, shake, or otherwise injure the root.

After the prominent parts of the crown shall have been
removed by means of the forceps above described, as nearly
as possible to the semi-circular arch of the gum, a round, ellip-
tical or half round file is employed to complete the process.

The file should be fine-cut, and ought to be used with de-licacy, as well to save the sensibilities of the patient, as to avoid agitating the root to such a degree as to produce inflammation of the investing membrane and surrounding structure.

7. When the file has reduced the root to the edge of the gum, and even a little beyond it, the next operation is to per-forate the fang, by enlarging the natural nervous tube by means of a broach or hand drill of something like the following con-struction.

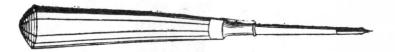

The point may be either square, or pentagonal like the com-mon watch-maker's broach, and should be of sufficient size to produce an orifice capable of receiving a pivot of the size of a large knitting needle. Several broaches of smaller sizes are necessary to enlarge the natural orifice by degrees to the re-quired diameter. The depth of the orifice should be one-fourth of an inch, in roots that will admit of it.

8. Select a mineral tooth as nearly as possible of the colour of the adjacent teeth, taking care that the shade never be lighter than that of the natural teeth in the same mouth. Let it be moreover of the proper length, breadth, and thickness, with as little grinding as possible. Some change of shape and di-mensions is however generally necessary, for which a suitable grinding apparatus is indispensable. Machines for grinding mineral teeth are of various kinds, of which a common grind-stone is the most obvious and simple. Small and portable

stones for the use of dentists, are prepared and mounted by
dental instrument-makers, of which the following is a draft:

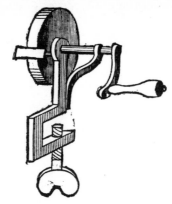

An improvement on this construction has been attempted by
Messrs. Royce & Esterly, ingenious dentists, resident in Pough-

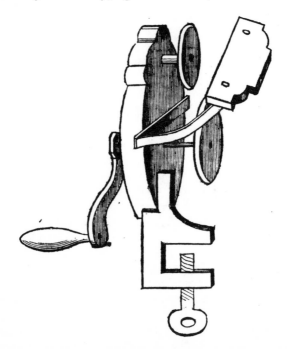

keepsie, in the state of New York.   This grinding apparatus
consists of simple system of cog-wheels by means of which

one of the two stones has an accelerated motion. This patent has the advantage of elegance of structure, neatness in the operation, and the easy change of stones of various dimensions; and is moreover well adapted to the use of a newly invented grinding wheel, which will be described hereafter.

The two foregoing machines for grinding teeth, are well adapted to the use of travelling dentists; but for those members of the profession who are stationary, foot lathes are much the most efficient. These may be of very simple construction, thus:

Lathes constructed on this principle may be enclosed in ornamental cases, and thus become articles of furniture not unbecoming the operating room of the genteel dental surgeon; but they are generally better fitted to the laboratory of the artificial workmen.

19

Of the stones or wheels employed in grinding mineral teeth, many varieties are in vogue. Some good workmen use wooden wheels about six inches in diameter, the circumferences of which are turned into convenient forms, and covered with hot glue and emery. These are commonly called emery wheels, and have been long used in the mechanic arts.

Many dentists still adhere to the use of grind-stones of small dimensions, but from recent experiments I am led to prefer a composition wheel made of shellac and emery, combined in certain proportions when hot, afterwards cooled in moulds of strong metal provided expressly for the purpose, in which the material is compressed by great mechanical force.

10. The evident advantages of this species of grinding apparatus are, first, its little liability to change of form from constant use; secondly, its capability of retaining sharp edges, corners and curves, longer than any other substance hitherto employed; thirdly, its economy, being exceedingly durable; and fourthly, the mechanical correctness of its execution, arising from its hardness and solidity.

The following are some of the convenient forms of the cutting edges of these wheels, as they come from the moulds.

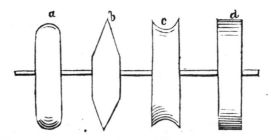

Although these edges, corners, planes and curves remain long with little apparent change, which is by no means true of any other wheels used for the purpose excepting copper ones; yet it must be evident that constant use will more or less change those original forms, unless the mode of grinding upon them shall be calculated to preserve the primitive shapes; a point to which ordinary ingenuity will direct the attention of the artist.

11. As the manufacture of these wheels is attended with considerable expense, in the way of moulds and presses to give form and compactness to the materials used, it is presumed that dentists will prefer to purchase rather than to make them, and therefore any farther description is deemed superfluous.

When the tooth has been carefully and accurately fitted to the stump or root by grinding, and made of the proper length, breadth and thickness, it may be fixed temporarily in its place with a pivot of white pine, poplar or other soft wood, for the purpose of affording the patient an opportunity of suggesting any alteration that may be desired.

12. When all parties are fully satisfied with the appearance of the artificial substitute, and when the antagonizing teeth in the opposite jaw meet with no obstruction on closing the mouth, the tooth is ready to be permanently fixed in its place; but before proceeding to establish it firmly on its pivot, an instrument may in some cases be employed with advantage to cut away the central portions of the root, in order to make a close fit of the crown to the stump.

_a_

When the point (_a_) of this instrument is inserted in the orifice of the root, a rotary motion files away the parts proper to be removed in order to perfect the joint.

By placing eight or ten thicknesses of gold foil between the crown and root, the fluids of the mouth may be wholly excluded.

13. The pivot which is to sustain the new crown in its position, should be made of the best of hickory, as no other wood proper to the American soil possesses so much strength and elasticity combined. Force the pivot, when properly rounded and smoothed with a file, into the orifice of the artificial crown, and cut the part of the pivot which projects from the crown to such length as the orifice in the root will admit; after which the size of the projecting portion of the pivot must be adjusted to the orifice of the fang. The force used to insert the pivot

in the root need not be great, inasmuch as the swelling of the wood, when saturated with moisture and heated to the temperature of the body, will secure it firmly in its place. The following are a front and a lateral view of a crown when thus prepared for insertion.

14. In some instances the cavity in the natural root has become, by decay, too large for a pivot of the description just given, in which case pivots of gold or platina of a square or flat form made jagged at the corners, must be substituted for the hickory, as follows: First fill the enlarged orifice of the root with a plug of soft wood, which must be trimmed neatly to correspond with the end of the fang. Then insert a similar plug into the mineral crown, into which plug screw the end of the metallic pivot after it has been passed through one or more of the holes of the following screw plate.

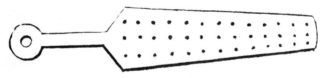

It will be evident that the metallic pivot just described will be round at one end and square or flat at the other, thus:

a *b*

The end (*a*) is inserted into the natural root, and the end (*b*) into the artificial crown.

15. The final adjustment of teeth set in either of the methods just described, may be effected by the aid of a wooden instrument somewhat of the form which follows, and should be made of very tough and soft wood.

If the strength of the hand should be found insufficient to force the pivot perfectly into its place, a slight blow on the end of the wood, when placed upon the end of the tooth, will complete the operation.

16. It sometimes happens that the position of the root is such that a crown placed upon it as above described, will not occupy the desired position in the mouth, being too far back or forward, or having too great a lateral inclination to the right or left. In these circumstances an entirely new course must be pursued; another kind of mineral crown must be procured, known as a *plate tooth,* in contradistinction to the former kind called a *pivot tooth.* The plate teeth are capable of being attached firmly to a metallic plate, and as gold is by far the best metal for this purpose, I shall denominate it, throughout this treatise, a *gold plate.*

In a case requiring to be treated in this manner in consequence of some unnatural condition of the root or of the adjoining teeth, after filing and preparing the root exactly as before, take common bees-wax and bring it to a pliable consistency by steeping it for a few minutes in warm water. When in the state of stiff dough or putty, place the wax in a frame made of tin, German silver, or other convenient metal, conformed to the arch of the jaw, as follows:

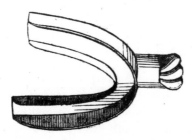

Of these frames the operator should be provided with various forms and sizes to suit mouths of different dimensions.

17. When a frame of the proper size and curvature has been filled with the softened wax, insert it cautiously into the mouth

of the patient, and press the wax gently but effectually against the cutting edges of the teeth adjacent to the space to be filled, until the teeth and gums are completely imbedded in the wax, which should be pressed against the gums both inside and out, by the thumb and fingers of the operator, holding the frame firmly in its proper position with the other hand. The frame and wax are next to be cautiously withdrawn from the mouth, in such manner as not to mar in the least the impression thus obtained. Let the wax cool, and then oil it with a soft brush and olive oil slightly; after which thrust a common pin or a small wire into the centre of each cavity made by the teeth in the wax, in order to render the plaster-cast taken from the wax less liable to injury.

Surround the wax thus prepared with a riband of paper two inches in width, secured to the wax by pins or twine, and then set the whole in a vessel of sand, which will secure the paper in its place.

18. Take calcined plaster of Paris or gypsum, ground and sifted, and mix with it a sufficient quantity of water to reduce it to creamy paste, the exact consistency of which is best determined by taking in a small vessel as much water as would nearly fill the wax mould and the paper rim, and dropping into it little by little as much superfine plaster as shall just absorb all the water, then stir the mixture for a moment and turn it into the mould.

After fifteen or twenty minutes, as must be determined by the quality of the plaster, and the lapse of time since its calcination, the paper may be removed, and the wax together with the plaster-cast immersed in warm water until they can be separated with ease and safety. Trim the cast with a sharp knife, being careful to give the whole such a form as will be easily withdrawn from the metal which is to be cast upon it. Dry the plaster thoroughly, and it is ready for use.

It is always best and sometimes necessary to take two similar casts in the manner just described, for distinct purposes, as will be seen hereafter.

19. Some good artificial workmen take their metallic castings in sand, after the manner of brass and iron founders, but I

have found the following process to be much more direct and explicit, and every way successful. Take an iron ladle of hemispheric shape, and capable of holding at least a pint and a half of fluid; melt in it as much lead as will nearly fill the ladle. Into this molten lead immerse one of the plaster-casts, and depress it by laying weights upon it till the points of the teeth shall be sunk about one inch below the surface of the melted lead in the ladle. When cool, immerse the whole in water, and carefully remove and wash away the plaster. Cover the surface of the lead with which the other metal is to come in contact, either with the smoke of a lamp, or with *whiting* laid on wet with a brush, in order to prevent the adhesion of the melted tin which is to be poured into it.

Dry the leaden mould well, and place it on a vessel filled with water or wet sand, so that the lead shall be sunk in the water or sand about an inch, to prevent its fusion when the tin shall be poured into it. Surround the impression of the teeth in the mould with a ring of tin, copper, or brass, an inch or more in width, as in the following cut:

(*a*) Denotes the metal ring. (*b*) Denotes the leaden mould. (*c*) Denotes the vessel with water or sand.

Fill the ring (*a*) with melted tin just at the point of fusion, or at such a temperature that it will not char dry pine chips or shavings; at any temperature higher than this there will be danger of fusing the lead, and thus of uniting the metals into one mass. But inasmuch as the tin fuses at a lower heat than lead, and as the cold water or wet sand will maintain the low temperature of the lead, there will be no danger of spoiling the cast, in case the foregoing rules are carefully regarded. The two metals when cool must be separated by means of a heavy hammer, assisted when necessary with wedges of iron. The two parts of the mould are now ready for use. Experience will soon instruct the beginner so to trim the plaster-cast, as that the tin may be withdrawn easily from the lead.

20. The operator is now provided with metallic casts similar to those which he will be frequently called upon to take in the exercise of his art, and between which his plate is to be struck.

Let him then in the next place, cut a piece of gold plate of the thickness of a smooth shilling into such shape as exactly to occupy the space on the tin cast in which the tooth is to be inserted. When the gold plate is adjusted in its position, and bent by the aid of a hammer or pair of pliers nearly into the shape desired, bring the tin and lead casts together upon it and with a smart blow with a heavy sledge-hammer, force the two metals into close contact, by which means the gold plate is wedged into the exact shape of the parts to which it is to be applied.

This latter operation is sometimes performed by means of a powerful vice, which perhaps effects the object with equal certainty.

21. Separate the casts once more, and place the gold plate on the second plaster-cast, which has been reserved for this part of the process. If the casts were equally perfect, the plate will fit the plaster-casts as it did the tin; and perhaps I may as well mention it here as any where, that if the operator wishes his plaster-cast to be clean and hard, it should be made warm and smeared with two or three coats of boiled linseed oil, applied in quick succession by means of a common paint brush, and then suffered to dry.

22. A plate tooth must now be selected of proper colour, form and size, and having platina pivots inserted during the process of its manufacture to attach it to the plate. At this point the operator finds the necessity for two implements of the description following:

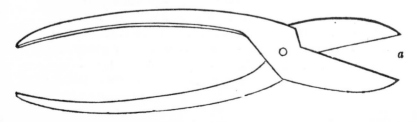

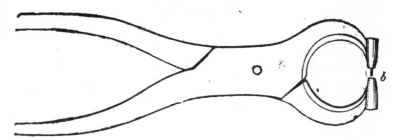

The shears (*a*) must be strong; and the plate-punch (*b*) of sufficient material to sustain the force required to perforate the plate without springing or breaking. With the use of these instruments together with a half round file, cut a plate of gold nearly as large as the back surface of the tooth; punch the holes as required, and insert the pivots as in the cut.

23. The process of soldering the tooth to the plate, must now be understood. To this end, procure a soldering lamp of something li ke the following form.

The orifice of the spout into which the wick is inserted, should be at least three-fourths of an inch in diameter, and the vessel capable of containing a quart or more of oil.

24. A large blowpipe sixteen inches in length must next be procured, having a large orifice, and yet capable of bringing a jet of flame to an exact focus when required. The long blow-pipe prevents a too great exposure of the eyes of the operator, and a pair of green glass goggles contribute to the same desirable result. Before lighting the lamp, cover the surface of the tooth on every side excepting that on which the plate is fixed, with a coating of plaster or Spanish white and water,

and when time will permit suffer the coating to dry before exposing it to the blowpipe.

25. The surface of the gold plate, already slightly riveted to the tooth, must be washed with a solution of borax (subborate of soda) ground with clean water, and laid on with a camel's hair brush, and care must be taken that every part of the work, where it is desired that the solder should take effect, should be touched with the solution. The best surface on which to grind or rub the borax is a common slate, such as children use at school.

The solder employed with plate twenty carats fine, may be prepared as follows: To one English sovereign or half an American eagle, add eighty grains of silver and forty grains of copper. Melt once with borax. In order to fit it for convenient use, it should be rolled into thin plate and well cleaned.

26. As some students may desire to understand the process of manufacturing their own plate in cases of necessity; Take an English guinea or sovereign, or an American half eagle, and alloy it with an American five cent piece of silver, which will reduce it to something less than twenty carat gold. Melt the two metals in a crucible with a small lump of borax and when cast into an ingot, hammer and roll for use. After being rolled the plate should be annealed by heating it to redness; and then cleaned by boiling in sulphuric acid diluted with water.

27. The foregoing hints are deemed sufficient to guide the student in the preparation of his own solder and plate when compelled to prepare them for himself; but as a rolling mill and other implements are necessary to this course, dentists generally procure their plate and solder ready prepared.

28. In submitting a piece of work to the action of the blowpipe, a piece of charcoal, cork or pumice stone is used to sustain the work and confine the heat. Charcoal is most readily obtained in masses of convenient size, but a large and flat piece of cork, or a block of pumice stone answers nearly the same purpose, and on some accounts are frequently preferred. When soldering whole sets of teeth or large pieces, a round block of charcoal four inches in diameter and six inches in length, hollowed in the form of a mortar, and having the outer surface

covered with plaster laid on smoothly with a knife or trowel, will be found very useful and durable.

29. When first bringing the flame of the soldering lamp upon a mineral tooth under the blowpipe, care must be taken to raise the heat slowly, lest a too sudden expansion of the surface of the enamel should crack it, and render the tooth useless; and a similar caution should be used when cooling the teeth after the operation of soldering has been completed.

30. The skilful use of the blowpipe requires that a constant blast should be given till the solder fuses; or at any rate the interruptions should be few as possible. To this end the operator must acquire the habit of breathing through his nostrils, while a stream of air is constantly projected from the blowpipe by the action of the muscles of the cheeks, which may be made to expel a current of air from the mouth even during the act of inhalation through the nostrils. This process requires some practice, but may be effectually acquired by determined perseverance: without it the process of soldering can be but imperfectly effected.

Doctor Black's self-acting blowpipe, in which the burning steam of alcohol is used instead of oil, may be managed successfully by a careful workman after a little practice; but the heat being very powerful, exposes the gold to fusion. For general use the soldering lamp just described will be found the most safely available to the mechanical dentist.

31. When the piece to be soldered has been brought to redness, the operator should watch the progress of his work carefully so as to be ready to remove the piece from the flame the moment the solder fuses and spreads as desired over the surface of the gold. This should be done for two reasons: first, that the plate itself may not be melted as well as the solder; and secondly, that the solder may not be too much dissipated by an excess of heat. The great art of soldering consists in knowing just the quantity of flame proper to be used in a given case, and the exact point of time when the heat should be withdrawn.

After the piece has become entirely cool, it may be placed in an earthen vessel containing equal parts of water and sulphuric acid. Indeed any *simple* acid may be used with safety and success, taking care that nitric and muriatic acid be not used together; for this mixture constitutes the *aqua regia*, which is the only sure solvent of gold.

The action of the diluted acid will be accelerated by heat, which requires a copper vessel: but if the water has been recently mixed with the acid, sufficient heat will be evolved by the chemical union of the two fluids, to accomplish the purpose of cleaning the gold in a few moments.

32. The surface of the solder may now be rendered smooth by the use of files, when the tooth and its plate will be ready to be united; but before this is done, a gold or platina pivot must be inserted in that precise point of the plate which corresponds with the orifice in the root of the tooth, and this pivot should be square or flat as described in section 14. When this pivot has been soldered into the plate so that it will exactly fit its place in the mouth, adjust the plate to the second plaster-cast, so that it will fit it as it does the place in the mouth where it is to be permanently worn. Then with files and the grinding apparatus fit the tooth to the plate, and give it the exact position desired as regards the adjacent teeth, and those in the opposite jaw. Support the tooth when rightly adjusted, by means of plaster of Paris mixed with equal parts of common sand, and applied in a state of paste to the surface of the tooth and the adjacent parts of the plaster-casts. The sand has the effect of preserving the plaster from cracking when heated by the blowpipe.

33. The piece is now ready when well dried for its final soldering; and as a great quantity of heat will be required to bring the plaster-cast to the temperature necessary for fusing the solder, the whole may be heated to redness in a ladle over a fire; or the concave piece of coal before described may be used for confining the blast of the blowpipe.

34. Use a liberal quantity of solder in joining the backs of the teeth to the principal plate, in order to give both strength and beauty to the work.

Indeed this is a part of the work which should never give way, because there is always room in this sharp angle to use a quantity of material which shall secure it from fracture.

35. If the work has been properly conducted thus far, all

that part of the plate not covering the end of the natural root, and connecting with the tooth, may be filed away; and then the whole should be polished on a lathe similar to that which has been described as a grinding apparatus in section 8, by means of a brush wheel, as follows:

Common sand, ground pumice stone, emery, the *debris* of a grindstone, or crocus, may be used on the brush with water, and the final polish may be given with a similar circular brush and dry whiting.

36. In case the tooth requires to be set farther forward than could be done on a wooden pivot, the piece constructed as already described, will have the following appearances when viewed laterally and from behind.

When the pivot requires to be placed on one side of the centre of the tooth, it may assume the following appearance.

As metallic pivots are liable to work loose when inserted in the naked bone of the root, a covering of floss silk or even of raw cotton wound upon the pivot, will have the effect of preventing the friction of the bony structure. Or in some instances, when the size of the root will allow it, a plug of soft wood may be first inserted, into which the metal pivot may be gently driven.

In concluding my directions for inserting a single mineral tooth upon a natural root, it becomes necessary to apprize the student of the propriety of so placing and shaping the artificial crown, that it may not come in contact with the teeth of the opposing jaw, inasmuch as constant agitation would soon either break or loosen the pivot, and thus render the work useless.

CHAPTER II.

Of the Insertion of several Teeth on natural Roots, in cases where the number of natural Roots does not equal the number of Teeth to be inserted.

37. It sometimes happens that several good roots remain in the mouth, fit to sustain artificial crowns, but that some one or more roots have been removed either from between or near the others, so that a complete arrangement cannot be effected on the principles laid down in the first chapter.

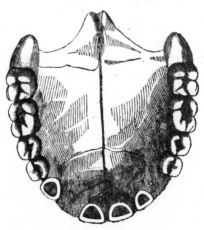

38. Let it be supposed that the crowns of the four upper incisores, and the two cuspidati, are lost, and also the roots of the right cuspidatus and left lateral incisor: as in the preceding cut.

In this case, although the four remaining roots would sustain four separate crowns independent of each other, yet there would still be two vacancies which are to be supplied; and though in the case supposed in the cut, there are back teeth which might be used to sustain a plate, with clasps, yet the patient might not consent to the use of them; and cases moreover often occur in which there are no back teeth in the mouth, leaving it imperative on the dentist to sustain the six front teeth on four roots, as in the cut.

39. Take a wax impression of the front part of the mouth, embracing at least the entire space to be supplied with teeth, as described in sections 16 and 17, from which proceed to obtain metallic casts, as explained in sections 18 and 19. To that part of the tin cast representing the space to be occupied with artificial teeth, fit a plate of tin or lead rolled to the thickness of drawing paper, so that it shall cover the ends of the roots together with the space left by the two teeth that have been extracted, extending back into the mouth three-fourths of an inch, and passing behind the first bicuspides on each side of the mouth. Bring the two casts together upon the soft metallic plate, and then trim it to the following shape.

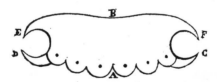

a is the front part covering the roots; b the back part extending to the roof of the mouth or palate; c and d are points of the plate which serve to retain it in its place while struck between the casts, but are afterwards cut away in case they are too much in sight; e and f are points extending behind the first bicuspides, which serve to sustain the piece steadily in its place; and especially prevent the whole apparatus from being pushed forward by the action of food, the tongue, or the antagonizing teeth.

40. Reduce the soft metallic plate to a plane surface under a planishing hammer, and employ it as a pattern by which to cut the gold plate, which must be struck between the casts as explained in sec. 20.   In swedging large plates which are to be much bent between the casts, care must be taken to anneal the gold plate once or twice during the operation, which is done by simply heating it to redness either under the blowpipe, or in a coal fire, care being taken that the gold be not melted by excessive heat.   The following instrument will be found very useful in bending gold plates into a shape approaching that given by the casts, in order to allow the casts to be brought together properly.

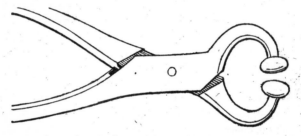

41. Pierce the gold plate with small pivot holes by means of the plate punch shown in section 22, exactly over the nervous orifices in the roots, into which solder pivots of gold or platina of the size of a small knitting needle, and one-fourth of an inch in length; after which clean the plate, file it smooth, and cut off the corners c and d of the plate, if the case requires it.

The plate and pivots will now assume the following appearance.

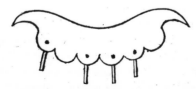

Adjust this plate to a plaster-cast which has been reserved for this purpose, in order that the artificial teeth may be ground and adjusted to the plate just as it is desired they should stand in the mouth. To this end support the teeth in their just position, by means of softened bees-wax placed behind them on the plate to which it may be made to adhere by warming the plate.

If the patient can be seen at this stage of the process, instead of fitting the teeth as just described, according to the best judgment of the operator, cover the plate with softened wax, which place in the mouth, and bring the ends of the teeth of the lower jaw against the wax till the mouth is shut in its natural position. The impression of the antagonizing teeth in the wax, will be a sure indication of the just position of the artificial substitutes. The wax may be cut away with a penknife as each tooth is adjusted in its place.

If, on the other hand, the operator finds it necessary to fit his teeth to their place before seeing his patient, the whole may be tried into the mouth, by proper care; or if sealing-wax be used instead of bees-wax, the trial will be attended with no difficulty.

42. When the mineral teeth have been set in the position required, and ground at the butts so as to fit the plate accurately, and project beyond it in order to touch and even press upon the gum, cover the enamelled faces of the teeth with a mixture of plaster and sand in equal parts reduced to a paste with water. This mixture is little liable to crack under the heat of the blowpipe, especially if secured by a few turns of fine iron wire, such as dentists frequently need in various parts of their work. This wire is little thicker than a bristle or coarse hair, and is so soft and pliable as to be little liable to break.

Remove the bees-wax from behind the teeth, which may be effected with a penknife, or by the aid of warm water.

43. Each tooth may now be removed from its place, and a gold back or stud may be fitted to it as described in section 22. Care should be taken that the gold back be fitted closely not only to the tooth but to the plate, and if, by accident, the junction with the plate should be imperfect, the vacancy may be filled with gold foil carefully introduced so as not to change the position of the tooth. Over this foil the solder will follow, and even incorporate itself with the foil, uniting the whole into

one solid mass, especially if a sufficient quantity of solder be
employed. When each tooth has its gold back thus properly
adjusted, the whole piece will have the following appearance
as seen from behind.

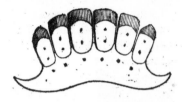

44. When the plaster has been thoroughly dried, which may
be done in an oven, provided the operator be in haste, or over
a fire in a ladle, provided the degree of heat used be not sufficient to *recalcine* the plaster, the piece is ready to be soldered.

In order to perform the operation of soldering with neatness,
solidity and beauty, apply the borax to the back of the tooth
only, quite down to the plate, by means of a flat, thin piece of
cane or soft wood. A sufficient quantity of the borax will run
down upon the plate without applying any to that, and if the
operator has any fear that the borax will carry the solder over
too great a portion of the plate, he may apply a thin coating of
whiting to all that part to which he wishes no solder to run,
leaving in all cases a semicircular spot behind each tooth,
which must be kept quite clean in order that the solder may
run over it unobstructed. Next, apply a quantity of solder to
the back of each tooth, nearly or quite equal to the weight of
the back itself. This may be in one or several pieces, at the
pleasure of the operator. Let the borax dry, if time will
permit, lest it should displace the solder during the sudden
conversion of the water into steam by too great a degree of
heat.

45. Before applying the blowpipe to a piece like this, the
hollow cup of charcoal mentioned in the first chapter should
be prepared as follows:—

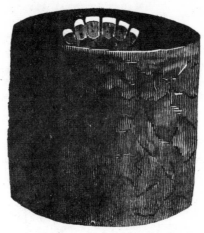

Let the operator not forget to apply the heat with caution, lest the teeth be cracked by sudden and unequal expansion, and let the heat be continued until the solder assumes the form best calculated to give strength and beauty to the work.   This form which the solder should assume, may be thus presented on a single tooth when seen laterally with a section of the plate.

Should the quantity of solder on any tooth be found insufficient, more may be added during the process of soldering, and the heat again raised to the point of fusion.

In soldering pieces like this, some advantage would be gained, if the right hand of the operator could be at liberty to make use of a rod of platina of the size and length of a knitting needle, with which he may move the melted solder about on the gold plate at pleasure, in order to bring it into the desired form.

To accomplish this object, it will be necessary to use one of Hook's self-acting blowpipes, which, with an improvement made by Dr. Jahial Parmly, of Bond Street, New York, will be found of great importance to the mechanical dentist.

This blowpipe, as is well known, consists of a brass globe composed of two hemispheres screwed firmly together, having an orifice at the top for the purpose of introducing alcohol, and a tube leading from the upper hemisphere to the flame of a lamp placed underneath the brass sphere. The whole may be supported on a stand as follows:—

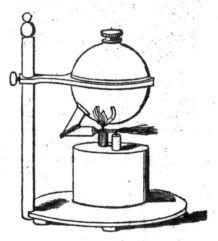

Without entering more minutely into the details of the formation of this instrument, I will merely add, that when the globe is partly filled with alcohol, and the lamp lighted beneath it, a part of the alcohol is soon converted into vapour, which finding no vent excepting through the small tube leading to the upper hemisphere of the brass globe, the vapour or steam of the alcohol is forced from the orifice of the tube directly against the flame of the lamp by which the alcoholic steam itself takes fire and forms a jet of flame of great intensity. Dr. Parmly's improvement consists in having two distinct wicks in the lamp with their appropriate tubes, so that one may act on the globe while the other is wholly diverted from it, or both may be directed upon the piece to be soldered when that may be *necessary.* With this instrument Dr. Parmly has succeeded in preserving the solder in a state of fusion for any required time, while with his platina rod he has given to the solder the form and position required, and all this without raising temperature enough to fuse the gold plate.

When the piece in question has been properly soldered, cleaned and polished as already described, the pivots may be wound with a little raw cotton, or floss silk, before fixing the plate firmly in the mouth, in order to avoid the wearing away of the roots by the metal; or when the cavities in the roots are very large, they may be filled with soft wood, and the pivots inserted into these wooden plugs.

Of the Insertion of a single Tooth in the Absence of a natural Root.

46. This is so nice and difficult an operation that I shall deem it expedient to present several examples, inasmuch as we find that many dentists who can construct a good double set—rarely ever succeed in setting a *single tooth* well.

Let us first suppose that the tooth to be supplied is a central incisor of the upper jaw; and that it is intended rather for show than mastication, inasmuch as the patient is unwilling to submit to an arrangement that would render the artificial substitute fit for general use.

After fitting a gold plate to the space to be occupied by the tooth, as already directed, solder a wire of fine gold or platina to each end of the plate, of sufficient length to embrace the two adjacent teeth as far as those next to them will permit, as follows:

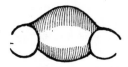

Such a plate with its clasps of wire, when well fitted to the gum and the two adjacent teeth, is found to sustain a tooth in its place with sufficient firmness for all purposes excepting that of masticating food; but if a tooth be desired for the performance of this latter function, another plan must be pursued.

Select two of the molares or bicuspides, one on each side of the mouth, around which clasps of gold may be adjusted, either with or without filing a passage for the clasps, as circumstances may require. To these clasps attach the extremities of a plate constructed as already described, and sustaining the tooth as follows:

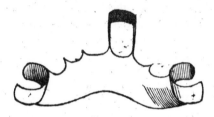

As the best methods of attaching a clasp to a plate in a neat manner, are of some importance to the student, I may state that winding with fine iron wire will sometimes succeed, yet the following mode is always most efficient and exact. The clasp which in most cases should be as wide as the tooth it embraces will admit, may be secured to the gold plate while both are on the model, by joining them with bees-wax, or, when necessary with sealing-wax. Then lift the whole carefully from the model, lay it on a piece of paper with the side on which the wax is downward, and pour plaster upon the upper side until both the clasps and plate are imbedded in the plaster. When the plaster is set, remove the wax, dry the plaster, apply the borax, and solder as usual.

In this as in all other cases when two pieces of gold plate are to be united with solder, if the two do not accurately meet, fill up the vacancy with gold foil before applying the borax and solder, as already directed.

This method of insertion, although more expensive than with one clasp only, has the advantage of greater firmness and durability.

The disadvantages of such a plate and clasps, are, the injury accruing by necessity to the teeth which are embraced by the clasps, and the inconvenience experienced by the tongue from the presence of a plate in the front of the mouth, which the tongue meets in articulating all the lingual sounds. Both these disadvantages, however, are generally preferred to the absence of a tooth from the front of the mouth.

In cases like the foregoing, for the purpose of preparing a metallic cast in such a manner that the gold plate struck upon it shall fit accurately to the natural teeth behind which it passes, cut away from the plaster model all the teeth nearly level with the gum, then after taking the metallic casts from this, strike the gold plate over the whole, and cut away the plate accurately with round files, where the natural teeth are to meet the plate.

47. It happens not unfrequently that, either on account of the loss of the teeth on one side of the mouth, or for some other solid reason, an attachment can be made to only one tooth, or to those on but one side of the jaw. In the former case a piece may be constructed as follows:

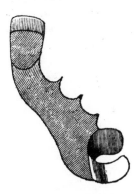

If the plate and spring, or clasp, are of considerable thickness and strength, this arrangement will be successful, even for purposes of mastication, but it is desirable in many cases, if practicable, to take two points of support, as follows:

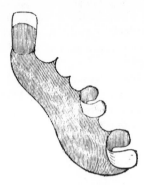

In all cases the clasps embracing natural teeth for the purpose of supporting artificial ones, should be as wide as possible, in order to avoid wearing away the teeth at the neck.

48. Let us next suppose that the second bicuspis has been removed, and the dentist is required to supply its place. The object in this and all other cases, being to throw the fastenings as far back into the mouth as possible, in order to be out of sight, let the clasp embrace one side of the first molaris, and both sides of the second, thus:

This method of fixing will prove very firm, provided the strength of the materials be justly proportioned to the use to which the artificial substitute is to be applied.

In those cases where the next tooth is the only one to which attachment can be made, it must be evident that no great dependence can be placed on the firmness of the work. If, however, the tooth which is to sustain the piece be either very flat like some bicuspides, or very strong and angular like some molars, the work will not fail to be of use. Take, for example, a first bicuspis and a first molaris.

In the former case, if the second bicuspis be very flat, the clasp will be little liable to a rotary motion. In the case of a first molaris, when the second is strong and angular, the most perfect success will attend the operation. In both these cases the strength of the material, together with the peculiar form of the supporting tooth, will secure the piece from being displaced by any other means than hard food, which must not be allowed to come in violent contact with so slight a fixture.

Of the Insertion of several Teeth on a Gold Plate with Clasps sustained by natural Teeth.

49. As cases of this description are very various, and not less in number than the arithmetical changes that can be rung on 32 bells, I shall deem it necessary to give only a few examples as specimens of the whole: and I begin with the most common and most important case of this kind, which presents itself in supplying the two central superior incisores.

Although there can be little doubt of the superior permanence and utility of a plate of this kind attached to some of the back teeth, thus:—

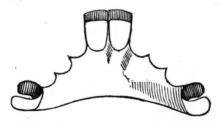

21

Yet many American dentists and most of the English practitioners would treat the case as follows:

Here the whole apparatus is secured in position by means of two small gold wires encompassing in part the lateral incisores. Some assistance, however, is rendered by the narrow neckings on that part of the plate which is adjacent to the neighbouring teeth. These neckings must fit with great exactness or they cannot be endured by the tongue. Pieces like these are less liable, perhaps, than some others to affect injuriously the natural teeth: which is certainly a great argument in their favour.

50. Sometimes when even four of the incisores are to be supplied, the same principle is successfully observed, thus:

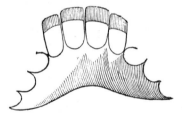

But in almost all cases of this kind, I should prefer an attachment to some of the back teeth when practicable, as follows:

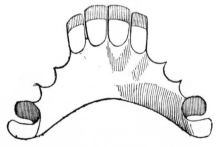

If two bicuspides are to be supplied, as is not unfrequently the case, let the following be a sample:

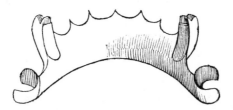

51. In cases where several teeth must be supplied, and only a few remain to sustain them, various mechanical contrivances become necessary to solve the problem with success.

Suppose, for example, that the two first molars are the only remaining natural teeth. It will be evident that the weight of a plate bearing the ten anterior teeth, would soon cause the two supporting teeth to swerve from their rectitude, and allow the front teeth to fall away from the gum.

In order to avoid this catastrophe, the plate must be extended as far as possible behind the supporting molars, in order to find a fulcrum or sustaining point to the lever here represented by the gold plate.

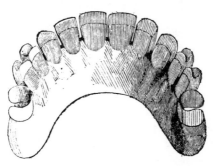

These extremities of the plate may be used to sustain artificial teeth, or they may be left unoccupied, but their presence is essential to the proper construction of the piece, inasmuch as the two supporting molars must be drawn perpendicularly from their sockets before the front can fall in

consequence of their motion; whereas a mere lateral decli-
nation of these supporters would produce that effect in the
absence of these extremities of the plate behind the two natural molars.

52. One of the most vexatious cases falling into the hands of
the dentist, is that in which a large plate must be supported by
a single tooth.

If this should chance to be a large and firm molaris, the
chances of success are somewhat enhanced; in which case the
piece will present the following appearance.

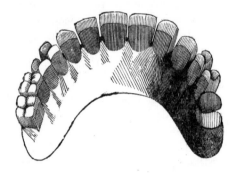

Cases of this character are so doubtful as to the permanence
of the supporting tooth, that unless it be very firm and sound,
it ought not to be trusted. When, however, the attempt is
made to construct such a piece, let the clasp be very strong and
the plate thin and light. The teeth also should be as slender
as possible.

53. The operator should always avoid laying plates over
roots of the natural teeth remaining in the mouth. Besides
the absolute certainty that these roots will prevent the perfect
fit of the plate to the gum, they are liable to be agitated by
the constant action of the plate upon them, by which they become loose, and often require extraction, after which the plate
no longer fitting the gum, becomes useless.

Although many patients are very averse to the removal of
these roots, and often allege examples among their acquaint-
ances in which plates have been laid over the roots of the
natural teeth, with perfect success, cases rarely occur in which

these persons cannot be persuaded to pursue a proper course of treatment, by judicious management on the part of the dentist. Sometimes he may succeed in inducing them to submit to the operation of extraction, by showing them that their money will be wastefully expended in procuring work which rests upon a foundation insufficient and precarious; at other times, by assuring them that he is wholly averse to executing work unless he can do it in what he knows to be a proper manner, by which he can do justice both to his patient and his own professional reputation.   Often he may succeed in his object by persuading the patient to permit him to remove one or two only of the loosest of the roots, after which, the charm being broken, no resistance will be made to the extraction of the rest.

At any rate, if the operator consents, in any instance, to lay a plate over the stumps of teeth, he owes it to himself to impress it on the memory of his patient that he does it in opposition to his judgment and experience, and does not consent to hold himself responsible for the result. If this statement should be entered on his books, with the patient's knowledge, it might prevent future complaints, for it happens not unfrequently that a dentist in extensive practice is blamed for operations, the failure of which is the result of the obstinacy of his employer.

54. Another precaution of which the young practitioner should be early apprized, is, never to lay a plate after teeth or roots have been extracted, until sufficient time has elapsed to allow the alveolar processes to be absorbed, and the gums fully healed, so that the teeth shall not become too short by subsequent absorption of the subjacent parts.

The dentist who neglects this precaution, will find himself frequently called on to substitute longer teeth, and will even sometimes be assured that they have been always too short from the beginning.

55. To avoid these unpleasant occurrences, let him, on the one hand, insist on allowing the gums sufficient time to become thoroughly healed and settled before constructing his work, and, on the other hand, let him never forget to leave the artificial teeth as *long* as circumstances will permit. In many instances, especially when the artificial substitutes are met on

their cutting edges by antagonizing teeth, the latter of these injunctions cannot be obeyed, and it is in such cases particularly, that the dentist should protect himself from both blame and loss, by keeping a record of the statements which he made to the patient on the subject.

56. It is very difficult to give any definite rule as to the period required for the absorption of the alveolar processes and the thorough healing of the gums after the removal of teeth or roots. In some cases a week may be sufficient, if only a single root, and that a short one, has been removed. A month even would be too brief a period for the majority of cases that occur in practice, and two or three months are sometimes required. Each case is modified so much by the condition of the patient's health; by the number and character of the teeth extracted ; and by the state of the natural teeth remaining in the mouth, that the period required in any given set of circumstances, is better learned by observation, than taught in theory; and this is one, among many reasons, requiring a patient apprenticeship of several years under suitable tuition, in order to enter understandingly upon general practice in dental surgery.

57. The dental operator owes it to his patient who has confided in his skill and integrity, and he owes it to justice and humanity, to inform all his professional friends who wear artificial teeth on metallic plates, of the great importance of not merely putting the mouth in a healthy condition before the introduction of artificial substitutes, but of the absolute necessity of keeping the mouth, and all it contains, perfectly clean afterwards.

Nothing is better established among physiological facts, than that filth lodged among the teeth, and left to ferment, decompose, and putrefy in the mouth, invariably destroys, sooner or later, all the remaining natural teeth; and thus renders useless all the clasps and fastenings of which we have treated at large in this chapter.

It may indeed be true that many patients will not comply with the instructions of the dentist on this subject, as it is unquestionable, that even some females of extreme neatness in other things, allow the mouth to be by far the most filthy place in all their habitations. They scrub their hearth-stones and require the chimneys of their houses to be now and then swept, but as to their mouths, they have really no time to keep them clean. But notwithstanding all this, the dentist who introduces artificial teeth, should urge the necessity of keeping the mouth absolutely clean.

58. It is known to every dental practitioner that although there is no single and simple acid that will corrode or dissolve gold, yet there are combinations of acid and other acrid substances allowed by some persons who wear metallic plates to remain so long and so constant in their mouths, as to destroy a thick plate of gold in a very few years.

This never could occur if the mouth were washed thoroughly with water and a brush several times a day; much less, if some slightly alkaline solution, or a good dentifrice were occasionally employed.

59. In order to aid the patient as much as possible in this duty of keeping the mouth free from impurities, the dentist should in all cases, if not impracticable, so construct his work that it may be readily removed from the mouth.

The springs or clasps which have been already described, should be made sufficiently fast to sustain the plate and teeth, but at the same time capable of being slipped from the natural teeth which they embrace, at the pleasure of the wearer.

To this end it may be sometimes necessary to restore the elasticity of the metal which has been destroyed by the heat employed in soldering. This is effected by the strokes of a small hammer; and by using a small anvil called a beck-horn, it may be done with ease, especially in those parts of the clasp where the elastic spring is most required.

60. This elasticity of the clasp is most required in those cases where the neck of the tooth which sustains the plate, is considerably smaller than the crown over which the clasp must be first passed. I have sometimes been compelled to obviate this difficulty by means of an elastic gold ferule made of very thin plate and wound in concentric circles in the manner of the mainspring of a watch. This should be so constructed that when encompassing the neck of the tooth, it shall embrace it firmly. Over this the clasp attached to the plate may be readily passed, if all parts be properly constructed.

CHAPTER III.

Of the Insertion of entire Sets of artificial Teeth, both upper and lower, on Plates of Gold, without Clasps or Springs.

61. It often happens, in this age of luxurious refinement, effeminate ease, and unnatural alimentation, that persons of both sexes, and of all classes of society, lose successively every tooth in both jaws; but more frequently in the upper maxillary arch. The dental operator who understands his business, although he deplores the folly or misfortune of his patient, is never more confident of ultimate success than in treating cases of this description, when he is permitted to exercise his best judgment in the employment of his utmost skill on the most suitable materials. As there is no longer a necessity of attaching his work to other teeth, which are liable to be soon removed either by decay or dislocations, he can construct an entire set of teeth, set upon a strong plate of gold, which shall fulfil all the reasonable expectations of the patient in regard to appearance, speech and mastication, and which shall moreover be so durable in its character as to render the annual expense of small amount for many years to come.

62. To secure entire success in the fabrication of these entire sets of artificial teeth, the utmost care must be taken to remove all the roots of the natural teeth, and to bring the gums and adjacent parts into a perfectly healthy condition. In ordinary cases, time alone, without any sanatary remedies, will effect this object, provided a sufficient period be allowed after the removal of the natural roots. Not only must the cavities which the roots occupied be wholly filled up, but the alveolar processes must be thoroughly absorbed, so that no material changes shall occur after the wax impression shall have been taken, from which the working models are to be made.

63. It is impossible to prescribe definite periods for all the cases that may occur in a promiscuous practice, during which this healing process, together with the absorption of the bone,

will be perfected. Much depends on the age, habits and health of the patient, and not a little on the circumstances under which the natural teeth are shed. In some subjects, the alveoli are nearly or wholly absorbed, before the roots of the natural teeth lose their hold upon the integuments: in others, several sound teeth are extracted, around which the alveoli were perfectly preserved. From all these causes it must be evident, that each distinct case possesses an idiosyncrasy of character peculiar to itself, and must be treated accordingly. It is proper to say here, that a few weeks will be sufficient for the preparation of some mouths for taking an impression; whereas, months will be required in a majority of instances.

64. When the operator becomes convinced that the gums are well healed and settled, and that no farther changes are to be feared, which will endanger the permanent and complete success of the operation, he should procure very ample metallic cases to contain his wax, so that the impression may extend to every part of the maxillary arch on which the plate must rest; taking care that the wax shall reach the extremity of either jaw towards the angle of articulation, and spread itself over at least two-thirds of the palatial concavity, when the upper teeth are to be restored, and moreover, that the wax come forward on the labial side of the arch as far as the muscles and integuments will permit. In taking these large impressions, let the wax be pure and without any admixture of olive oil, and just soft enough to receive the impression without too great pressure on the parts, and yet not so soft as to be injured while withdrawing it from the mouth. The proper consistency of the wax and the necessary shape and strength of the metal case, which contains it, are of great moment in the attempt to secure a satisfactory result; but in this case, as in many others, experience is the only competent instructor.

65. Inasmuch as the pieces which I am now describing, are those which by some have been called "suction plates," and by others are said to be retained in position by *atmospheric pressure*, I deem it proper in this place, to express an opinion on the subject, resulting not only from conversation with distinguished dentists, but from years of personal experience and observation, during which I have had occasion to inspect

pieces of this description constructed by some of the most distinguished artists of both hemispheres.

66. One result of my inquiry and observation has been, that few pieces of this kind are fixed firmly upon the gum, and used successfully for purposes of mastication, by mere suction, or atmospheric pressure, without any aid from the tongue, lips, cheeks, and antagonizing jaw. There is indeed, in favourable cases, a very firm adhesion of the plate to the subjacent parts after it has been some time worn, and thus closely fitted to the gum and palate. But this adhesion, which is that of two well adapted surfaces, from between which the atmosphere is excluded either by impact, or by liquids, or both combined, could never be effected unless the plate were held firmly in its place, for a season, either by the bold relief of the alveolar projection, or by the lips, tongue, teeth and opposing jaw; and in fact, these surrounding parts—together with the contained convexity of the projecting gum, contribute not merely *partially*, but *mainly*, to the preservation of the piece in its just position. The manner in which the surrounding parts operate to secure such a plate *in situ*, are too well known to need any illustration even to the youngest student of our art; but the manner in which the bold *bas relief* of a prominent alveolar projection, may and often does operate to sustain a plate, from beneath which the atmosphere has not been excluded, shall be explained by a simple diagram.

Let *A B* in the above figure, be a cylinder of wood, metal or any other substance, not more yielding than the alveolar ridge of the human mouth when denuded of its teeth; and let *C D* be a plate of metal so bent as to embrace the cylinder firmly in the parts adjacent to its two straight sides. It is very manifest, that such a plate might be sustained very firmly in its connexion with the cylinder, even though a stratum of air of any supposable thickness, intervened between the cylinder and plate.

It is indeed quite certain, that the firmness of this adhesion would be much increased if the cylinder were so fitted to the plate, as that the air were wholly excluded, and this only proves what I wish to impress strongly on the mind of the dental student, that even when all other circumstances are most favourable to the success of his operation, the perfect adaptation of plates like this to the subjacent parts, is of the utmost importance. The fact that a *perfect fit,* as it is called, excludes the particles of food, and also renders the plate more tolerable to the tongue, would of itself impel every neat and finished operator, to give to his plate the best possible adaptation to the parts beneath.

67. Another fact, with which observation has furnished me is, that inasmuch as the lips and cheeks contribute greatly to the stability of the position of an entire set; the artificial teeth should extend as far back as possible on the plate, in order to present as large a surface as convenient to the sustaining action of the muscles of the cheek. For a similar reason, the portion of the gold plate resting upon the palate directly over the tongue, in what is vulgarly called the roof of the mouth, should be as broad as circumstances will permit, in order that the superior surface of the tongue may lend its important aid, when required, in sustaining the artificial fixture in its place.

68. Experience and observation teach, moreover, that the gold plate must pass upwards as high as the muscles will permit, on the anterior and outer surface of the gum, between the cheeks and the maxillary arch. This not only increases the surface, thereby augmenting the force of adhesion, but it assists in preventing the plate from moving either laterally or backwards, in the act of mastication.

69. A proper thickness of the gold plate is matter of primary consideration, in these entire sets of teeth; and the thickness must vary in the direct ratio of the flatness or prominence of the alveolar ridge. The rule invariably is, that the plate shall be as light as is compatible with the strength required. Very flat gums require thicker plates than those which are more convex and protuberant, on the simple principle that a flat riband of metal of any given breadth and thickness, will bend in the direction of its length more readily than the same plate bent laterally into the semi-segment of a hollow cylinder.

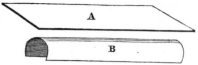

If *A* represent a flat metallic plate of any length and breadth, and *B* a cylindrical plate of equal dimensions, the strength of the latter will be many times greater than that of the former, in proportion to the convexity of its curvature. Hence it follows that the deeper the convexity of any gold plate for the mouth, and the broader its superficial area, the thinner may be the plate. And, on the other hand, when the plate is narrow and flat, it must be increased in thickness until it shall possess sufficient strength to resist the ordinary forces to which it must be necessarily subjected.

70. Since, as we have already said, every plate worn in the mouth should be as light as the strength demanded will permit, we have another among many solid reasons for preferring gold to any other metal for setting artificial teeth. Platina would resist the action of corrosive agents better than gold, but a much greater weight and bulk of this metal would be required, to give the strength of a similar gold plate.

71. The following is a drawing from a cast of one of the most prominent gums, to which I have been called upon to adjust a suction plate during the period of my professional practice.

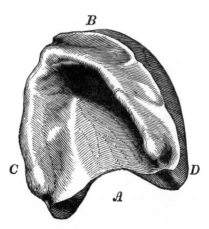

The depression at *A* below the prominence at *B C D* is full three-fourths of an inch. To a mouth like this there can be no difficulty in adjusting a suction plate with the most perfect success. If the model be correctly taken, the plate rather thin, and proportionally broad, it will require no more than ordinary mechanical skill to construct a piece which will remain firmly in its place, even in the act of masticating the hardest kinds of food.

72. But the ability of such a piece, to sustain the office of an implement of mastication, depends greatly on the position of the teeth, which are set upon it, and on the manner in which they meet those of the lower jaw. If the front incisores should be set too far forward on the plate, and if there should be no molar teeth in the lower jaw to countervail their action on the lower incisores, it will be manifest that the whole will be thrown forward, in closing the mouth.

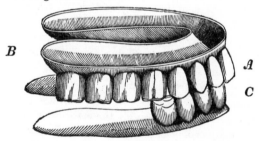

In the cut here given, if we suppose the upper incisores at *A*, to strike wholly over and in front of the lower incisores at *C*, inasmuch as there is nothing to sustain the point of the plate at *B*, it will inevitably fall away from the gum, whereupon the whole will be projected forward whenever the mouth shall close, and render the piece useless. Such an arrangement could be made available only by supplying the deficiencies in the lower jaw. If this is not done, the front teeth of the artificial piece must be removed backward until they strike perpendicularly upon the lower incisores, in which case the centre of gravity of the artificial piece will, in most instances, be so supported as to render the work available for all the important uses to which the teeth are usually applied.

73. After the dental operator has formed his plan as to the

22

position which he wishes the teeth to assume on the plate, and also as to the manner in which he intends the substitutes shall meet the natural teeth of the lower jaw, the best method of proceeding is as follows: After striking the plate as heretofore described, and after fitting the gold backs to the teeth which have been selected for the purpose, cover the outer surface of the plate which may be called the *lingual* surface, with softened bees-wax, equal in thickness to the length of the teeth, and adjust the teeth as nearly as possible in the required position, taking care to grind each tooth down to the plate with the greatest accuracy, in such manner that the gold back of each tooth shall touch the plate. There are some advantages, in certain cases, in using sealing-wax instead of bees-wax; in thus temporarily attaching the teeth to the plate. When this is used the flame of a lamp or candle may be employed to melt the wax as it shall be needed for each tooth.

74. In this stage of the progress, try the whole into the mouth of the patient, and correct the position of the several teeth so that in all respects they shall stand as desired. This process of adjusting will be readily effected, while the wax is preserved by heat in a softened state. When all the teeth stand exactly as all parties desire, remove the whole from the mouth carefully, and encompass all the teeth, together with the plate, with plaster of paris, leaving the wax uncovered. When the plaster shall become thoroughly hard, immerse the whole in warm water, in order to soften the wax, or cut it away with a penknife, leaving the teeth and plate firmly imbedded in the plaster. In this as well as other cases where the plaster must be subjected to the action of the blowpipe, sand should be mixed with the plaster to prevent its cracking, or if this precaution should have been neglected, the plaster may be encompassed with a few turns of fine iron wire, as already directed.

75. After the gold plate and backs of the teeth have been divested of the wax, they should be well washed in clean water, when the piece will be ready for soldering. In large pieces like this, where great strength and durability are required, the utmost care must be used to employ solder enough not only to render the work beautiful, but to give the stability required; for, as I have already remarked, a good piece of work never

gives way at the junction of the plate with the backs of the teeth, inasmuch as that is by far the strongest part of a good piece. In soldering large plates of this sort, the flame of the blowpipe should be applied cautiously at first, and afterwards augmented gradually till the whole mass is heated to redness; after which a concentration of the jet of flame should be brought to bear upon the back of each of the teeth successively till the solder has all assumed the desired form and position, throughout the entire range. After cooling, cleaning, and polishing, the piece will be ready for insertion.

76. As the cleaning and polishing of such large plates, is an important operation as regards their beauty, I will recapitulate the process, and describe it a little more minutely than I have yet done. When the piece has been boiled for a few seconds in diluted sulphuric acid, or suffered to lie a few minutes in diluted muriatic acid, without boiling, let the edge of which rests on the palatial arch be a little bent upwards by the use of a small riveting hammer, while the plate rests on the end of a steel rod half an inch in diameter, rounded at the end in the form of a hemisphere.

The shape of the rod, and the form and size of the hammer, are represented in the following wood-cut.

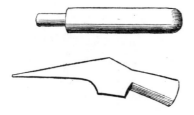

The sharp and broad edge of the hammer must be applied with repeated strokes and a skilful hand to the lingual side of the inner edge of the plate until it shall effect the object to the extent desired. There is but one method of avoiding the necessity of this operation, which is to pare away the plaster cast upon which the metal casts are to be made, along the inner edge of the plate, so that the plate in being struck between the me-

tal casts, shall be properly bent upwards without the use of
the hammer afterwards.   This trimming of the cast, however,
will be more difficult than the method first described, especially
to the inexperienced.

77. Let the plate in the next place be filed very smooth, in
all parts, commencing with coarser gold-files and finishing with
very fine ones.   In the next place, rub the plate smooth with
a silver-smith's polishing stone, which may be cut with a fine
saw into any shape desired.   After this, use rotten-stone and
sweet oil, applied with leather attached to the end of a piece
of soft wood; afterwards apply dry Spanish white, crocus, or
rouge, and finish by washing in clean water.   To those portions of the plate which cannot be reached with the leather,
the above-named substances may be applied on threads of silk,
flax, hemp or cotton.   When threads are thus used they may
be fastened at both ends to some fixed points in the manner of
the horse-hair of the bow of a violin, and motion may be given
to the piece along these filaments to which the polishing substances have been previously applied.   When the whole is
finished and ready to be inserted in the mouth, it presents the
following appearance.

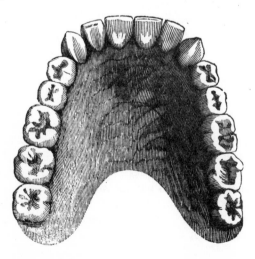

78. It sometimes happens that the maxillary ridge is so flat, that the action of the lips, cheeks and tongue, together with the slight degree of adhesion which takes place when the plate is first inserted, are incapable without a little practice of keeping the piece in its place, whereupon being left to the action of gravitation, it falls whenever the mouth is opened. To remedy this difficulty, which is removed by a little experience, and which is felt less and less as the gum becomes adapted to the plate, it is sometimes necessary to wear a piece of soft leather, either that of the chamois goat, or well-dressed lamb-skin, cut to the exact size of the gold plate, and moistened with water. By this means the adhesion is promoted to such a degree, that the piece may be worn with little comparative difficulty. It is often true, in the case of aged persons, that the alveolar processes become so completely absorbed, and the parts upon which the plate must rest, so nearly flat, that the difficulty of wearing a suction plate is greatly increased. In such cases the use of springs must be adopted, such as will be hereafter described, or the patient must dispense with artificial teeth altogether.

79. As the foregoing description of a suction plate, is applicable only to the upper jaw, inasmuch as the principle of cohesive attraction or atmospheric pressure, does not apply to any great extent, to plates worn upon the narrow alveolar ridge of the lower jaw, it may be proper here to remark, that the attraction of gravitation necessarily operates in some degree to counterbalance this defect in the lower plates. These pieces will of course remain in their places by gravitation alone, provided the food, the tongue, the lips, and the cheeks do not displace them. But all these causes are so apt to render lower plates useless without some artificial means to keep them in position, that I shall deem it necessary to employ springs in most instances; but as there are a few cases in which under pieces can be worn without springs, I shall present a drawing of one of them as follows:

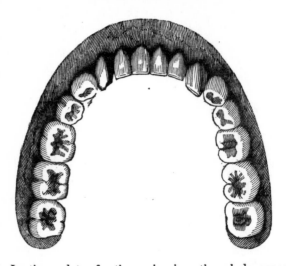

80. In these plates for the under jaw, the whole process of construction, will be similar to that already described, with the difference, that as the edges of the plate must approach as near as possible to the muscles on either side of the alveolar ridge, without wounding them, and as the plate at least can be but narrow, it becomes imperative that it should be much thicker than plates for the upper jaw. This increased thickness will both impart the required strength, and present a less trenchant edge to the muscles and integuments that necessarily move upon it. There is an excellent method of removing this difficulty of the sharp edges of the lower plate, when the condition of the mouth will admit of it. In many cases the absorption of the parts becomes so considerable, as to leave sufficient room in the mouth, to construct the lower plate *double*, especially that portion of it which pertains to the back part of the mouth, sustaining the molar teeth. The following method of procedure will enable the operator to construct a double plate with facility. After the ordinary plate has been completed agreeably to directions already given, cover the upper or lingual surface with beeswax, and mould or cut it into such form as shall represent the exact position which it is desired that the upper plate shall assume. Lay the whole on the tin-cast upon which the plate was struck, and after oiling the surfaces of the wax,

plate and mould, with olive oil, cover the whole with plaster, sufficiently thick to give it the required strength.   This will form the basis of a new set of metallic castings, upon which a second plate may be constructed, which, being soldered to the first plate, and carefully filed and polished, will present very smooth and cylindrical surfaces to the tongue, cheeks and lips. This sort of double plate, which has long been familiar to the profession, is quite unlike those patented machines of modern invention, provided with flute-holes like the lamprey, for the storage of all kinds of filth, both solid and fluid, which can be collected from the mouth, fomented by heat, and rendered exe-crable by fermentation.   But as these portable nuisances have gone, for the benefit of posterity, to the tomb of the Capulets, I have resuscitated their memory merely to say, that those double plates which I here recommend, in certain cases, are wholly unlike them, inasmuch as they are merely air vessels, and not depositories of garbage.   One advantage of these double plates for the lower jaw, in addition to that already mentioned, is that they enable the artist to use teeth of uniform length, giving greater symmetry and beauty to the work—and besides this the strength of the piece will be augmented many-fold. It should be moreover known to the profession generally, that the market is now supplied with *gum-teeth*, as they are techni-cally called, of great beauty, which are very useful in those cases of considerable alveolar absorption, where double plates are not employed.

81. Before entering upon the subject of double sets with springs, which will engage our attention in the next chapter, it may, perhaps, be useful to the student to say a few words in relation to the several kinds of mineral teeth which have been offered to the profession from time to time by the principal manufacturers of Europe and America.   Until a few years ago the French dentists took the lead in this branch of manufacture, and supplied not only their own country, but foreign markets. If we are to judge of the French teeth from the specimens sent to this country while there was a demand for them, it must be confessed that although the material of both the body and the enamel, was exceedingly well calculated to resist the action of the blowpipe, and although they were in some instances

well coloured, yet as to beauty of form and the method of attachment to metallic plates, they were vastly inferior to those of
American fabrication which have now wholly supplanted them.
And in relation to two of these points of superiority, I am compelled to acknowledge that I have never yet seen any artificial
mineral teeth, so elegantly formed, and coloured so perfectly
to nature, as those manufactured by Mr. C. Ash, of London,
who has kindly forwarded to me a few sets to be exhibited
next summer at the meeting of the American Society of Dental
Surgeons in Boston.   But, as these teeth manufactured by
Mr. Ash do not resist the action of the blowpipe in such a
manner as to be capable of being soldered to plates with solder
of sufficient firmness to resist the action of the fluids of the
mouth, I am confident that some of our American dentists,
among whom I am happy to rank Mr. Samuel W. Stockton,
of Philadelphia, and Mr. James Alcock, of New York, have
presented to the profession the best specimens of incorruptible
teeth, of which we have any account in the history of our art.
And yet when I contemplate the undeniable superiority of the
teeth fabricated by Mr. Ash, of London, as regards beauty of
form and perfection of colouring, I cannot allow myself to
doubt that higher points of perfection are still to be attained
in the production of this species of manufacture, as regards all
those particulars in which the teeth now in market are found
deficient.   There is scope enough to call into activity the energies of the most exalted genius, and a field in which enter-
prise and perseverance will reap a harvest of gold, when the
profession confess that they are wholly satisfied with the quality
of this article now so essential to the perfection of our art.
But I should esteem myself chargeable with manifest injustice
and ingratitude towards those who have done so much for the
improvement of mineral teeth, for having spoken thus of the
defects of the present fabrics, did I not also express my joy
and astonishment that so much has been done already during
the present century for this manufacture.

82. Of the various modes of constructing what are techni-
cally called *plate teeth*, I shall deem it necessary to introduce
but three on this occasion, as being the most conspicuous among
the many kinds in vogue.

The French plate teeth so long as they continued to come to our market, were constructed as follows:

Each tooth had a longitudinal groove on its posterior surface, with three points or pivots of platina set firmly in the body of the tooth during its fabrication, to which a gold or platina wire might be soldered. To this wire when ground to the level of the surface of the tooth, a metal back was to be attached by soldering. Teeth thus constructed possess a good degree of strength, but are not easily replaced in case of accident, and therefore the dentists of the United States adopted the following improvement.

Two small platina pivots of wire, are inserted firmly in the body of the tooth during the manufacture, designed to be inserted into two corresponding holes in the metal plate. These pivots can be both riveted or soldered to the metal packs. Dr. Harrington, of Philadelphia, has recently secured a patent for an improvement in these pivots, which consists in forming a head on that end of the pivot which is inserted into the tooth, as well to prevent it from being drawn out, as to enable the tooth to sustain the strokes of the riveting hammer. In the fabrication of the American teeth just described, many individuals of eminent mechanical genius, have been for some years ardently engaged. Many of these dentists manufacture only for their own use, and succeed in producing teeth of good quality. Among those who have manufactured for the market, Mr. S. W. Stockton, of Philadelphia, has been most generally patronised, and has received more frequently than any other individual, the medals and diplomas of the American Institute. Mr. James Alcock, of New York, has also succeeded, after years of persevering experiment, in fabricating beautiful teeth, and has likewise obtained the medal of the Institute.

83. The only remaining kind of mineral teeth of which I propose to speak, is that from the manufactory of Mr. C. Ash, of London. His teeth differ from those already described, in having a central, longitudinal cavity or orifice, bushed with gold, for the reception of a pivot of the same metal, as follows:

One of the advantages of this method of construction, is that teeth of this kind are adapted as well for insertion on roots as on plates of metal. Their great excellency is their surpassing beauty of form and colour; and when these properties can be made compatible with a material capable of resisting the action of the blowpipe, little will be left to be resolved by future generations in the problem of constructing artificial teeth. But the period when this desirable object will be attained, is left to conjecture, and I deem it not too much to say that, the fortunate individual who successfully resolves this difficult problem and unites the separate excellencies of those three kinds of teeth, will not only insure to himself and his family an ample fortune, provided he conduct the exclusive manufacture with spirit and skill, but will deserve the general thanks of the profession and the gratitude of mankind.

CHAPTER IV.

Manner of preparing Teeth with spiral Springs.

Both jaws are often, to a certain extent, supplied with teeth without aid of spiral springs; but it is only when the springs are employed, (whether any natural teeth remain or not,) that the sets are denominated double. Spiral springs, however, may be required for securing a single set, or a set for a single jaw. But this can rarely happen, except for the fastenings of sets for the lower, since those for the upper can, generally, or always be confined in a more convenient manner.

In the preparation of a double set, the plate for the upper jaw should be made about five-eighths of an inch wide; the width of the lower must be regulated by the height and width of the alveolar ridge for which it is designed.

The alveolar ridge of the lower jaw, is, in some instances, so much absorbed as to be scarcely perceptible, and is covered over with the integuments of the lower part of the mouth, lying in loose folds upon it. The utility of false teeth, especially as regards mastication, can never, under such circumstances, be very great. The moving about of the teeth, which, on account of the narrowness of the ridge, it is impossible wholly to prevent, and the pressure upon the loose integuments always produce irritation; so that the teeth, instead of contributing to the comfort of the wearer, are a source of almost constant annoyance. It would, therefore, be better, in cases of this kind, wholly to dispense with their use. Should, however, an individual whose mouth is thus circumstanced, still persist, after he has been apprized of the true state of the case, in desiring the insertion of teeth, we should endeavour, as much as possible, to obviate the difficulty, by making the plate narrow, and rounding its under edges. But when the plate is very narrow, it should be made thick, in order that it may not be easily bent.

Teeth inserted with springs, must be arranged, mounted and antagonized, and have their plates fitted and adapted, in the same manner, as those that are to be fastened with clasps.

In order that the teeth, upon the upper and lower plates may antagonize properly, we use what has been denominated *antagonizing models:* they are obtained in the following manner:—

When both plates have been properly adjusted to the mouth, soft bees-wax is to be placed between them, so as to occupy the position that the teeth are to assume; to ascertain the proper height of the wax, which is to be the length of the teeth, we must be governed by the lips and profile of the face: the centre of the mouth is now marked upon the plates or wax, and the whole may then be withdrawn.

The lower plate must be filled with calcined plaster mixed with water to a proper consistency, and extend posteriorly two or three inches beyond the plate, and in which two depressions are made: these are intended as articular cavities for the plaster, which is to be poured into the upper plate and extended over this. The plaster poured into the lower plate should be allowed to set, and then be oiled previous to filling the upper plate: this will prevent the two parts from adhering.

Fastenings for the springs must be attached to the plate before we solder the teeth. These are sometimes fixed at the ends of the plate, but the proper place for them is on the sides, between the bicuspides and molares; for when the springs are fastened here, they keep the teeth much more firmly in their places, than when fixed at the ends of the plate. These fastenings consist of small studs of gold, each about the sixth of an inch in length, soldered upon the plates near their outer edges, and on a line with the outer surfaces of the teeth, having a gold pivot or pin, about the thickness of a fine knitting needle, and an eighth of an inch in length, projecting at right angles, from the outer side of each, towards the cheeks, with a small screw and nut on its end.

The springs are formed either by winding a piece of gold wire upon a small round spindle, or by wrapping it upon another piece of wire of the proper size, made fast in a vice. The former, however, is the better mode of making them. After the gold wire has been wound in this manner, the spindle is drawn from it, and the coil that remains, cut to the proper length. Another piece of gold wire having a flat head, with a hole rather larger than the pins attached to the studs and being of the thickness of the spindle, and about half an inch in length, is next to be inserted in each end of the coil, so as to form a kind of eyelet or swivel.

Springs are then attached to the upper and lower plates, which being thus connected, are placed in the mouth and held in their proper places by the action of the springs.

The wire used for the construction of springs, should be no thicker than is absolutely necessary to give to them the requisite power; and the diameter of the coil should never exceed the seventh or eighth of an inch. Their length must be regulated by the peculiarities of the mouth. In some cases they will have to be much longer than others; the usual length, however, is about an inch and a quarter, but in some instances I have found it necessary to make them an inch and three quarters.

When a single set is to be confined in the mouth in this manner, fastenings for the springs at one end are to be attached to one of the natural teeth, on each side in the other jaw. These consist of gold caps placed on the teeth, and furnished with a pivot or pin, fixed on each of their outer sides, like those before described. Where caps are employed, the artificial teeth, which are to antagonize with those upon which they are placed, should be shorter than any of the others. Gold bands are in some cases substituted, with advantage for caps.

ALPHABETICAL TABLE.

incorruptibles. Paris, 1821, in-8°, 4 fr.—Quelques réflexions sur
le procès intenté au lord Égerdton, comte de Bridgewater, par M.
Dubois de Chemant, 1826.—Un mot sur la réfutation du sieur
Dubois de Chemant, dentiste.

AURIVILLIUS. Dissertat. de dentitione difficili. Upsal, 1757.

AUSSANT. Sur les soins à donner aux dents de seconde dentition. (*Dissertation inaugurale.*) Paris, 1828, in-4°.

AUVITY (*Ant.*) Première dentition et sevrage. (*Dissertat. inaugur.*, Paris, 1812, in-4°.)

AUZEBI. Principes d'odontologie. Description des différentes
maladies qui affectent la bouche, et des moyens de les guérir.
Lyon, 1771, in-12.

B.

BAUHINUS. Dissertat. de odontalgiâ. 1660.

BAUMES. Traité de la première dentition et des maladies, souvent
très graves, qui en dépendent. Paris, 1806. Un vol. in-8°,
6 fr.

BEAUPREAU. Dissertation sur la propreté et la conservation des
dents. Paris, 1764.—(*Voyez* aussi *Journal de mèdecine*, t. XXI.
p. 477.—Lettre à M. Cochois sur les maladies du sinus maxillaire. Paris, 1769.

BECKER. Sur les dents, etc.—La Manière la plus sûre, etc.
Leipzig, 1807, 1810.

BENNET. A Dissertation on the teeth. London, 1779, in-8°.

BERDMORE (*Th.*) A treatise on the disorders and deformities
of the teeth and gums, illustrated with cases and experiments.
London, 1770.

BEURLIN. Dissertat. de dentitione difficili. Altd., 1720.

BEW (*Charles.*) Opinions on the causes and effects of diseases
in the teeth and gums, etc., etc. 1819.

BLAKE. Dissertat. de dentium formatione et structurâ in homine
et variis animalibus. Edimb., 1798.

BLUMENTHAL (*C. A.*) Nahere prüfung der ætiologie der zah-
narbeit der kinder gegen Wickman. Stendal, 1799, in-8°.—Sur
les Connaissances naturelles des dents. Stendal, 1800.

BOLLET. Manière de conduire les enfans depuis leur naissance
jusqu'à l'âge de sept ans, et d'éviter les convulsions, le croup
et la coqueluche. Paris, 1820. In-8°.

BOTOT. Le Chirurgien-dentiste, etc. Paris, 1786, in-12.—Avis
au peuple sur les soins nécessaires pour la propreté de la bouche.
Paris, 1789. In-12.—Moyens pour conserver les dents, 1802.

BOURDET. Lettre à M. D., Paris, 1754, et Éclaircissemens au sujet de cette lettre. Paris, 1754.—Recherches et observations sur toutes les parties de l'art du dentiste. Paris, 1756, in-12, 2 vol., 5 fr. Feutsch, 1762.—Soins faciles pour la propreté de la bouche et la conservation des dents. Paris, 1759.—Manière simple de maintenir les dents saines et la bouche fraîche. Leipsick, 1762.—Dissertation sur la propreté et la conservation des dents. Paris, 1764, in-8°.—Dissertation sur les dépôts du sinus maxillaire. Paris, 1764.

BRACHMAEND. De Ulceribus dentium fistulosis. Lipsiæ, 1733.

BRENDEL. Dissertat. de odontalgiâ, 1697.

BRING. Observ. in hodiernam de dentibus præcipuè hominum doctrinam. Lond., 1793.

BROUWER. Dissertat. de odontalgiâ. Leyd., 1692.

BRUNNER (*J. B.*) Einleitung zu den wissenschaften eines Zahnarztes. Wien und. Leipzig, 1766, in-8°.

BRUNNER (*Ad. Ant.*) Abhandlung von der hervobrechung der milchzæhne. Wien, 1771, A. D. B., XVI, B., p. 619.

BUCHNER. Dissertat. de curâ dentium. Hales, 1752.

BUCKING. Traité complet sur l'art d'arracher les dents. 1805.

BUNON. Dissertation sur un préjugé concernant les maux de dents des femmes grosses. Paris, 1741, in-4°.—Essai sur les maladies des dents, où on propose de leur procurer une bonne conformation dès la plus tendre enfance, et d'en assurer la conservation pendant tout le cours de la vie. Paris, 1743, in-12. Expériences et démonstrations faites à l'hôpital de la Salpétrière et à Saint-Côme, en présence de l'Académie de Chirurgie, pour servir de suite et de preuves à l'Essai sur les maladies des dents. 1746, in-12.

BURLIN (*R. Ph.*) Dissertat. de dentitione difficili, etc. Altdorf, 1720.

C.

CAIGNÈ (*Francois.*) Sur la dentition des enfans du premier âge. (*Dissertat. inaugur.*, Paris, 1802, in-4°.)

CAMPANI (Λ.) Odontalgia, ossia trattado sopra i denti. De Denti e loro cura, e la maniera di estrarli. Fior., 1789.

CAPURON. Essai sur la luxation de la mâchoire inférieure. (*Dissert. inaugurale.*) Paris. an 9, in-8°.

DE CASTRILLO (*F. Mart.*) Colloquium de dentitione. Valladolid, 1557, et Madrid, 1570.

CATALAN. Mémoire, rapport et observation sur l'appareil propre
à corriger la difformité qui consiste dans le chevauchement de
la mâchoire inférieure en avant de la supérieure; difformité vul-
gairement nommée *menton de galoche*, 16 pages. Paris, 1826.

CHEMANT *(Dubois de.)* *Voy.* Dubois.

COLONDRE. Essai sur les plus fréquentes maladies des dents et
les moyens propres à les prévenir et à les guérir. Genève, 1781.

CONRING *(Herm.)* Dissert. de naturâ et dolore dentium. Helm-
stadt, 1672.

CORNELIO (*Vittorio.*) Statistica odontalgica del Piemonte et in
especie di Torino per l'anno 1817. Torino, 1818.

COURTOIS. Le Dentiste observateur, etc. Paris, 1775.—Sur l'état
et les maladies des dents. Gotha, 1778.

CRAUSE. Dissert. de dentium sensu. Jéna, 1704.

CRAUSIUS. Dissert. de odontalgià. Jéna, 1681.

CRON (*Ludw.*) Der beym Aderlassen und Zahnausziehen ges-
chikte Barbiegesell. Leip., 1717, in-8°.

CUMME. Dissertatio de dentium historià physiologice, pathologice
et therapeutice, pertractatâ. Helmst., 1716.

CURTIS. A Treatise on the structure and formation of the teeth.
London, 1769.

CUVIER (*F.*) Des dents des mammifères considérées comme
caractères zoologiques. Paris, 1822—25, un vol. in-8°. avec 100
pl., 40 fr.

D.

D * * *. L'art du dentiste joint à l'anatomie de la bouche, in-12.

DEFRITSCH. Dissert. de dentibus. Vienn., 1772.

DELABARRE. (Chirurgien-dentiste.)—Dissertation sur l'histoire
des dents. In-4°, 1806.—Odontologie, ou Observations sur les
dents humaines, suivies de quelques idées nouvelles sur le mé-
canisme des dentiers artificiels. Paris, 1815, in-8°, fig., 2 fr. 50
c.—Discours d'ouverture d'un Cours de médecine dentaire. 1817,
in-8°.—Traité de la partie mécanique de l'art du chirurgien-dentiste. Paris, 1820, 2 vol. in-8°, avec pl. 16 fr. Traité de la
seconde dentition, et méthode nouvelle de la diriger, suivie d'un
Aperçu de séméiotique buccale. Paris, 1819, in-8°, fig., 10 fr.
Discours d'ouverture d'un Cours de stomatonomie. Paris, 1825,
in-8°.—Méthode naturelle de diriger la seconde dentition. Paris,
1826, in-8°, fig., 3 fr.

DELMOND. Mémoire sur un nouveau procédé pour détruire le
cordon dentaire des six dents antérieures et éviter leur extraction,

Paris, 1824, petite broch.—Epitre à M. Marmont, à l'occasion de son poëme sur l'odontotechnie, 1825, petite broch.

DESCHAMPS le jeune. Traité des maladies des fosses nasales et de leurs sinus. Paris, 1804, in-8°, 4 fr.

DESIRABODE. Je ne puis me taire, ou mémoire de M. Désirabode. Paris, 1823, in-8°, 75 c.

DESPRE. Dissertat. de dentitione difficili. Erf., 1720.

DEVAUT. Essai sur la nature et la formation des dents. (*Dissertat. inaugur.*, Paris, 1826, in-4°.)

DOWNING (*Richard.*) A Popular essay on the structure, formation, and management of the teeth. London, 1815, in-8°.

DROUIN. Sur les Maladies des dents. Strasbourg, 1761, in-8°.

DUBOIS. Esquisse sur l'hygiène dentaire, ou Analyse des moyens propres à la conservation des dents et des gencives. Paris, 1823.

DUBOIS DE CHEMANT. Dissertation sur les avantages des nouvelles dents et rateliers artificiels, incorruptibles et sans odeur. Paris, 1789.—Lettre sur les dents artificielles. Paris, 1790. Dissertation sur les avantages des dents incorruptibles de pâte minérale, etc., Paris, 1824, broch. in-8°.—Mémoire pour M. Dubois de Chemant contre le lord Egerdton, comte de Bridgwater. Réfutation des assertions fausses et calomnieuses contenues dans un libelle dirigé par Audibran, dentiste, contre M. Dubois de Chemant, sous le prétexte d'un procès intervenu entre le lord Egerdton et M. de Chemant. 1826, in-4°.

DUBOIS-FOUCOU. Expose de nouveaux procédés pour la confection des dents dites de composition. Paris, 1808, in-8°.— Lettre adressée à MM. les dentistes. Paris, 1808, in-8°.

DUCHMIN. Sur la Carie de dents de lait. (Journal de Trévoux, 1759, février.)

DUPONT. Remède contre le mal des dents. Paris. 1633, in-8°.

DUVAL. Des Accidens de l'extraction des dents. Paris, 1802, petite broch. in-8°. Réflexions sur l'odontalgie, considérée dans ses rapports avec d'autres maladies. Paris, 1803, broch. in-8°. Expériences et observations pratiques sur les dents plombées, qui sont susceptibles de l'influence galvanique. Paris, 1807, broch. in-8°.—Recherches historiques sur l'art du dentiste. Broch. in-8°, Paris, 1808. Conseils des poètes anciens sur la conservation des dents. Paris, broch. in-8°. (*Mémoire imprimé dans le Magasin encyclopédique*, année 1805.)—Mémoire sur la position relative à l'ouverture externe du canal maxillaire, pour servir à la démonstration de l'accroissement de la mâchoire

inférieure.—Propositions sur les fistules dentaires, précédées
des Observations sur la consomption de l'extrémité de la racine
des dents. Paris, 1810, broch. in-8°.—Observations sur l'état
des os de la mâchoire, dans les ulcéres fistuleux des gencives
et dans les fistules dentaires. (Extr. du *Bulletin de la Faculté
de Médecine de Paris*, 1814, n°. IV.)—Observation sur quelques
affections douloureuses de la face, considérées dans leur rapport
avec l'organe dentaire. 1814.—Notice historique sur la vie et les
ouvrages de M. *Jourdain*, dentiste. Paris, 1816, broch. in-8°.
Le Dentiste de la jeunesse, ou Moyens d'avoir les dents belles
et bonnes. Paris, 1807, in-8°, 3 fr. 50 c., deuxième édition.
De l'Arrangement des secondes dents, ou Méthode naturelle de
diriger la deuxième dentition, soumise au jugement de la raison
et de l'expérience. Paris, 1820, in-8°, 2 fr. 25 c.—Extrait d'un
mémoire sur l'atrophie des dents. Paris, in-8°.—Notice des travaux entrepris sur les dents en France depuis 1790. Paris, 1825
(1.)

E.

EHINGER. Dissertat. de odontalgiâ. Altdorf, 1718.
ELOY. Dissertat. de remediis anti-odontalgicis. Viennæ, 1772.
ERASTUS. Disputat. de dentibus in disp. et epist. Tigur., 1595.
EUSTACHIUS. De dentibus. (V. *Opusc. anatom.*) Venet., 1574,
in-4°.

F.

FAUCHARD. Le Chirurgien-dentiste. Paris, 1786, 2 vol. in-12,
fig., 5 fr.
FAY. A description of the mode of using the forceps invented for
the extraction and excision of teeth. London, 1827, broch. in-8°.
FICHER. Sur les diverses formes des os de la mâchoire dans
plusieurs espèces d'animaux. Leipsick, 1800.
FINOT (*C. F.*) Maladies de la première dentition. (*Dissert. inaug.*
Paris, 1813, in-4°.)
FLEURIMON. Moyens de conserver les dents belles et bonnes.
Paris, 1682, in-12.
FONZI. Rapport sur les dents artificielles, terro-métalliques. Paris,

(1.) Il serait à désirer pour la science, que ce savant dentiste et habile
opérateur réunît en un seul ouvrage les nombreux travaux qu'il a publiés
depuis près de trente ans, et dont il est presque impossible de se procurer la
collection complète.

1808, 8 pages.—Réponse à la brochure de Dubois-Foucou, Paris, 1808, 6 pages.

FOUCHON. Propositiones de dentium vitiis. Paris, 1775.

FOUCOU *(Dubois.) V.* Dubois.

FOX *(Joseph.)* An account of the diseases which affect children during first dentition. Append. natural history of the human teeth. London, 1803.—The history and treatment of the diseases of the teeth, gums, etc. London, 1806, in-4°.

FRANK. Dissertat. de odontalgiâ. Jenæ, 1692.

G.

GALLETTE. Réflexions sur la cure des dents. Mayence, 1810. Sur l'art dentaire. Mayence, 1803.—Chirurgien dentiste, 24 pag., 1813. Broch. in-12.

GARIOT. Traité des maladies de la bouche, Paris, 1805. in-8°. fig., très-rare.—Système de la physiologie, pathologie et thérapeutique de la bouche, avec plusieurs avis de Angermann. Leipsick, 1806.

GENLIS *(Z. C.)* Progr. observ. de dentitione tertiâ. Lips., 1786.

GEOFFROY-SAINT-HILAIRE. Système dentaire des mammifères et des oiseaux, Paris, 1824, 23 pages.

GERAUDLY. L'art de conserver les dents. Paris, 1737.

GERBAUX. A practical treatise on the most frequent diseases of the mouth and teeth specially on the accidents of the first dentition, etc. London, in-8°., 1823.

GESHENCK. Sur persononn beiderlet geschlechts die zaichne gesmedmed tchonzu. Herrhatten. Francf., 1796.

GILLES *(Arnauld.)* La fleur des remèdes contre le mal de dents. Paris, 1622.

GIRAUD *(J.)* Die gute mutter, oder abandlung von den mitteln, seinen kinderueinen starken, danerhalten kœrper, besondersein glückliches zahnen zu verschaffen. Brannschw, 1790, in-8°. A. D. B. III. B. p. 411.

GLAUBRECHT. Dissertat. de odontalgiâ. Argentorati, 1766.

GOBLIN *(D.)* Manuel du dentiste à l'usage des examens, Paris, 1827, in-8°, 5 fr.

GOECKEL (Eberb.) Epitome theoriæ practicæ de odontalgiâ, oder Bericht vondem. Zahnweh, nordl. 1688, in-8°.

GOGUELIN *(J. G.)* Mémoire sur le scorbut. S.-Brieuc, 1804, 1 vol. in-8°, 2 fr. 50 c.

GRACBNER *(Carl. Auq.)* Gedanken, über das. Hervorkommen und Wechseln der Zahne.

GRASSO. De dentitione difficili. Erfordiæ.

GROUSSET. De la dentition ou du développement des dents chez l'homme. (*Dissert. inaugur.* Paris, 1803, in-8°, 1 fr. 50 c.)

GRUN. Dissert. de odontalgià. Jena, 1795.

GUERTIN. Avisos tendentes a conservaçao dos dentes e sua sub-stituiçao. Paris, 1819, 8 pages in-8°.

H.

HEBENSTREIST (*J. E.*) De dentitione secundâ juniorum. Lips., 1738, in-4°.

HEBERT. Le citoyen dentiste, etc. Lyon, 1778. in-8°.

HEISTER. Dissert. de dentium dolore. Altd., 1711.—Epistola de pilis, ossibus et *dentibus* in variis corporis humani partibus repertis. Helmst., 1743.

HEMARD (*Urbain.*) Recherches sur la vraie anatomie des dents, etc. Lyon, 1582. in-8°.

HERNANDEZ. Mémoire sur les questions suivantes, faites par la société de médecine de Lyon, en frimaire an 14.—*Quels sont les signes diagnostiques et prognostiques que peuvent fournir dans les maladies aiguës et chroniques, l'état de la langue, des lèvres et des dents ?—Quelle conséquence doit-n en déduire dans la pratique?* Toulon, 1808, broch. in-8°, 3 fr.

HERTZ (*J. P.*) A familiar dissertation on the causes and treat-ment of the diseases of the teeth, etc., Lond. 1815, in-8°.

HESLOPP. Dissert. de dentitione infantum difficili et laboriosâ. Leid., 1700.

HEURNIUS. Tractatus de morbis oculorum, aurium et *dentium.* Leid., 1602.

HEYE. Dissertat. de dolore dentium. Helmstadii, 1672.

HILSCHER. Dissertat. de odontalgià, Jen., 1748.—Remarques sur les dents, fondées sur la pratique. Jena, 1776 et 1801.

HOFFMANN. Dissertat. de dentibus eorum morbis et curâ. Halæ, 1698 et 1714.—Dissertat. de remediis odontalgicis. Halæ, 1700.

HORSTIUS. De aureo dente. Lips., 1595, in-8°.

HUNTER. Natural history of the teeth and their diseases. Lon-don, 1771 ; traduct. latine, 1773 ; allem., 1780.

HURLOK (*J.*) A Practical treatise upon dentition. London, 1742, in-8°.

I.

INGOLSTETTER. De aureo dente Silesiaci pueri. Lipsiæ, 1795.

J.

JACKSON. Dissertat. de physiologià et pathologià dentium erup-
tionis. Edimb., 1778.

JANKE. Dissertat. de dentibus evellendis. Leps., 1751.—De ossibus mandibulæ puerorum septennium. Leps., 1751.

JERON (J.) Practische darstellun aller operationem der Zahnazt
neykunst. Berlin, 1804.

JETUZE. De difficili infantum dentitione. Erfordiæ, 1732.

JOSSE. Analyse de l'émail des dents. Paris, an 10. (*Journal de
Médecine.*)

JOURDAIN. Traité des dépôts dans les sinus maxillaires, des
fractures et des caries, suivi de réflexions sur toutes les opérations de l'art du dentiste. Paris, 1761.—Essai sur la formation
des dents comparée avec celle des os. Paris, 1766.—Traité
des maladies et des opérations réellement chirurgicales de la
bouche et des parties qui y correspondent, suivi de notes, d'observations, consultations intéressantes, tant anciennes que mo-
dernes, 2 vol. in-8. Paris, 1756.—Nouveaux élémens d'odontologie. Paris, 1756.

JOURDAN et MAGGIOLO. Manuel de l'art du dentiste. Nancy,
1807, in-8°, fig. 2 fr. 50 c.

JUNKER. Dissertat. de dentium affectibus. Halæ, 1740.—Dissertat. de dentitione difficili. Halæ, 1745.—Dissertat. de quatuor
præcipuis infantum morbis. 1746. Dissertat. de odontalgià. Halæ,
1758.

JUNCKER. Sur les maladies des dents et les maux de tête, et
l'art de les guérir. Braumschweig, 1802.

K.

KEMME. Dissertat. sistens dentium historiam, physiologice, pathologice et therapeutice pertractatam. Helmst. 1740.

KOECKER (*Léonard.*) Principles of Dental surgery, exhibiting
a new method of treating the diseases of the teeth and gums, etc.
London, 1826, in-8°.

KOENEN. Dissertat. de præcipuis dentium morbis. Francof.,
1793.

KRANSE (*R. W.*) De odontalgià. Jenæ, 1780.

KRAUTERMANN (*Val.*) Sicherer Augen und Zahnarzt. Arnstadt,
1732, in-8°.

KREBEL (*J. L. Cottis.*) Dissertatio inauguralis de dentitione
difficili. Lipsiæ, 1800. In-4°.

KUCHLER. Dissertat. de ulceribus dentium fistulosis. Lips., 1733.

KULENKAMP. Dissertat. de difficili infantum dentitione. Harderow, 1788.

L.

LAFORGUE. Dix-sept articles relatifs aux maladies des dents. Paris, an 8. Broch. in-8°.—L'art du dentiste. Paris, 1802, in-8°. fig.—Théorie et pratique de l'art du dentiste. Paris, 1810, 2 vol. in-8°. fig.—De la Séméiologie buccale, et Buccamancie. Paris, 1814, in-8°.—Le Triomphe de la première dentition, almanach nouveau et curieux pour l'an bissextile 1816. Paris, 1816, in-32.

LAUBMEYER. Dissert. de dentibus. Regiom, 1745.

LAVIGNA (*Fr.*) Osservazioni odontalgiche sulle cause della carie. Turin, 1813, in-8°.

LAVINI (*Guisippe.*) Tractado sopre la qualita di denti colmodo di cavargli. Fiorenza, 1740.

LECLUSE. Traité utile au public, où l'on enseigne la méthode de remédier aux douleurs et aux accidens qui précèdent et qui accompagnent la sortie des premières dents des enfans, de procurer un arrangement aux secondes, enfin de les entretenir et de les conserver pendant le cours de la vie. Nancy, 1750, 1753, Paris, 1754.—Nouveaux élémens d'odontologie. Paris, 1754 et 1782.—Eclaircissement pour parvenir à préserver les dents de la carie, etc. Paris, 1755.

LEGROS. Le conservateur des dents. Paris, 1812.

LEICHNER (*Richard.*) Dissert. de atrocissimà dentium dolore. Erfort, 1678.

LEMAIRE (*Joseph.*) Le dentiste des dames. Paris, 1812, in-12.— Deux observations d'anatomie pathologique sur les dents. Paris, 1816. Cinq pages in-8°.—Histoire naturelle des maladies des dents de l'espèce humaine. (Translated from the English work of Joseph Fox. Paris, 1821, in-4°, avec pl. 20 fr.)—Traité sur les dents, *physiologie, pathologie.* Paris, 1822 et 1824, 3 vol. in-8°, 12 fr. 50 c.

LEMAITRE. Rapport fait à la société des inventions et découvertes, sur les dentiers perfectionnés. Paris, 1784.

LEMONIER. Dissertation sur les maladies des dents. Paris, 1753 et 1783, in-12.—Lettre à M. Mouton. Paris, 1784, in-8°.

LENTIN (*Leber Benjam.*) Bekerungen von der Wirkung der electrischen Erschütterung im Zahnweh, 1756.

LEROY (DE LA FAUDIGUERE.) Manière de prévenir et de guérir les maladies des gencives et des dents. Paris, 1806, in-8°.

LÉVEILLÉ. Mémoire sur les rapports qui existent entre les premières et les secondes dents, et sur la disposition favorable de ces dernières au développement des deux mâchoires. (*Société médic. d'émulation*, tom. 7, pag. 394.)

LEVÉQUE. Notice sur la nécessité de diriger la dentition des enfans, les soins que réclament les dents à tous les âges, et les moyens à employer pour prévenir, arrêter ou ralentir les progrès des maladies qui affectent ces organes. Strasbourg, 1823, in-8°.

LEWIS. An essay on the formation of the teeth with a supplement containing the means of preserving them. London, 1772, in-8°.

LICHTENSTEIN (*J. M.*) Deber die porgfalt für zahnfleisch und zahne bremen in-8°. A. Jh. L. Z. 1812, n°. 31.

LIDDELINS. Tractatus de dente aureo pueri Silesiaci. Hamb., 1626. (App. ad artem medicam.)

LIMA. Plusieurs observations sur un nouveau moyen de guérir certaines douleurs de dents. Lyon, 1788.

LOESELIUS. Dissertat. de dolore dentium Regiom (1639.)

LOESCHER. Dissertat. de dentibus sapientiæ, eorumque morbis. Witteb. 1728.

LONGBOTTOM. A treatise on dentistry. Baltimore, in-12.

LUDOLF (*H.*) Disputat. de morbis gingivarum. Erfort, 1708 et 1822.

LUDWIG. Programma de cortice dentium. Lipsiæ, 1753.—Diss. de dentitione difficili. Leps., 1800.

M.

MAGGIOLLO. Le Manuel de l'Art du dentiste. Nancy, 1807, in-12, fig., 2 fr. 50 c.

MAHON. Le Dentiste observateur, Paris, an VI, in-12, 1 fr. 50 c.

MARMONT (*J.*) L'Odontotechnie, ou l'Art du Dentiste, poème dictatique et descriptif, en quatre chants, dédié aux dames, Paris, 1825, in-12.

MARTEL (*N. M.*) Sur l'Odontalgie et les affections qui la simulent. (*Dissert. inaugur.* Paris, 1807, in-4°.)

MARTIN. Dissertation sur les dents. Paris, 1679, in-12.

MAURY (*J. G. F.*) Manuel du Dentiste, pour l'application des dents artificielles incorruptibles, suivi de la description de divers instrumens perfectionnés. Paris, 1820, in-8°. 2e. *édit.*, principalement augmentée du mode de fabrication des dents incorruptibles. Paris, 1822, in-8°, fig., 3 fr.

24

MEKEL. Dissertat. An morbi, qui Dentium translationem sequuntur, venerei sint necne ? Hal., 1792.

MEYER (*J.*) Abhandlung von der gewohnhichen Zahnkrankheiten. Hanau, 1778, in-8°.

MIEL. Note sur la manière dont les dents sortent des alvéoles et traversent les gencives, lue à la *Société médico-pratique.* 1810. Quatre pages in-8°.—Description d'un nouvel instrument pour exécuter facilement une opération occasionée par la fracture des pivots des dents artificielles dans les racines qui les reçoivent ; et quelques vues sur la forme la plus avantageuse à donner à ces pivots. Paris, 1808. Huit pages.—Quelques idées sur le rapport des deux Dentitions et sur l'accroissement des mâchoires dans l'homme ; Paris. Vingt-cinq pages in-8°.—Recherches sur l'Art de diriger la seconde dentition en général. Paris, 1826, in-8°, fig., 4 fr. 50 c.

MŒBIUS. De Odontalgiâ seu de dentium statu naturali atque præternaturali. Jenæ, 1661, in-4°.

MONAVIUS. De dentium affectibus. Basil., 1578.

MONGIN. Ergo prægnanti mulieri acutissimo dentis dolore laboranti ejusdem evulsio, 1740.

MONIER (*G. Ph. L.*) Dissertation sur les maladies des dents. Paris, 1783, in-12.

MORTET. Extraction des dents, à l'aide d'un instrument nouvellement inventé. (*Dissert. inaugur.*) Paris, 1802, in-8°. 1 fr. 50 c.

MOUTON. Essai d'Odontotechnie, ou Dissertation sur les Dents artificielles. Paris, 1786, in-12.

MURPHY (*Joseph.*) A Natural History of the human teeth with a treatise on their diseases from infancy to old age, etc. London, 1811, in-8°.

MYRRHEN. Dissertat. de Odontalgiâ, Giess, 1693.

N.

NEDHART. De Affectibus Dentium.

NICOLAI. Dissertat. de variis dentium affectibus eorumque in sanitatem influxu. Jenæ, 1799.

O.

OETINGER. Dissert. de Ortu Dentium, etc. Tub., 1770.

ORTLOB. Dissert. de Dentitione puerorum difficili. Lips., 1694.

OUDET. (*J. L.*) Expériences sur l'Accroissement continué et la reproduction des dents chez les lapins, considérées sous le rapport de leur application à l'étude de l'organisation des dents humaines. Paris, 1823, broch. in-8°·

P.

PACHEUS. Dissert. de Dentium dolore. Basil., 1707.

PALDAMUS. Dissert. de Dentium morbis. Hal., 1799.

PALLU. An Dentium dolori conferat tabacum? Turonib., 1642, in-8°.

PARMLY (*L. S.*) A Practical guide to the management of the teeth, comprising a discovery of the origin of caries, or decay of the teeth with its prevention and cure. London, 1818. in-12.— Lectures on the natural history and management of the teeth, etc. London, 1820, in-8.

PARMILY (*Eléazar.*) An Essay on the disorders and treatment of the teeth. In-8°. London, 1821.

PASCH (*Jos. Ge.*) Abhandlung von den Zahnen, des Zahnfleisches-der-Kiefer, Krankheiten und Heilart. Wien, 1767.

PAULI. Dissert. de Dolore dentium. Hafniæ, 1639.

PESTORF. Dissert. de dentitione difficili. Ultr., 1699.

PLANER. Dissert. de Odontalgiâ. Tul., 1695.

PLENCK (*J.-J.*) De Dentium et gingivarum morbis. Wien, 1778. Neapel, 1781. Tentsch. Wien, 1779. In-8°.

PLISSON. Observation sur une maladie extraordinaire des gencives. Lyon, 1781.

PLOUCQUET. Dissertat. Odontidis primæ lineæ. Tub. 1794.

POLH (*Pr.*) De Difficili infantum Dentitione. Lips., 1776.

POSEWITZ. Semeiologie aphtharum idiopaticarum et symptomaticarum. Vetrib., 1790.

R.

RAN. Dissertat. de Ortu et Generatione dentium. Lugd. Bat., 1694.

REGNART. Mémoire sur un Nouveau moyen d'Obturation des dents. Paris, 1818. Petite broch.

RENGELMANN (*Carol. Jos.*) De ossium morbis, eorumque in specie dentium, carie. Arnstadt, 1805.

RICCI. Principes d'Odontotechnie, ou Réflexions sur la Conservation des dents et des gencives. Paris, 1790.—Mémoire sur les dents raciformes ou racisubériques. Paris, 1816, in-8°.—Instruction sur l'Entretien des dents et des gencives, sur les propriétés d'une liqueur utile pour la guérison de leurs affections et pour un grand nombre d'autres cas maladifs. Paris, 1816, in-8°.

RINIÈRE. Instructions pour conserver les dents. Paris, 1811.

ROLFINCK. Dissert. de Odontalgiâ. Jena, 1669.

ROSSET. Sur la Dentition. (*Dissert. inaugur.* Paris, an XII.)

ROUSSEAU (*Em.*) Dissertation sur la première et la deuxième dentition. Paris, 1820, in-4°.—Anatomie comparée du Système dentaire chez l'homme et les principaux ; Paris, 1827. Grand in-8°, avec 30 pl., 30 fr.

ROUX (*Ph. Jos.*) Mémoire sur la Staphyloraphie ou Suture du voile du palais. Paris, 1825, in-8°. fig. 2 f. 50 c.

RUBICKI. Dissert. de Dentitione difficili. Regiom., 1803.

RUSPINI (*Barth.*) A treatise on the teeth, their structure and various diseases. London, 1779, in-12.

S.

SCARDOVI. Dissert. de dentibus. Argent., 1645, in-4°.

SCHEERS. Dissert. de dentibus. Traject., 1772.

SCHELHAMMER. Dissert. de odontalgiâ tactu sanandâ. Jena, 1711.

SCHMIDT. L'art de maintenir les dents depuis l'enfance. Gotha, 1801.—Le moyen de soigner et maintenir les dents saines. 1805. —Théorie et pratique des dents. Leipsick, 1806.—Quelques mots à ceux qui désirent maintenir leurs dents dans un bon état. Leipsick, 1801.

SCHMIEDEL. Dissert. de Dentitione, præsertim infantum difficili. Erf., 1751.

SEBIZ (*Melch.*) Disput. IV de dentibus. Arg., 1645.—De dentibus, urinâ et morbis contagiosis, etc. Argent., 1664. In-4°.

SENNERTUS. Dissertat. de dentium dolore. Witteb., 1629.

SERRES (E. R. A.) Essai sur l'anatomie, la physiologie des dents, ou Nouvelle Théorie de la dentition. Paris, 1817, in-8°. 4 fr. 50 c.

SIGMOND. A practical and domestic treatise on the diseases and irregularities of teeth and gums, with the methods of treatment. Bath., 1825, in-8°.

SKINER. A treatise on the human teeth concisely explaining their structure, and causes of diseases and decay. New York, 1801.

STISSER. Dissert. de odontalgiâ. Lugdun. Batav., 1675.

STRASBURG. Dissert. περι οδονταλγιας. Regiomonti, 1651.

STREITLEIN. Dissert. de dentitione. Altd., 1688.

STROBELBERGER (*Joh. Steph.*) De dentium podagrâ, sive de odontalgiâ. Lipsiæ, 1630, in-8°.

T.

TAVEAU (*O.*) Hygiène de la bouche. Paris, 1826, in-12, 3 fr.— Conseils aux fumeurs sur la conservation de leurs dents. Paris, 1827, in-8°. 2 f. 50 c.

TIMAEUS. A treatise on the tooth-ache. London, 1769, in-8°.

TOIRAC. Sur les dents considérées sous le rapport de la santé, de la physionomie, de la pronunciation. (*Dissert. inaugur.* Paris, 1823, in-4°.)

TOLVER (*A.*) A treatise on the teeth. London, 1752, in-8°.

TOUCHARD. Description d'un obturateur dentier présenté à la *Société de médecine de Paris:* suivie de remarques sur les dents artificielles. Paris, 1814, in-8°.

TRASTUS (Th.) Disput. de dentibus in disp. et epist. Tiguri, 1595, in-4°.

TROUBAT. Accidens d'une dentition difficile ou laborieuse : moyens certains d'y remédier. Mayenne, 1824, in-8°.

TRECURTH. Dissertat. de odontalgià. Hal., 1688.

TULLER. A popular essay on the structure, formation and management of the teeth, illustrated by engravings. (DOWNING, surgeon dentist, new edition, 1815.)

V.

VACHER. Dissertat. de dentium accidentibus. Paris, 1764 et 1767.

VALENTINI. Dissertat. de vacillatione, casu et reparatione dentium. Giess., 1727.

VAN DER BELEN. Dissertat. de odontalgià. Lavan, 1782.

VAN DER MAESSEN. Sur la nécessité de soigner les dents et les gencives. Gotha, 1802.—Le Dentiste pour tous les états. Leipsick. 1803.—Comment les parens peuvent-ils faciliter les moyens de faire les dents aux enfans. Pyrna, 1807.

VASE. Ergo hæmorrhagia ex dentium evulsione, chirurgici incurià, lethalis ? Paris, 1735.

VATER. Dissertat. de odontalgià. Witteb., 1683.

VESTI. Dissertat. de odontalgià. Erf., 1697.

VIGIER (*J.*) Tractatus de catarrho, rheumatismo, vitiis dentium, Genev., 1620, in-8°.

VAUQUELIN. Rapport sur le tartre des dents, fait à *la section de Pharmacie de l'Académie royale de Médecine.* Paris, 1825.

W.

WAGNER. Dissert. de dentitione difficili a dubiis C. L. Wichmann vindicata. Jén., 1798.

WALKEY. On the diseases of the teeth, their origin explained. Lond., 1793.

WARENIUS. Dissert., de catarrho et ex eo descendentibus, *odontalgiâ*, etc. Rostoch, 1663.

WEDEL. Dissert. de dentitione infantum. Jen., 1678.

WEYLAND (*Fr. S.*) Disput. de ozenâ maxillari cum ulcere fistulosa ad angulum oculi internum complicato. Argentorati. 1771, in-4°.

WOOFFENDALE. Practical Observations on the human teeth. London, 1788, in-8°·

Z.

ZAKBOCKJEN. Bevattende de middelen om de gezondheit der tanden te berwaaren, derzelver Zieklyke toevalle te voorkomen en te keer to gaan Arnheim. 1804, in-12.

ZBONATREIT. De Dentitione secundâ juniorum. Leipsig, 1738. in-4°.

ZEIDLER. Dissertat. de dolore dentium. Lepsiæ, 1631.

ZIEGLER (Fr.) Disputat. de morbis præcipuis sinuum ossis frontis maxillæ superioris et quibusdam mandibulæ inferioris. Rinteln, 1750.

ZIEGLER. Diss., 1613.—Dissert. de odontalgiâ. Uttraject., 1695.

Journals and Periodicals, containing interesting documents upon the Structure of the Teeth, their diseases, and the Therapeutical means of remedying these.

Académie royale de Médecine.

Acta Eruditorum Lipsiæ.

Acta Helvetiæ.

Acta Naturæ Curiosorum.

Acta (*Nova*) Naturæ Curiosorum.

Bulletin de la Faculté de Médecine de Paris.

Commercium litterarium.

Encyclopédie par ordre de matières.

Ephémérides des Curieux de la nature.

Journal de Médecine et de chirurgie.

Journal général de Médecine.
Journal der Practischen Heilkunde (*Hufeland.*)
Journal der Erfindungen, etc.
Physical and medical Journal.
Journal des Savans.
Mémoires de la Société médicale d'Emulation.
Mémoires de la Société royale de Médecine.
Recueil périodique de la Société de Médecine.
Medical Repository.
Transactions philosophiques.

APPENDIX TO LIST OF AUTHORS, &c.

BY THE TRANSLATOR.

American Journal of Dental Science, 8vo. vol. 1, 1840-'1, New York, C. A, Harris. M. D. and Eleazar Parmly, M. D., Editors. Do. vol. 2, 1841-'2.

Baltimore, C. A. Harris, M. D., D. D. S., Solyman Brown, M. D., D. D. S., Editors.—Do. vol. 3. 1842-3.

(Now issuing,) C. A. Harris, M. D., D. D. S., Solyman Brown, M. D., D. D. S. Leonard Mackall, M. D., Editors.

ASHBURNER J. M. D., on Dentition, 12mo. London, 1834.

BLANDIN, P. F., Anatomie du Systeme Dentaire, 8vo. Paris, 1836.

BROWN, SOLYMAN, M. D., Dentologia, a Poem on the Diseases of the Teeth, and their proper Remedies, 8vo. 1833. New York.

BURDELL, J. & H. On the Structure, Physiology, Anatomy and Diseases of the Teeth, 8vo. New York, 1838.

CLARK, J. P. A practical and familiar Treatise on the Teeth and Dentism, 8vo. London, 1836. A new System of treating the human Teeth, 12mo. London, 1841.

CHANNING, F. B. Remarks on the Importance of the Teeth, &c., &c., 8vo. Richmond, 1833.

DE LONDE, S. C. On surgical, operative and mechanical Dentistry, 8vo. London, 1840.

ETTMULLER, C. F. B. Medizenisch Chirurgische Abhandlung uber die Krankheiten der zhne, &c. Leipzig, 1798.

FLAGG, J. F., M. D. Family Dentist, 12mo. Boston, 1832.

FULLER. Popular Essay on the Structure, Formation and Management of the Teeth, 12mo. 1815.

GRAY, JOHN. Preservation of the Teeth, 12mo. London, 1840.

HARRIS, C. A., M. D., D. D. S. Dental Art, a practical Treatise on Dental Surgery, 8vo. Balt., 1839.—Essay on the Characteristics of the Teeth, Gums, &c., 8vo. Baltimore, 1841.

HITCHCOCK, D. R. Preservation of the Teeth, a Family Guide, 12mo. Boston, 1840.

IMRIE, W. The Parents' Guide, &c., 8vo. London, 1835.

JAMET, C. A. Traité des Dents, 8vo. Paris, 1839.

JOBSON, D. M. Treatise on the Anatomy and Physiology of the Teeth, &c., 8vo. London, 1835.

KOECKER, L., M. D. Essay on artificial Teeth, Obturators, and Palates, 8vo. London, 1835.

KOECKER, L., M. D. Essay on the Diseases of the Jaws, 8vo. London, Philadelphia, 1834.

LINTOD, W. On the Structure, Economy and Pathology of the human Teeth, 12mo. London, 1841.

LEFOULON, J. Nouveau traité Theorique et Pratique de l'Art du Dentiste, 8vo. Paris, 1841.

LINDERER, C. J. & J. Handbuck der zachnheilkunde enthaltend Anatomie und Physiologie Materia Medica Dentaria und Chirurgia, &c., 8vo. Berlin, 1842.

MURPHY, J. L. Popular Treatise on the Structure, Diseases and Treatment of the human Teeth, 12mo. London, 1837.

MALLAN, JOHN. Practical Observations on the Physiology and Diseases of the Teeth, 8vo. London, 1835.

NICHOLLES, JOHN. On the Teeth, 8vo. London, 1833.

NASMYTH, A. Three Memoirs on the Developement and Structure of the Teeth and Epithelium, 8vo. London, 1841.—" Historical Introduction to the Anatomy, Physiology and Diseases of the Teeth," 8vo. London, 1839.

PARMLY, L. S., M. D. A practical Guide to the Management of the Teeth, 8vo. 1819, New York.

PURLAND. Practical Directions for preserving the Teeth. London, 1831.

PLOUGH, A. L. Observations Generales sur l'importance des Dents. New Orleans, 1836.

ROBERTSON, W. A practical Treatise on the human Teeth, 8vo. London, 1839.

SPOONER, S., M. D. Guide to sound Teeth, or a popular Treatise on the Teeth, 12mo. New York, 1836.

SAUNDERS, E. Advice on the Care of the Teeth, 12mo. London.

SNELL, J. A practical Guide to Operations on the Teeth, 8vo. London—Philadelphia, 1832.

SCOTT, J. Every Man his own Dentist, 8vo. London, 1838.

SPOONER, S. Dissertatio medica inauguralis de generis humani Dentium Philologia et morbis, 8vo. New York, 1835.

SCHANGE, J. M. A. Precis sur le Redressement des Dents, etc. etc. 8vo. Paris, 1842.

TRINOR, J., M. D. Physiological Inquiry into the Structure or Organization and Nourishment of the human Teeth, 8vo. New York, 1828. Observations on Neuralgia, 1830.

WAITE, G. Surgeon Dentist's Manual, London—Philadelphia, 1830.—On the Gums, 8vo. London—Philadelphia, 1838.

WARDROPER, W. On the Structure, Diseases and Treatment of the Teeth, 8vo. London, 1838.

EXPLANATION OF PLATES.

EXPLANATION OF PLATE I.

FIGURE 1. A head exhibiting the muscles of the face.

2. A head exhibiting the distribution of the superficial temporal nerve, and the superior and inferior maxillary nerves.

Pl. 1.

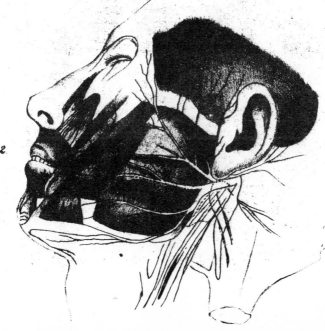

EXPLANATION OF PLATE II.

FIGURE 1. Superior and interior jaws, the external plate of bone removed to exhibit the roots of the teeth and the nerves penetrating them.

2. Superior and inferior jaws, the internal plate removed to exhibit the arteries and veins that are distributed to the dental pulp. (The arteries are designated by dots, the veins by lines.)

Pl. 2.

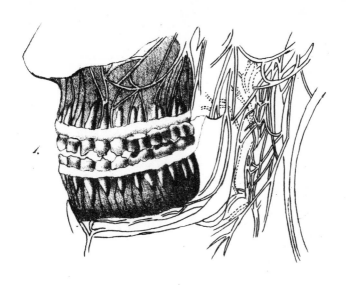

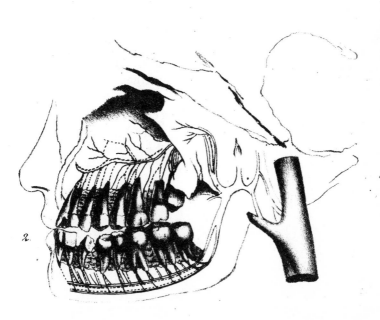

EXPLANATION OF PLATE III.

First Dentition.

Superior Teeth.

Figure 1. Central Incisor of a child of three months.
2. Lateral   "   "   "
3. Cuspidatus   "   "
4. First Molar   "   "
5. Second Molar   "   "
6. Central Incisor of a fœtus of eight months.
7. Lateral   "   "   "
8. Cuspidatus   "   "
9. First Molar   "   "
10. Second "   "   "

Inferior Teeth.

11. Central Incisor of a fœtus of eight months.
12. Lateral   "   "   "
13. Cuspidatus   "   "
14. First Molar   "   "
15. Second "   "   "
16. Central incisor of a child of three months.
17. Lateral   "   "   "
18. Cuspidatus   "   "
19. First Molar   "   "
20. Second "   "   "

Second Dentition.

Superior Teeth.

21. Central Incisor of a child of seven years.
22. Lateral   "   "   "
23. Cuspidatus   "   "

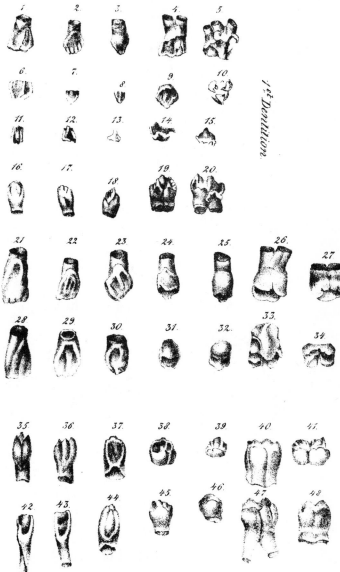

Pl. 3.

1ᵗ Dentition.

2ⁿᵈ Dentition.

FIGURE 24. First bicuspis of a child of seven years.
     25. Second   "   "   "
     26. First Molar   "   "
     27. Second   "   "   "
     28. Central Incisor of a child of five years.
     29. Lateral   "   "   "
     30. Cuspidatus   "   "
     31. First bicuspis   "   "
     32. Second   "   "   "
     33. First Molar   "   "
     34. Second   "   "   "

Inferior Teeth.

     35. Central Incisor of a child of five years.
     36. Lateral   "   "   "
     37. Cuspidatus   "   "
     38. First Bicuspis   "   "
     39. Second   "   "   "
     40. First Molar   "   "
     41. Second   "   "   "
     42. Central incisor of a child of seven years.
     43. Lateral   "   "   "
     44. Cuspidatus   "   "
     45. First bicuspis   "   "
     46. Second   "   "   "
     47. First Molar   "   "
     48. Second   "   "   "

EXPLANATION OF PLATE IV.

FIGURE 1. A preparation showing the dental matrices of two central incisores of second dentition, and their communication with the gum by a conduit called iter dentis.

2. Dental matrix containing the crown of a central incisor of second dentition.

3. A decayed tooth, exhibiting a cyst at the extremity of its root.

4. A central incisor of second dentition of a child of seven years, sawed longitudinally, the dental pulp having fallen out.

5. The half of figure 4, showing the situation that the dental pulp had occupied.

6. A bicuspis exhibiting stationary decay.

7. A central incisor sawed in two, showing the obliteration of the dental canal at about the age of sixty.

8. Profile of a person fourteen years old, having an inversion of the dental arch. (*Menton de Galoche.*)

9. The same profile at fifteen years of age showing the teeth after having been well arranged.

Pl. 4.

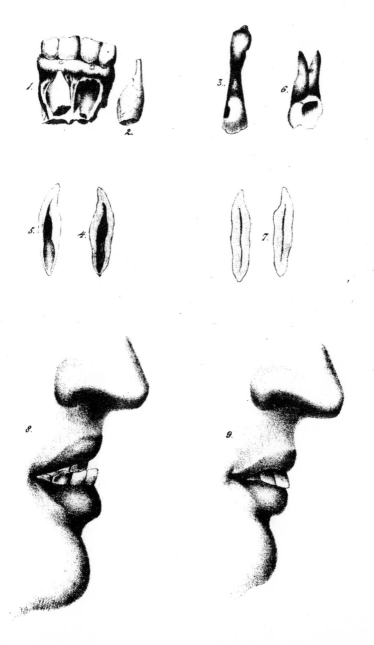

EXPLANATION OF PLATE V.

FIGURE 1. The half of the inferior jaw of a child at birth, the exterior plate removed, showing the dental gums.

    2. The same at eight months, the incisores beginning to appear.

    3. The same at sixteen months, the incisores being entirely through the gums.

    4. The same at 23 months, the cuspidatus commencing to appear.

    5. The same at 31 months, the first molar having commenced to appear.

    6. The same at 40 months, the first and second molares of first dentition having appeared.

Pl. 3

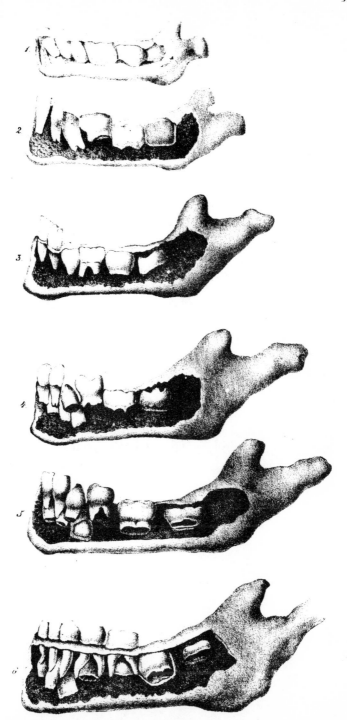

EXPLANATION OF PLATE VI.

FIGURE 1. The half of the inferior jaw of a child from six to seven years old, the central incisor of second dentition commencing to appear. (The first molar also appears at this age.)

2. The same, from 11 to 12 years of age, the second molar nearly out, and the germ of the wisdom tooth exhibited.

3. *Adult*, dentition being complete.

4. *Old age*, all the teeth being removed, the alveoli are obliterated so as to form a solid border, which serves in a measure for mastication.

Pl. 6.

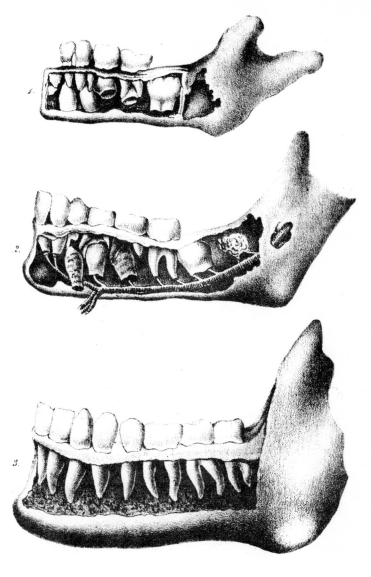

EXPLANATION OF PLATE VII.

THE FORMS OF THE TEETH OF FIRST DENTITION.

Superior Teeth.

FIGURE 1. Central Incisor.
2. Lateral Incisor.
3. Cuspidatus.
4. First Molar.
5. Second Molar.

Inferior Teeth.

6. Central Incisor.
7. Lateral Incisor.
8. Cuspidatus.
9. First Molar.
10. Second Molar.

THE FORMS OF THE TEETH OF SECOND DENTITION.

Superior Teeth.

11. Central Incisor.
12. Lateral Incisor.
13. Cuspidatus.
14. First bicuspis.
15. Second bicuspis.
16. First Molar.
17. Second Molar.
18. Third Molar.

Inferior Teeth.

19. Central Incisor.
20. Lateral Incisor.
21. Cuspidatus.
22. First bicuspis.
23. Second bicuspis.
24. First Molar.
25. Second Molar.
26. Third Molar.

Pl. 7

1.   2.   3.   4.   5.

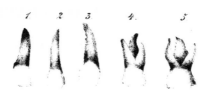

1st Dentition.

6.   7.   8.   9.   10.

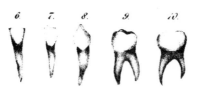

11.   12.   13.   14.   15.   16.   17.   18.

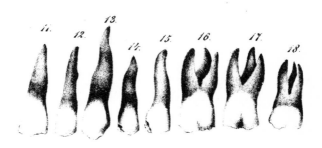

2d Dentition

19.   20.   21.   22.   23.   24.   25.   26.

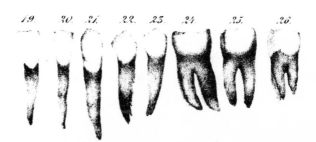

EXPLANATION OF PLATE VIII.

FIGURE 1. A molar tooth with a speck of enamel on its root.

2. A wisdom tooth of the inferior jaw having four roots and diminutive tooth adhering to it.

3. First superior molar with a diminutive tooth adhering to it.

4. Two superior incisores united.

5. A superior central incisor with its root curved obliquely.

6. Supernumerary tooth.

7. Second and third inferior molares united.

8. A lateral incisor having a diminutive tooth upon its heel.

9. A drawing of two incisores of a child three years old, each having a young tooth upon its heel.

10. The form of a supernumerary tooth and a diminutive of the wisdom tooth, which grow near the last superior molar.

11. A supernumerary tooth.

12. The first superior molar having a bicuspis embraced between its roots.

13. A superior incisor having a root in the form of a bayonet.

14. A first superior bicuspis having three roots.

15. Two inferior central incisores of first dentition united.

16. Form of a supernumerary tooth growing between the superior central incisores.

17. The root of a molar having in its centre a diminutive tooth.

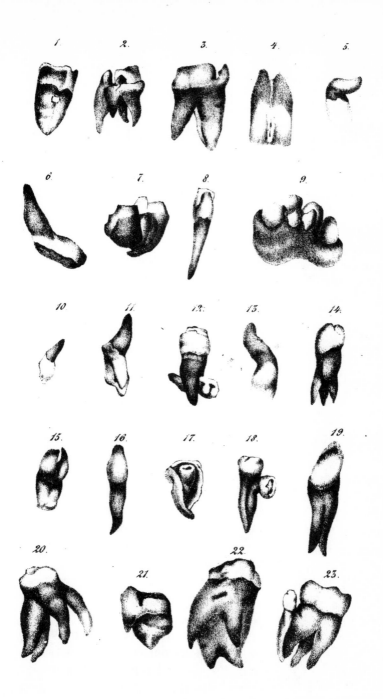

T. Sinclair's lith. Phila

18. Two inferior bicuspides united to a single root.

19. An inferior cuspidatus bifurcated.

20. First superior molar having four divergent roots.

21. A superior wisdom tooth having a very large crown, and scarcely any root.

22. The second superior molar of very large size.

23. A superior molar, having a supernumerary tooth united to its root.

EXPLANATION OF PLATE IX.

FIGURE 1. A superior jaw in which is developed in the substance of the bone two supernumerary teeth which made their appearance under the nasal fossa. They are inverted.

2. The right supernumerary tooth forming a part of figure 1.

3. The left supernumerary tooth forming part of figure 1.

4. The central incisor of figure 1, its root formed like a bayonet.

5. The right side of a superior jaw viewed internally; the left central incisor directed toward the wing of the nose.

6. Position of the two central incisores of figure 5.

7. Central incisor of figure 5 viewed anteriorly.

8. Central superior incisor having a diminutive root.

9. A supernumerary tooth situated between the two central superior incisores.

10. A lateral superior incisor having its root in the form of a bayonet.

Pl. 9.

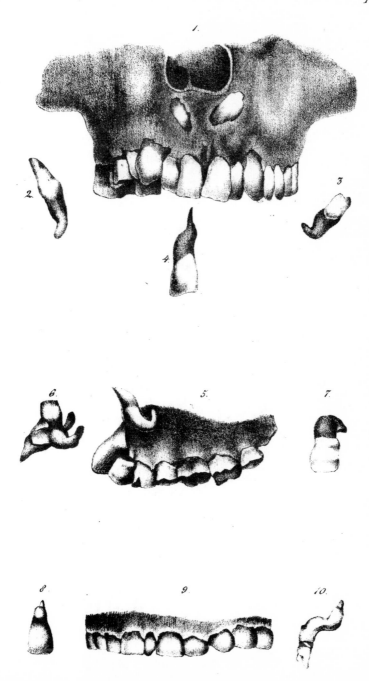

EXPLANATION OF PLATE X.

FIGURE 1. A superior jaw in which are seen two wisdom teeth, one above the other.

2. Drawing of a superior jaw, having a congenital depression about nine lines deep, in the form of the figure 8. The subject from whom it was taken spoke and sang well.

3. An inferior jaw, the six anterior teeth projecting outwardly. The corresponding teeth of the superior jaw having been lost.

4. A molar tooth having osselet or deposition of bone in the place occupied by the dental pulp.

Pl. 10.

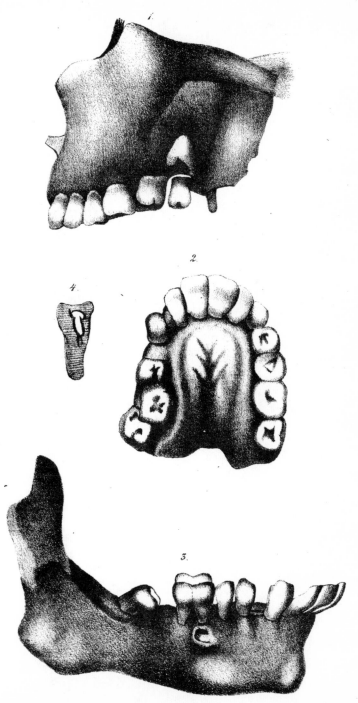

EXPLANATION OF PLATE XI.

FIGURE 1. Superior lateral incisores growing within the dental arch, a ligature attached to bring them into their proper positions.

2. A small platina band with two curves and a hook, used with the ligatures to turn a central superior incisor, having its lateral surface presented anteriorly.

3, 4, 5, 6. Various hooks used to prevent ligatures slipping down on the gums.

7. A ligature and hook adjusted to regulate a central incisor above the level of the other teeth.

8. Inversion of the dental arches: ligatures placed upon the inferior teeth to adjust them.

Pl. 11.

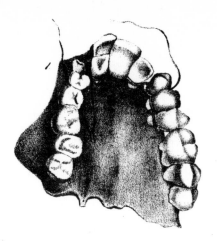

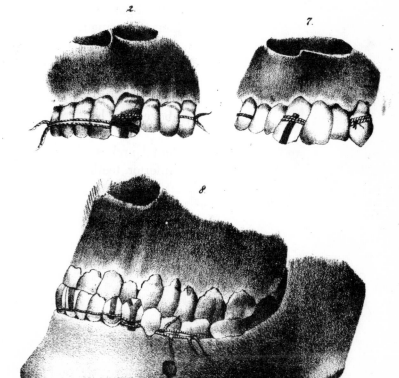

EXPLANATION OF PLATE XII.

FIGURE 1. Calcareous decay of a central incisor.

2. Peeling decay.

3. Diruptive decay.

4, 5. Black decay.

6. Perforating decay.

7. Erosion upon the roots of the inferior incisores.

8. Erosion upon an inferior molar.

9. Erosion upon a superior molar.

10. Destruction of a part of a root above which existed an epulis.

11. Stationary decay upon the crown of a molar.

12. Several lines of erosion upon twelve teeth of the same subject.

13. The destruction of a portion of the root of a lateral incisor produced by inflammation of the alveolo-dental membrane, the nerve remaining healthy.

14. Commencement of external decay, progressing toward the dental nerve.

15. Internal decay making its appearance upon the external table of the crown of a tooth.

16. Exostosis on one root of a molar.

17. Exostosis on an inferior lateral incisor, involving the whole length of the root.

18. Exostosis on a central incisor.

19. Exostosis of the root of a molar.

20. Exostosis of an inferior bicuspis.

21. Exostosis of a superior cuspidatus.

Pl. 12.

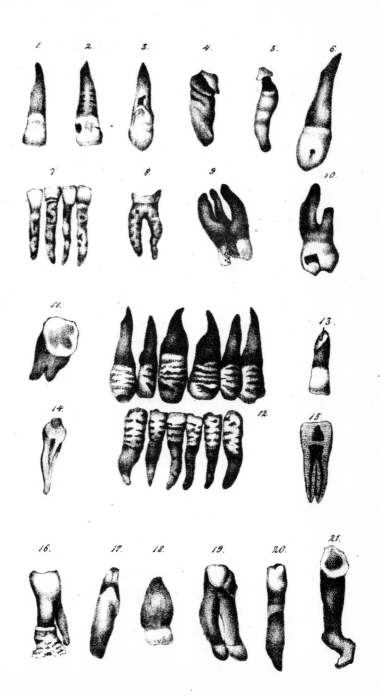

EXPLANATION OF PLATE XIII.

FIGURE 1. Sequestra of a branch of the inferior jaw, decayed in consequence of the unskilful extraction of a tooth.

2. Cutting edge of a central incisor fractured by a blow.

3. The internal face of a central incisor entirely worn away by the friction of the inferior teeth.

4. A central incisor, the crown of which is nearly worn away by the perpendicular friction of the corresponding inferior teeth.

5. An incisor worn away by the continued use of badly prepared dentifrices and hard brushes.

6. A cuspidatus tooth worn away by the clasp of an artificial piece.

7. An oblique fracture of the crown of a tooth.

8. Decay of the maxillary bones, the teeth remaining sound.

9. Inferior incisores and cuspidati covered with tartar to the extremities of their roots, all of which came out together.

10. First inferior molares extracted at the ages of thirteen and fourteen years respectively.

11. An inferior wisdom tooth situated obliquely in the substance of the maxilla.

12. A superior central incisor with a very crooked root.

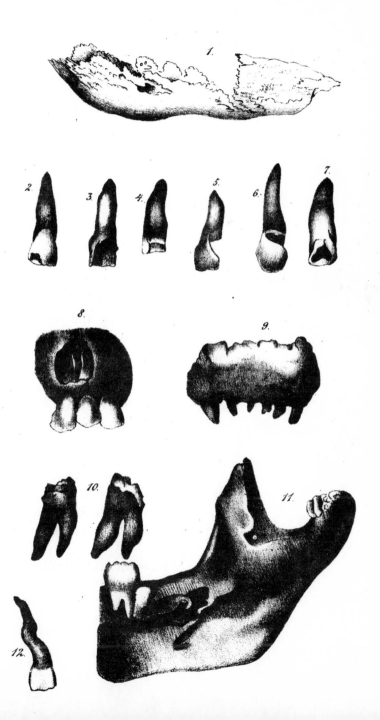

Pl. 13

EXPLANATION OF PLATE XIV.

FIGURE 1. The fish-tongue adapted to a handle.
2. An elevator for the extraction of teeth.
3. A blade of a lancet somewhat curved, mounted upon a shaft, and constructed so as to assume various positions.
4. The straight blade of a lancet adapted to the handle of figure 3.
5. Two small steel semitubes terminating in a saw, the opposite extremities adapted to a shaft, and this inserted in a socket-handle.
6. Half of a tube (figure 5) viewed internally.
7. Two steel spiral branches adapted to the uses of figure 5.

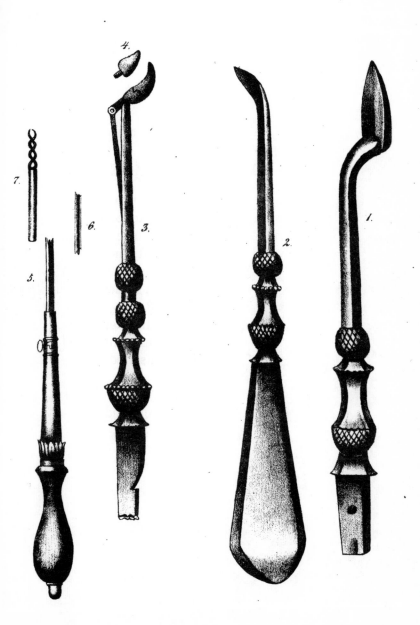

Pl. 14.

EXPLANATION OF PLATE XV.

FIGURE 1. A pair of curved excising forceps.
       2. A pair of straight excising forceps.
       3. The curved forceps grasping a tooth to be excised.
       4. A molar excised at its neck with number 1.
       5. The crown of this molar viewed internally.
       6. A piece of wood used as a fulcrum or support for instruments in the extraction or excision of teeth.

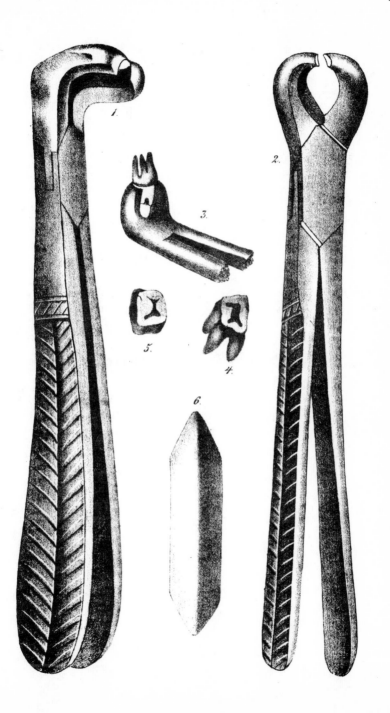

Pl. 15.

1.

2.

3.

5.

4.

6.

EXPLANATION OF PLATE XX.

FIGURE 1. Obturator with branches adapted to figure 4, pl. XIX.

    2. Superior and inferior dentures with spiral springs.

    3. A part of the inferior denture intended for the support of the superior denture.

    7. Obturator with branches.

    8. Palatine roof upon which is indicated by lines the situation for an obturator.

    9. An obturator secured by means of sponge.

    10. An obturator secured by a button.

    11. An obturator with teeth attached.

THE END.

EXPLANATION OF PLATE XIX.

FIGURE 1. Form of a superior alveolar ridge with only the wisdom teeth remaining.

2. Form of an inferior alveolar ridge with only the wisdom teeth remaining.

3. The superior and inferior jaws with complete artificial dentures.

4. A palatine roof, exhibiting the partial loss of the osseous and soft parts.

5. Portion of the necrosed bone taken from the palatine roof figure 4.

Pl. 19.

Pl. 18

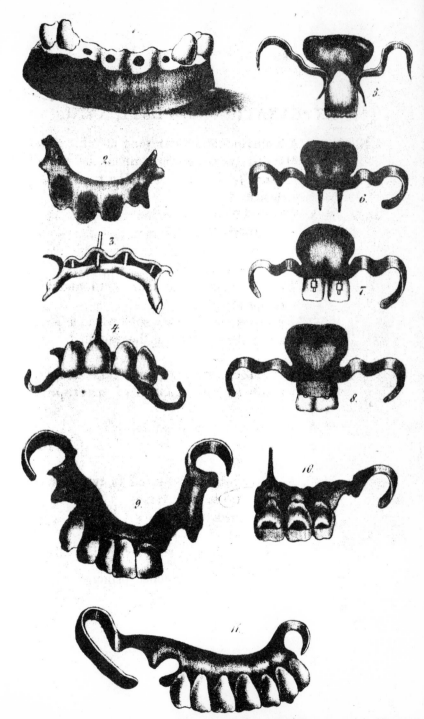

EXPLANATION OF PLATE XVIII.

FIGURE 1. A metal mould for stamping metallic plate.

2. Metallic plate stamped upon the mould figure 1, and prepared to be tried in the mouth.

3. The same plate provided with a pivot to be attached to the root, and four small pivots to which the incorruptible teeth are to be soldered.

4. The same plate, the four teeth and two clasps attached.

5. An incorruptible tooth soldered to a plate, and to be retained in the mouth by two clasps.

6. A metallic plate with two clasps and two pivots for the reception of incorruptible teeth.

7. Figure 6, the two teeth attached.

8. Figure 7, a small plate soldered behind the teeth.

9. Five teeth to be adjusted to two molares by means of two clasps.

10. Three incorruptible teeth to which are attached metal heels.

11. Seven teeth to be attached principally by one long clasp.

17. A sea-horse tooth base prepared to re-
    ceive two incisores to be adjusted upon
    screws.

18. The incisores previous to being attached
    as above.

19. Two incorruptible teeth mounted upon a
    plate to be secured by means of clasps.

20. Incorruptible piece of three teeth, to be
    attached by ligatures to adjacent teeth.

21. Inferior dentures of sea-horse nearly de-
    composed by long retention in the mouth.

Pl 17

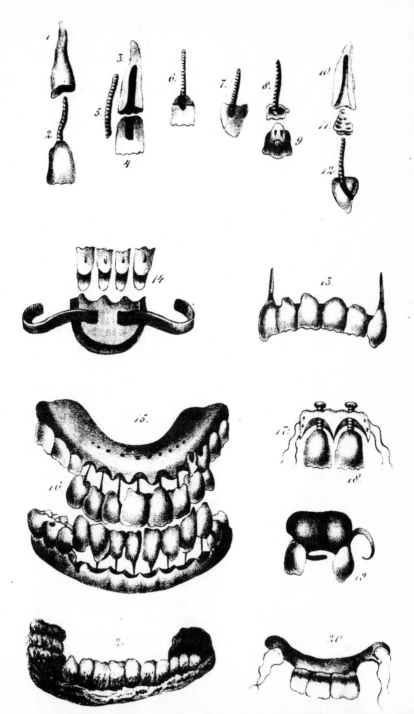

EXPLANATION OF PLATE XVII.

FIGURE 1. The root of a tooth prepared to receive an artificial crown.

    2. An artificial tooth with the pivot adjusted to it.

    3. The half of a root, showing the manner in which it should be drilled for the reception of an artificial crown.

    4. The half of a natural tooth viewed internally, representing the screw-tap to receive the pivot.

    5. A pivot furnished with a screw at one end and slight notches at the other.

    6. The half of a natural tooth seen posteriorly, in which is a pivot through which a pin passes.

    7. A pivot screwed into a tooth.

    8. A pivot to which is soldered a metallic heel.

    9. An incorruptible tooth previous to being soldered to the pivot in figure 8.

    10. The root of a tooth, its canal nearly destroyed.

    11. A funnel or tube intended to partially fill up the root of figure 10.

    12. A natural tooth with a pivot attached previous to being adjusted to figure 10 by means of the tube figure 11.

    13. Six incorruptible teeth mounted upon a plate secured in the mouth by two pivots.

    14. A piece of sea-horse tooth carved for the reception of several natural crowns.

    15. Superior and inferior dentures of sea-horse tooth, having sixteen natural anterior teeth adjusted to it.

    16. Sixteen natural teeth riveted and prepared for attachment as above.

Pl. 16.

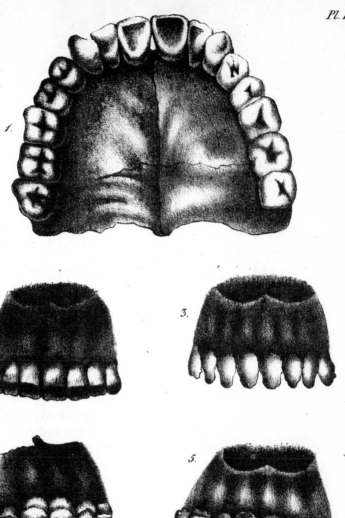

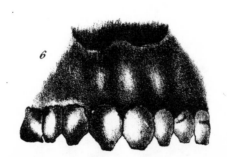

Lith. of Thos Sinclair, Phila.

EXPLANATION OF PLATE XVI.

FIGURE 1. A well developed superior jaw of a Hottentot.

2. Teeth of an African, a portion of them near the cutting edge properly removed.

3. The teeth of a Soosoos (African) separated to their necks, according to the custom of that people.

4. The teeth of a Madurian, cut away on the anterior side, forming transverse gutters.

5. Teeth of a native of Cabinda, upon the coast of Africa, carved in such a manner as to give to eight the appearance of four.

6. Teeth of a Mandingue, on the coast of Africa, carved like the teeth of a saw.

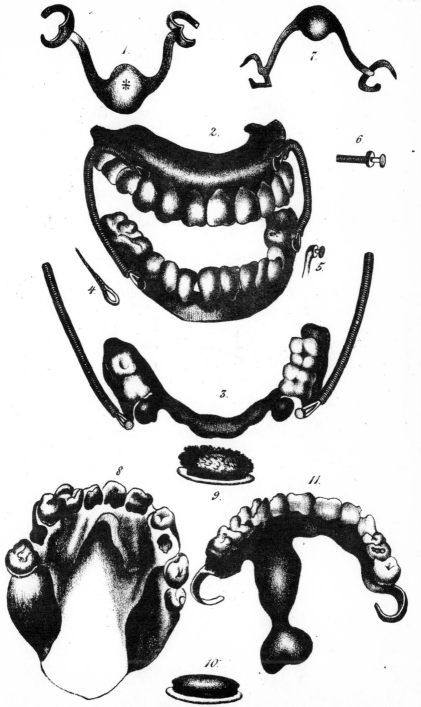

Pl. 20.